Second Edition

W9-BHS-798

ADVOCACY
AND OPPOSITION
An Introduction
to Argumentation

Karyn C. Rybacki
Donald J. Rybacki

Northern Michigan University

PRENTICE HALL
Englewood Cliffs, New Jersey 07632

Library of Congress Cataloging-in-Publication Data

Rybacki, Karyn C. (Karyn Charles), [date]
    Advocacy and opposition : an introduction to argumentation / Karyn
  C. Rybacki, Donald J. Rybacki.—2nd ed.
    p. cm.
  Includes bibliographical references and index.
  ISBN 0-13-016130-6
1. Persuasion (Rhetoric) 2. Debates and debating.   I. Rybacki,
Donald J. (Donald Jay), [date]. II. Title.
P301.5.P47R93   1991
808.53—dc20   90-48088

Editorial/production supervision: *Edith Riker*
Cover design: *Patricia Kelly*
Prepress buyer: *Debra Kesar*
Manufacturing buyer: *Mary Ann Gloriande*

 © 1991, 1986 by Prentice-Hall, Inc.
A Division of Simon & Schuster
Englewood Cliffs, New Jersey 07632

Printed in the United States of America

10 9 8 7 6 5 4 3 2 1

ISBN   0-13-016130-6

Prentice-Hall International (UK) Limited, *London*
Prentice-Hall of Australia Pty. Limited, *Sydney*
Prentice-Hall Canada Inc., *Toronto*
Prentice-Hall Hispanoamericana, S.A., *Mexico*
Prentice-Hall of India Private Limited, *New Delhi*
Prentice-Hall of Japan, Inc., *Tokyo*
Simon & Schuster Asia Pte. Ltd., *Singapore*
Editora Prentice-Hall do Brasil, Ltda., *Rio de Janeiro*

CONTENTS

PREFACE *xi*

1

WHAT IS ARGUMENTATION? *1*

THE NATURE OF ARGUMENTATION *1*
THE USEFULNESS OF ARGUMENTATION *4*
LIMITATIONS ON THE USE OF ARGUMENTATION *6*
APPLICATIONS OF ARGUMENTATION *7*
THE HISTORICAL DEVELOPMENT OF ARGUMENTATION *8*
ETHICAL STANDARDS FOR ARGUMENTATION *10*

The Research Responsibility *10*
The Common-Good Responsibility *11*
The Reasoning Responsibility *12*
The Social Code Responsibility *12*

LEARNING ACTIVITIES *13*
SUGGESTED SUPPLEMENTARY READINGS *14*

2

WHAT DO I NEED TO KNOW BEFORE I CAN BEGIN TO ARGUE?   15

PRESUMPTION   *15*
BURDEN OF PROOF   *19*
THE NATURE OF PROPOSITIONS   *20*

>   Selecting Terms for Definition   *21*
>   Specifying Direction of Change   *22*
>   Identifying Key Issues   *25*
>   Summary of the Nature of Propositions   *27*

THE CLASSIFICATION OF PROPOSITIONS   *27*

>   Propositions of Fact   *28*
>   Propositions of Value   *28*
>   Propositions of Policy   *29*
>   Summary of the Classification of Propositions   *31*

PHRASING THE PROPOSITION   *31*

>   Summary of Rules for Phrasing Propositions   *32*

LEARNING ACTIVITIES   *33*
SUGGESTED SUPPLEMENTARY READINGS   *34*

3

WHAT AM I GOING TO ARGUE ABOUT?   36

THE PRIMA FACIE CASE   *36*
STOCK ISSUES AND PROPOSITIONS OF FACT   *40*
STOCK ISSUES AND PROPOSITION OF VALUE   *42*
STOCK ISSUES AND POLICY PROPOSITIONS   *44*
THE TOULMIN MODEL OF ARGUMENT   *46*

>   Claims   *46*
>   Grounds   *50*
>   Warrant   *52*
>   Summary of the Elements of the Primary Triad   *53*
>   Backing   *54*
>   Qualifiers   *55*
>   Rebuttals   *56*
>   Summary of the Elements of the Secondary Triad   *56*

LEARNING ACTIVITIES   *57*
SUGGESTED SUPPLEMENTARY READINGS   *58*

4

HOW ARE PROPOSITIONS OF FACT AND VALUE ARGUED?   59

SIMPLE, CHAIN, AND CLUSTER ARGUMENTS   *59*
ADVOCATING PROPOSITIONS OF FACT   *61*

Building the Prima Facie Case   *61*
Preempting Opposing Arguments   *62*
Summary of Fact Advocacy   *62*

OPPOSING PROPOSITIONS OF FACT   *63*

Evaluating the Inference   *63*
Using Presumption to Dispute the Inference   *63*
Refuting by Denial and Extenuation   *64*
Responding to Preemptive Arguments   *65*
Summary of Fact Opposition   *65*

VALUE ADVOCACY IN ACTION   *66*
ADVOCATING PROPOSITIONS OF VALUE   *68*

Define the Value Object   *68*
Identify the Hierarchy   *69*
Specify the Criteria   *69*
Measure the Object   *71*
Summary of Value Advocacy Strategies   *72*

VALUE OPPOSITION IN ACTION   *73*
OPPOSING PROPOSITIONS OF VALUE   *74*
Establish Strategy   *75*
Examine Definitions and Hierarchy   *75*
Challenge Criteria   *76*
Refute Measurement   *76*
Summary of Value Opposition Strategies   *77*

LEARNING ACTIVITIES   *78*
SUGGESTED SUPPLEMENTARY READINGS   *78*

5

HOW ARE PROPOSITIONS OF POLICY ARGUED?   80

ADVOCATING POLICY PROPOSITIONS   *80*

Advocacy of the First Stock Issue   *81*
Advocacy of the Second Stock Issue   *82*
Advocacy of the Third Stock Issue   *83*

Patterns of Organization   *85*

POLICY ADVOCACY IN ACTION   *86*

Summary of Policy Advocacy   *89*

OPPOSING POLICY PROPOSITIONS   *89*

Establish Strategy   *90*
Examine Definitions   *90*
Refute the Reason for Change   *91*
Refute the Consequences of Change   *92*
Offering Counterproposals   *94*
Patterns of Organization   *94*

POLICY OPPOSITION IN ACTION   *94*

Summary of Policy Opposition   *98*

LEARNING ACTIVITIES   *99*
SUGGESTED SUPPLEMENTARY READINGS   *99*

6

HOW DO I ANALYZE PROPOSITIONS?   *101*

LOCATING THE IMMEDIATE CAUSE   *102*
INVESTIGATING HISTORICAL BACKGROUND   *104*
DEFINING THE KEY TERMS   *107*

Rules of Definition   *107*
Terms Needing Definition   *108*
How to Define Terms   *110*

DETERMINING THE ISSUES   *113*
LEARNING ACTIVITIES   *116*
SUGGESTED SUPPLEMENTARY READINGS   *117*

7

HOW DO I PROVE MY ARGUMENT?   *118*

TYPES OF EVIDENCE   *118*

Evidence of Fact   *119*
Evidence from Opinion   *123*
Summary of Types of Evidence   *124*

TESTS OF EVIDENCE   *125*

Tests of Facts   *125*
Summary of Tests of Factual Evidence   *129*
Tests of Opinion Evidence   *130*
Summary of Tests of Opinion Evidence   *130*
General Tests of Evidence   *131*
Summary of General Tests of Evidence   *133*

THE DISCOVERY OF EVIDENCE   *133*

Books   *134*
Periodicals   *134*
Newspapers   *135*
Government Documents   *135*
lmanacs, Fact Books, and Other Resources   *137*

RECORDING EVIDENCE   *138*
LEARNING ACTIVITIES   *140*
SUGGESTED SUPPLEMENTARY READINGS   *140*

8

HOW DO I REASON WITH MY AUDIENCE?   *143*

ARGUMENT FROM CAUSE   *144*
Summary of Argument from Cause   *148*
ARGUMENT FROM SIGN   *148*
Summary of Argument from Sign   *150*
ARGUMENT FROM GENERALIZATION   *150*
Summary of Argument from Generalization   *152*
ARGUMENT FROM PARALLEL CASE   *152*
Summary of Argument from Parallel Case   *153*
ARGUMENT FROM ANALOGY   *154*
Summary of Argument from Analogy   *155*
ARGUMENT FROM AUTHORITY   *155*
Summary of Argument from Authority *158*
ARGUMENT FROM DEFINITION   *158*
ARGUMENT FROM DILEMMA   *159*
LEARNING ACTIVITIES   *160*
SUGGESTED SUPPLEMENTARY READINGS   *163*

9

WHAT SHOULD I AVOID?   165

FALLACIES IN REASONING   *166*

Hasty Generalization   *166*
Transfer   *167*
Irrelevant Arguments   *168*
Circular Reasoning   *169*
Avoiding the Issue   *169*
Forcing a Dichotomy   *170*
Summary of Fallacies in Reasoning   *170*

FALLACIES OF APPEAL   *171*

Appeal to Ignorance   *171*
Appeal to the People   *172*
Appeals to Emotions   *172*
Appeal to Authority   *173*
Appeal to Tradition   *174*
Appeal to Humor   *175*
Summary of Fallacies of Appeal   *175*

FALLACIES IN LANGUAGE   *176*

Ambiguity and Equivocation   *176*
Emotionally Loaded Language   *177*
Technical Jargon   *178*
Summary of Fallacies of Language   *178*

LEARNING ACTIVITIES   *178*
SUGGESTED SUPPLEMENTARY READINGS   *180*

10

HOW DO I PRESENT MY ARGUMENTS TO AN AUDIENCE?   181

AUDIENCE ANALYSIS   *182*

The General Audience   *182*
The Specific Individuals in Your Audience   *183*

LANGUAGE CHOICE AND STYLE   *184*

Words as Symbols   *184*
The Elements of Style   *185*

BRIEF WRITING *188*
DELIVERY TECHNIQUES *196*

   Use of Voice *196*
   Use of Body *198*
   Use of Visual Aids *199*

BUILDING CREDIBILITY WITH AN AUDIENCE *200*

   External Credibility *200*
   Internal Credibility *201*
   Managing Your Credibility *201*

LEARNING ACTIVITIES *203*
SUGGESTED SUPPLEMENTARY READINGS *204*

APPENDIX 207

DEBATE FORMATS *207*
SPEAKER RESPONSIBILITIES *209*
BURDEN OF CLASH *212*
CROSS-EXAMINATION *212*
FLOW SHEETING *214*
DEBATE JUDGES *215*

REFERENCES 217

INDEX 219

PREFACE

Since the publication of the first edition of *Advocacy and Opposition* in 1986, there has been a renewed interest in argumentation from a pedagogical and theoretical perspective. The realization that critical thinking skills are a necessary part of education at all levels has increased the number of students taking argumentation courses. More colleges and universities have a critical thinking or reasoning skills course as a graduation requirement. A new international journal, *Argumentation,* began publication in 1987, focusing on the theoretical aspects of the subject. Additionally, national and international interest increased the number of seminars and professional meetings devoted to probing both the theory and the teaching of argumentation.

In 1986, our goal was not only to approach argumentation in a way that preserved the essential theory and practice of competitive debate, but to tailor the concepts to fit the needs of the student who is not a member of the debate team. In the second edition we are also committed to offering a practical approach to critical thinking for the beginning student. For instructors who want something more than a traditional approach to policy debating in an argumentation or critical thinking class, *Advocacy and Opposition* offers a theoretical view of the nature of argument in our society, a discussion of ethical principles of arguing as a form of communication, a focus on how arguments are created using the Toulmin model of argument, and end-of-chapter exercises for classroom discussion and argumentation assignments that may be completed as either oral or written projects. For those instructors whose focus is on debating, an Appendix with rules and formats for debate is provided.

WHAT IS NEW IN THIS EDITION?

1. Chapters have been reorganized, moving concepts of the prima facie case and stock issues in value and policy argumentation into the first half of the text. This responds to a problem many have encountered in teaching argumentation, how to get students actively involved in thinking about and analyzing issues early in the semester. The traditional pattern of chapter organization that teaches research early on, equips students to head for the library where they have no idea what to look for, or why to look for it.

2. A new chapter has been added on presentation skills to assist students in turning theory into practice. The first edition taught argumentation theory, but not enough about "how to present" arguments to an audience. This edition remedies that problem.

3. An expanded discussion of how and why one constructs an argumentative brief gives students a better model to follow in turning individual units of argument into a persuasive message. Since so many students enter the course in argumentation with little understanding of how to structure information and ideas, we have devoted more attention to explaining how to organize individual units of argument into chain and cluster arguments and how to combine these into a case.

4. Dated examples have been replaced and real-world "Argument in Action" examples replace the artificial ones in the first edition. Taken from the Senate Hearings on lyrics in rock music and the House of Representatives Hearings on the proposal to compensate American citizens of Japanese ancestry interned during World War II, "Argument in Action" in Chapters 4 and 5 shows students how issues are developed and argued in value and policy debate. The two issues were selected for their interest value and because they can be used to stimulate discussions about fact, value, and policy argumentation; the use and misuse of reasoning techniques and evidence; and the delivery strategies that are part of argumentation as it exists in the real world.

5. The relationship between argumentation and persuasion has been clarified in Chapter 1 and the new Chapter 10 on presenting arguments before an audience. How argument functions as a form of instrumental communication that is the rational element in persuasion and why argumentation is necessarily an audience-centered activity were more implied than discussed in the first edition. The discussion of argumentation as part of persuasion, adapted to a group of listeners or readers, now enables students to understand more easily how critical thinking skills are part of the process.

6. The discussion of researching evidence has been expanded to include information on using the new computerized search techniques. Most college libraries have computerized card catalogs and periodical indexes. To help students learn the benefits of this technology, we have included a discussion of how to find evidence using indexes on CD-ROM.

As you may have inferred from the foregoing six points, we did more than just update the examples in producing this second edition. Chapter 1 defines the nature of argumentation, the uses of argumentation in our society, and the ethical responsibilities of arguers. Chapter 2 examines the concepts of presumption and burden of proof and introduces propositions of fact, value, and policy as the determinant of which side in a controversy has the benefit of presumption and the burden of proof. Proper phrasing of propositions is also discussed. Chapter 3 introduces the student to the concepts of the prima facie case; stock issues in fact, value, and policy; and the Toulmin Model of argument as they relate to issue analysis and issue development in response to the imperatives of presumption and the burden of proof. Chapter 4 discusses how individual units of argument are organized in chains and clusters, and applies this to how advocates of change and their opponents argue propositions of fact and value. Stock issues and argumentation strategy are covered in detail. Chapter 5 focuses on policy propositions and the necessary requirements for developing proposals to change behavior. The advocate's and opponent's roles in policy argumentation are discussed. Emphasis is given to the different systems for approaching policy development and the strategies an opponent may employ in responding. Chapter 6 starts the student down the road to preparing his or her own argumentative case by introducing a four-step process for analyzing any proposition of fact, value, or policy. The student learns to think in terms of why the proposition is important now, how it has been regarded in the past, what the key terms in it mean, and what issues would comprise a prima facie case in support of it. Armed with this knowledge, the student is ready to read Chapter 7 and head for the library. Chapter 7 explains the types of evidence, rules for testing evidence, and how to search for evidence. An expanded discussion of scientific evidence is included. Chapter 8 reviews reasoning patterns and critical thinking; arguments from cause, sign, generalization, parallel case, analogy, authority, definition, and dilemma. Chapter 9 examines breakdowns in the reasoning process by reviewing the common fallacies committed in creating arguments. In addition, this chapter examines fallacies of appeal and language use. Chapter 10 covers techniques used in presenting arguments before an audience. Audience analysis, language use and style, brief preparation, delivery, and managing credibility are discussed. An Appendix summarizes rules and formats in competitive debate, and discusses the duties of the speakers and cross-examination.

We would like to thank John Lyne of the University of Iowa, whose suggestions for improving the first edition have shaped this revision.

We also thank the editors and production staff at Prentice Hall for their assistance. We thank our colleagues who have used the first edition and offered their advice on what we might do to improve upon it. Finally, we thank our students who have openly shared with us their thoughts about what they liked and found frustrating in the first edition. Their input has assisted us in turning this text into what we hope is a better approach to teaching and learning about the process of argumentation.

1

WHAT IS ARGUMENTATION?

The way you feel about "having an argument" may influence your attitude toward this textbook and the course in which it is being used. Having taught argumentation for many years, we never cease to be amazed at the misconceptions that exist about its value. Recently a student asked us to fill out recommendation forms for employment with a certain organization. One category on the form concerned perceptions about whether this person was "argumentative" in nature. As you read this textbook, we hope you will discover being "argumentative" is not necessarily a negative trait, as the recommendation forms from that organization's personnel office suggested.

THE NATURE OF ARGUMENTATION

To discover argumentation, all you have to do is look at the daily attempts to influence your beliefs and behavior. Some efforts will be aimed at your emotions, prejudices, and superstitions, but some will use information and reasoning in an attempt to influence you. Almost every person we encounter, friends, family, teachers, employers, the mass media, advertisers, editorialists, and politicians, offer arguments imbedded in persuasive appeals to encourage us to think as they do or behave as they wish. From the apparently trivial matter of choosing a breakfast cereal to the more vital decision of what career to pursue, we are constantly exposed to the argumentation of others.

Every day of our lives, each of us authors dozens of written and oral messages intended to influence the beliefs or direct the behavior of others. If you have ever asked a friend to lend you five dollars, a teacher to let you turn in a paper a week after it was due, or if you have ever written a letter to the editor, you have probably engaged in argumentation. Some of your appeals may have been aimed at the emotions, prejudices, or superstitions of the persons you were trying to influence, but some probably targeted the more rational sides of their beings. It may not be unreasonable to say that were it not for argumentation, we would not have nearly as much to hear or say, read or write. As a matter of fact, what you have just read is an example of argumentation.

Argumentation is a form of instrumental communication relying on reasoning and proof to influence belief or behavior through the use of spoken or written messages.

Examination of this definition allows us to begin to understand argumentation's purpose, targets, and methods, and its relationship to persuasion. Hart and Burks (1972) suggest that all communication falls into one of two categories: expressive or instrumental. Expressive communication is the ventilation of feelings. The expressive communicator articulates personal feelings and desires, and may not be terribly concerned about the effect of that expression on others. Expressive communication focuses on the "self" of the communicator. By comparison, instrumental communication is designed to influence the beliefs and behaviors of others. The instrumental communicator is very concerned with how those he seeks to influence will respond to his message. Argumentation is a form of instrumental communication because it is focused on the audience and is intended to influence its beliefs, behaviors, or both. Because it is "other-oriented," instrumental communication is the superior approach when the communicator's purpose is to influence belief or behavior.

Anyone who has witnessed or participated in the following sort of dialogue will understand why we claim that instrumental communication, or argumentation, is the superior method of influencing belief or behavior. Consider these two expressive youngsters:

BARTHOLOMEW: Can I play ball with you?
CHADWICK: No!
BARTHOLOMEW: Why?
CHADWICK: Cause.
BARTHOLOMEW: But why?
CHADWICK: Mom! Bartholomew is bugging me. Make him leave me alone!

In many ways, this fictitious dialogue possesses superficial characteristics which might suggest that it is argumentation. Verbal messages are employed in an attempt to promote changes in belief and behavior. But this encounter is not an example of argumentation because its method of communication is predominantly expressive. Bartholomew and Chadwick know in their hearts that they are right, and they do not consider what the "other" might be thinking or why he might be thinking it. Even Chadwick's solicitation of aid from a nominally neutral third party reflects a concern only for "self" and its free expression. The probable result:

MOM: Chadwick, be nice to your little brother. Now, you take him along, and let him play. Do you hear me?

Both youngsters learn something from this experience. Chadwick is probably less likely to take such problems to Mom in the future, since her neutrality has become suspect in his eyes. Bartholomew, however, may develop a strategy which renders even this defense useless: Go straight to Mom whenever the prospect of a ball game arises. Chadwick's only defense rests on his discovery of instrumental communication and his ability to adopt an other-orientation. At that point he discovers argumentation and possibly the winning argument.

CHADWICK: OK, Mom, it's just that the guys I play with are all my age and some of them are bigger than me. I was just worried that Bartholomew might get hurt since we play tackle.

The need of the "self" to be free of Bartholomew is still addressed by this argument which arouses two conflicting beliefs of the "other." First, Mom's concern for her younger son's safety is addressed directly. Second, her desire that her older son not be deprived of socializing experiences with his peer group is imbedded in the subject of the entire conversation. While she may decide that tackle football is too dangerous for both of them, Chadwick's use of instrumental communication gives him a chance to engage her belief in the benefits of socializing and constrain Bartholomew to stay behind.

Argumentation takes place in situations where people disagree, and is characterized by the controversy created by two opposing views. Because arguers want their views to be the ones that prevail, argumentation is always directed to some "other." Typically, we label this other the *audience*. The audience for argumentation consists of one or more people who have the power or ability to assure the future influence of a belief or pattern of behavior the arguer seeks. Sometimes we characterize the audience as a nominally disinterested third party, like Mom in Chadwick's dispute with Bartholomew, who will act as a decision maker after hearing both sides of the argument. The self can also be an audience for argument on occasion. In the process of intrapersonal decision making, we frequently engage in an internal dialogue, listing the pros and cons of accepting a particular belief or following some course of action. Whether the audience is the self or some other person, argumentation provides a framework for helping that audience determine whether changing or maintaining existing belief or behavior is more reasonable.

The concept of reasonableness helps us understand the relationship between argumentation and persuasion. Arguers are also persuaders. Persuasion is an attempt to move an audience to accept or identify with a particular point of view. Like argumentation, persuasion is also instrumental communication. Although we will often call your attention to the persuasiveness of arguments in this textbook, our primary purpose is to introduce you to the principles for effective argumentation, the rational subset of persuasion.

What differentiates argumentation from the larger category of instrumental communication, persuasion, is that persuasion operates on both the emotional and the rational levels in communication. Recall our earlier discussion of your role as both consumer and creator of messages intended to influence belief and behavior. We indicated that these appeals might be directed at emotions, prejudices, superstitions, or reason. Some persuasive messages depend more on eliciting an emotional reaction from the receiver than a logical one. Persuasion includes the study of the emotional properties of messages and how receiver psychology plays a part in determining how influential a message will be. The study of argumentation focuses on how proof and reasoning are used to appeal to the rational side of human nature.

A final characteristic of argumentation is that it is rule-governed communication behavior. When you communicate, you are engaged in rule-governed behavior. One set of rules is the grammar of English. In addition to the rules we learn in acquiring our native tongue, individual communication contexts have their own particular rules, which may be as broadly applicable as those which pertain to public speaking or as narrow as those that govern communication in a particular family. We learn these communication rules through formal instruction or through informally imitating the behavior of those around us. Because argumentation may occur in a variety of communication contexts, the rules for effective argumentation you will learn from this textbook will be appropriate in several contexts beyond the classroom.

THE USEFULNESS OF ARGUMENTATION

In drawing a distinction between argumentation and persuasion, it is not our purpose to suggest that argumentation is the superior form of communication behavior when your goal is to encourage or discourage a change in belief or behavior. We do believe there are good reasons to study and employ methods of argumentation in many everyday situations, because beliefs and behaviors often have serious consequences. For both pragmatic and philosophic reasons, argumentation studies are well worth your time and effort.

First, argumentation is a reliable method for arriving at the probable "truth" of something in dispute. Beliefs and behaviors arrived at through argumentation result from careful examination of facts and expert opinion, not from responses colored by emotion and prejudice, or by habitual predetermined responses caused by triggering stimuli (Ehninger, 1974). Beliefs and behaviors resulting from emotion, prejudice, or triggering stimuli stand the test of time only by serendipity. When you reach a decision through argumentation, you are more likely to feel good about it because it will stand up to your scrutiny and the criticism of others. To test this premise, pretend you are going to buy a new car. Which decision-making process will produce the most satisfaction in the long run—buying a car because the color appeals to you or buying the car with the best track record for safety , mileage, performance, and factory support?

Second, the use of argumentation increases personal flexibility (Ehninger, 1974). When you base belief or behavior on the dictates of an authority figure, tradition, custom, or prejudice, you may be unable to adapt to environmental changes that challenge that belief or behavior. Beliefs and behaviors arrived at through argumentation are less inclined to rigidity. The practitioner of argumentation searches out and develops new patterns of belief and behavior as new situations and new problems arise, rather than relying on traditional patterns. Developing argumentation skills is a means of coping with a future in which new knowledge and new ideas may make old "truths" crumble like the Berlin Wall.

The third pragmatic reason for the use of argumentation is found in the willingness of the listener or reader to change belief or behavior because of the role he plays in the process. When you change as a consequence of an argument you have heard or read, you are acting of your own volition, not because the argument's author has imposed his will upon you (Ehninger, 1974). Because argumentation is a two-way process, a dialogue between you and those whose beliefs or behaviors you wish to influence, much of the resistance that would be present if you attempted to force change upon them is defused.

There are also philosophical reasons for the use of argumentation that supplement the pragmatic reasons. First, communication is generally regarded as a liberal art. When we discuss the liberal arts, we are typically concerned with those disciplines that civilize and humanize us. Argumentation is a civilizing, humanizing process, since its practitioners must respect both their own rationality and that of their reader or listener. Argumentation treats people as rational beings rather than objects, incapable of thought.

A second philosophical justification for the use of argumentation is apparent when we examine the use of persuasion in our society. Listen to network news or read a national news magazine. It will not take long to find references to "mere rhetoric," "presidential rhetoric," or "a public relations ploy." What the media are really criticizing is not rhetoric or persuasion but how they are practiced. We are suspicious of persuaders who seek knee-jerk responses based on emotions, prejudices, or superstitions. Argumentation overcomes one of the objections to contemporary persuasion by treating its consumer as a rational person. The arguer does not manipulate the receiver, but offers her the opportunity to participate in the process by respecting her ability to think.

For the humanizing influences of argumentation to occur, its practitioners must accept substantial personal risk. Argumentation occurs in response to controversy. The potential arguer must make a choice: to retreat from controversy by taking refuge behind his established beliefs, or to confront the controversy and expose his beliefs to challenges that might result in their disconfirmation and alteration (Eisenberg & Ilardo, 1980). Realizing the risks involved, some decide that the payoffs from successful argumentation and the probability of achieving success are insufficient to warrant taking the risk.

One of the ways in which the individual grows is through confronting new ideas and change. As is true of any encounter in which a portion of the self is disclosed, argumentation carries risks that, if confronted, can result in substantial personal growth. Philosopher Henry Johnstone, Jr. (1965) sees argumentation, and its attendant risks, as an essential part of the development of a healthy, fully functioning self. For Johnstone, there is self only when there is risk, and the risk found in argumentation "is a defining feature of the human situation" (p. 17). Thus, accepting the risk of engaging in argumentation is not only a means of making our ideas acceptable to others and thereby achieving interpersonal goals, but it is also a vehicle for intrapersonal growth, testing our ideas so that we may reject those we discover to be unsound or irrelevant.

LIMITATIONS ON THE USE OF ARGUMENTATION

It is possible to find negative examples of argument, such as the demagoguery of a Hitler. Argumentation does have limitations, since it is practiced by fallible human beings whose motives may not always be above reproach. To achieve its fullest humanizing potential, argumentation depends on the ethics of its practitioners. An unsound argument or one based on shallow or inadequate proof can, through skillful oral and written presentation, be made to appear valid. Thus, as with other means of influencing belief or behavior, argumentation can be subject to abuse.

Ever since the first textbooks on argumentation and persuasion were written, scholars have been concerned with the use of argumentation to promote the selfish ambitions of the individual rather than the good of the group or society. Plato, concerned with the practice of rhetoric in ancient Athens, urged his students to practice *dialectic*, the use of questions and answers to arrive at truth, instead of argumentation and persuasion. Plato felt that arguments were mere flattery in the guise of rational thought. Aristotle, influenced by Plato, also warned students that appeals based solely on emotions were unethical. Two thousand years later, the problem remains. Automobiles are sold on the basis of sex appeal, household cleansers are marketed on the basis of social disapproval, and politicians campaign on the basis of form rather than substance.

Since we have listed the virtues of argumentation as a means of influence, you may wonder why the manufacturers of automobiles and household cleansers and the campaign managers of political candidates do not insist on carefully reasoned arguments to gain the public's acceptance. The second limitation of argumentation explains why. The process of argumentation is time-consuming. In subsequent chapters, you will learn about the process of phrasing propositions, defining terms, conducting research, and constructing arguments. Influencing belief or behavior through rational processes takes time. Although the ethics of resorting to emotion to transmit the message may be questionable, it can be achieved in a thirty-second spot or in a single picture. After all, would you want your favorite TV program interrupted for a half hour while someone proves why "ring around the collar" will make you a pariah?

Frustration over the second limitation of argumentation can cause its practitioners to engage in ethically questionable behavior. The time necessary to marshal sufficient evidence to support a position and ensure its logical consistency can make the siren song of stimuli that trigger an emotional response all the more alluring. In subsequent chapters dealing with the evidence and reasoning on which argumentation is based, we will provide a set of minimal standards, rules for sufficiency. As a creator of arguments, you should apply these standards rigorously in evaluating your own work. As a consumer of argumentation, you should be equally rigorous in using them. Test what you hear and read to ensure it is not emotive discourse masquerading as argumentation.

The potential abuses of argumentation notwithstanding, we need the ability to argue in order to communicate successfully. We have poked fun at commercials that seem to misuse persuasion and argumentation because these are familiar examples. Realize that these same techniques, which seem creative or merely annoying in commercials, create serious problems when they are used to "sell" a point of view on public-policy issues such as nuclear weapons, the environment, or education.

APPLICATIONS OF ARGUMENTATION

The most common applications of argumentation are found in situations where the individual discovers goals to be achieved or tasks to be completed that he alone is incapable of accomplishing. To implement new programs or change existing ones, to gain support for developments in thinking and theory building, to create new laws or alter existing legislation, an individual with an idea is dependent on the support of others. In seeking this support, he must communicate not only his goal but the evidence and good reasons that make it worthy of the support of others. To do this, people commonly engage in argumentation. Real-world examples demonstrate this and reinforce our earlier claim that argumentation is an instrumental rather than an expressive form of communication.

The first example, which affects a large number of Americans each year, is found in the criminal justice system. While both prosecuting and defense attorneys have goals, albeit conflicting ones, concerning the conviction or acquittal of the defendant, they are incapable of achieving these goals without the assent of a nominally disinterested third party, the jury. The disinterest of the jury may be more than nominal, since *voir dire* is used to weed out potential jurors who have already formed an opinion or who might be predisposed to make a decision based on some triggering stimulus, such as the race or age of the defendant, rather than the facts of the case. Because the system rests on societal values concerning the right to a fair trial, the presumption of innocence until guilt is proven, and the preferability of freeing a possibly guilty individual to convicting an innocent one, the defense is given certain advantages, not the least of which is *pretrial discovery*.

Pretrial discovery allows the defense to request to see the evidence on which the prosecution's case rests. After inspecting the basis, in evidence and in reasoning, for the case against her client, the defense lawyer may choose among alternative defenses, instrumentally determining which best serves her client's interests. The concepts discussed in the next chapter—presumption and burden of proof—are applied in criminal and civil proceedings every day. Although you may have no intention of becoming a lawyer, serving on a jury, being a criminal, or a victim, the second example represents the kind of argumentation to which we are regularly exposed and may even engage in ourselves.

Political campaigns, especially presidential campaigns, afford us an opportunity to observe political argumentation practices. In a larger sense, political campaigns are persuasive because they deal with the images of candidates in addition to the issues. However, one aspect of political campaigning emphasizes argumentation—candidate debates. Debates allow voters to hear the candidates' stand on important issues of the day. The tradition of political debating began with the series of debates between Abraham Lincoln and Stephen Douglas in the 1858 race for the Illinois Senate seat. In those debates, a single issue, slavery, dominated argumentation. Recently debates between presidential candidates have become common.

In 1960, Richard M. Nixon and John F. Kennedy met in the first televised debates between presidential candidates. In 1976, Gerald Ford and Jimmy Carter participated in a series of televised debates; the 1980 presidential campaign offered debates between Ronald Reagan and John Anderson, while Anderson's independent candidacy was still viable, and later a Carter-Reagan debate. The 1984 presidential campaign featured extensive televised debating among the Democratic contenders for the nomination, debates between Ronald Reagan and Walter Mondale, and a debate between the vice-presidential candidates. These traditions were carried forward into the 1988 contest between George Bush and Michael Dukakis.

Presidential debates have emphasized broad consideration of both domestic and foreign policy issues. America's role overseas, the use of military force, and the support of repressive regimes friendly to the United States, have been important foreign policy issues in these debates. Economic and industrial policy, defense spending, and social issues such as abortion and the rights of women and minorities have been debated in election years.

Argumentation is also employed in society's attempt to deal with controversies such as the one between the scientific explanation that life on earth evolved and the view that life appeared as an act of divine creation. Issues such as this, about which people disagree, abound in our society and we have the opportunity to observe or participate in argumentation about a variety of subjects. While we do not deny that a fair amount of expressive communication surrounds such controversies, to achieve change, instrumental argumentation is an effective means of communication which plays an important part in the persuasive process.

THE HISTORICAL DEVELOPMENT OF ARGUMENTATION

In this text we emphasize a model of argument developed by the English logician Stephen Toulmin. It is offered primarily as a means of organizing ideas in a form that listeners or readers will find most appropriate. As evidenced by our references to Plato and Aristotle, the study of argumentation has an extensive historical foundation. To gain a better understanding of contemporary argumentation theory and its evolution, it is worthwhile to review some of the earliest theories of argumentation and the societal forces that precipitated them.

The formal study of argumentation began in ancient Greece. Citizenship in the democracy of Athens required communication skills. Each male freeborn citizen might be called upon to serve the state in the deliberative processes of the assembly or the judgmental processes of the courts. He might also find himself acting as prosecutor or defense attorney, since the Greek judicial system required each party to the action to represent himself. The Greeks also engaged in public speaking on ceremonial occasions.

The study of communication skills necessary to fulfill these requirements— *rhetoric*—was an important part of formal elementary education. The foundations of argumentation, as studied today, were laid in those ancient schools. Rhetoric was conceived as a humane discipline, grounded in choice, that was primarily designed to persuade or change the listener. The communicator's purpose was to influence choice by developing meaningful probabilities, or arguments, in support of a claim being contested. Emphasis was placed on the claims that occurred in the courts, since so much speaking involved arguing one's own case.

One of the greatest of the Greek rhetoricians, Aristotle, viewed the practice of argumentation as central to human nature, "for to a certain extent all men attempt to discuss statements and to maintain them, to defend themselves, and to attack others" (Roberts, trans., 1954, p. 19). Aristotle had defined rhetoric as the ability to find, in a given situation, all the means of persuading an audience to believe a proposition. This involved more than just building workable arguments. The responsibility of the communicator was to investigate everything his audience might be moved by—their emotions, their political beliefs, and those sources of information which they respected most. The responsible communicator would choose the most ethical, the most probably true, of all of these available means of persuasion.

In their refinement of Greek rhetoric, Roman authors identified four kinds of questions crucial to legal disputes: (1) questions of fact—did the accused commit a crime? (2) questions of definition—if the accusation is theft, might not the act have been borrowing? (3) questions of justification—if the act were theft, did the accused steal out of dire need? (4) questions of procedure—was the charge properly made (Fisher & Sayles, 1966). The nature of these legal controversies, and the need for judges to determine which party to the dispute more nearly represented the "truth," was a driving force behind the development of rhetoric in Greece and Rome. While rhetoric was developed in the legal context, its study produced workable theories of argumentation and persuasion applicable to controversies in other contexts as well.

Theories of communication, then as now, included the content of the message, its context, and its potential consequences. In studying argumentation, we are concerned with that part of rhetorical theory relating to message content, its logic, form, and structure. From the body of classical writings on communication, the following identifying characteristics of argumentation emerge: (1) It involves offering a series of logically related statements or arguments; (2) These arguments involve the use of reasoning in writing and speaking; (3) Reasoning is used in arguments to induce belief;

(4) Arguments constitute a means of persuasion; and (5) For arguments to have social utility, their authors must fulfill certain ethical responsibilities.

ETHICAL STANDARDS FOR ARGUMENTATION

Because the audience for argumenation often lacks the time or resources to verify every statement made, the creators of arguments bear a heavy ethical burden, since that which is made to seem most probable or believable is that which is most likely to gain acceptance. Like other forms of communication, argumentation can be used to advance the cause of good or evil. Communication is a social act that implies moral obligations to one's audience (Nilsen, 1974), whether that audience is the whole of society or a single individual. Our audience often judges our communication as good or bad on the basis of how well we meet those moral obligations. This is the essence of speaker credibility.

Like other forms of communication, argumentation is a matter of choosing what to say. In preparing argumentative cases, you will research a topic, decide which claims and proofs to offer, and decide how to arrange your materials for the most impact. Whether your end product is deemed ethical or unethical will ultimately be determined by your audience. Because we live in a society that holds freedom of thought and speech as a cardinal value, ethical communication protects the rights of free speech while at the same time respecting the rights of audiences.

Stanley G. Rives (1964) suggests that those who engage in argumentation in a democratic society have three ethical obligations: "(1) the responsibility to research the proposition throughly to know truth, (2) the responsibility to dedicate his effort to the common good, and (3) the responsibility to be rational" (p. 84). To these we add a fourth obligation: the responsibility to observe the rules of free speech in a democratic society.

The Research Responsibility

An ethical arguer will thoroughly research the proposition to discover, insofar as possible, what is probably true about the subject. Although no one expects you to learn everything about a given subject, ethical argumentation requires you to be well informed. Your responsibility is to prepare your arguments as thoroughly as you can. This means knowing the subject not only from your viewpoint but from opposing viewpoints as well. It means using the resources available to you to your best advantage.

The research responsibility also requires you to use facts and the opinions of others honestly. Remember that when you think something through, something you have witnessed, read, or heard, you filter the information through your cognitive maps of experience. You decide how you will interpret reality. In deciding, you have the ability to distort or confuse the facts. Your ethical obligation is to avoid consciously distorting information to mislead your audience.

What is wrong with distortion, especially if it is done in pursuit of a worthy goal? Simply this, you violate the trust of your audience and create the possibility of not being considered a credible source in the future. During the 1960s and 1970s, the arguments used by government officials to justify the Vietnam War and the Watergate coverup created a crisis of belief that caused many Americans to question the veracity of any government official on any subject.

Beyond being honest in reporting facts and opinions, you should never fabricate research. Making up information is deceptive and unethical. With information available on almost any subject, a diligent exploration of printed resources will yield what you need to prove your arguments.

Realize that probable truth may exist on both sides of a controversy. Issues in human affairs are seldom one-sided. Indeed, we define something as controversial when at least two conflicting points of view exist. Just because information does not jibe with your point of view does not mean that such information is a "lie."

The Common-Good Responsibility

An ethical arguer has as her objective the welfare of the society. Many issues argued involve resolving which policy is best, which course of action should be taken. The responsible arguer always creates argumentative positions that stress the benefits of a course of action to society, attempting to determine the course of action that best serves the common good. In controversies over values, argumentation focuses on which value or value system ought to prevail for the common good.

The responsibility to seek the common good is a tricky ethical proposition. What appears good to one individual may appear evil to another. The issue of abortion on demand illustrates the problem. For some, the right to an abortion is an essential right of choice, consistent with the societal value of freedom. For others, abortion constitutes murder of the unborn, a violation of the rights of the fetus. Which set of rights is preeminent? The answer is ultimately up to the individual based on his or her values. This issue illustrates the importance of thorough research because determining the common good is not always an easy task. While research may not provide answers in every instance of conflicting values, it will at least help you better understand the values or policies in conflict.

Ethical behavior demonstrates one's character, and the tradition in communication is that a prerequisite of good character is placing the audience's welfare above your own interests. Therefore, ethical argumentation attempts to satisfy acknowledged public wants and needs. You rarely hear a presidential candidate state, "Vote for me because I want to be president." Rather, the candidate asks for votes on the basis that he best represents the interests of the electorate.

One aspect of ethical argumentation that promotes the common good is that we live in a society of laws and are obliged to respect these laws. Changing a law is often the motivation for debate and discussion and the responsible arguer advocates changing laws rather than breaking them. Although it is possible to point to exceptional cases, such as the civil rights protests of the 1960s in which "morally repugnant" segregation laws were violated for the purpose of drawing attention to their unjustness, generally the responsible argumentative position is to advocate change. You may, for example, believe that laws against the possession and use of marijuana, laws requiring the wearing of safety equipment, or laws regulating the purchase and consumption of alcoholic beverages are unjust, but to encourage violating them is to advocate anarchy. A responsible arguer makes a case by demonstrating a law's injustice, rather than deprecating the concept of the rule of law in society.

The Reasoning Responsibility

An ethical arguer uses sound reasoning in the form of logically adequate arguments supported by facts and expert opinions. Good or sound reasons are the premiere rule of argumentation and rhetoric according to modern theorists (Golden, Berquist, & Coleman, 1989). To engage in communication is to use and to respect its rules. When translated into practice, this requires the arguer to assume responsibility regarding the form her message takes. The rules of argumentation will be discussed in subsequent chapters on research practices, and constructing arguments, testing their quality, and organizing them into a case. While you do not need to be a slave to rules, ethical argumentation requires that you know and use them to ensure that you properly address your audience's rationality.

The Social Code Responsibility

An ethical advocate respects the rights of other arguers and the audience in order to preserve freedom of speech in a democratic society. Freedom of speech means everyone is entitled to a point of view, even if it is different from your own. Those with opposing viewpoints have an equal right to be heard and deserve the courtesy you expect for yourself. This is a form of the Golden Rule appropriate to communication. Remember, sometime you may be the one who has the unpopular view and your right to be heard will be jeopardized if only majority opinions are allowed free expression.

One social code of argumentation is that while criticism and refutation are important parts of the process, they should be directed toward the arguer's reasoning and proof, not his person. Character assassination is not good argumentation because it diverts attention from the issues and does nothing to further the rationality of your position. Point out the misinterpretations or mistakes in the other person's position but do not accuse him of little intelligence for having offered them.

Earlier we said that communication was rule-governed behavior. In addition to rules telling us about word order, idea organization, and rational thinking, there are rules of social custom that govern acts of communication. Discover these for the context in which you are arguing and avoid violating them. Because a word is in your vocabulary does not mean its use is appropriate in every communication context. Social customs include dressing appropriately and avoiding slang expressions and poor jokes.

A social code that is becoming increasingly important in a number of different communication contexts is avoiding language that discriminates on the basis of age, sex, race, ethnic origin, or personal characteristics. Because social customs vary greatly, being ethical means being flexible and determining what conduct is appropriate before a given audience. Remember, you will be judged on the basis of how well you operate within the social customs of the group you are addressing.

Many different standards of ethical behavior may be in operation at one time. Rules of law, religious codes of conduct, situational ethics, and professional codes of behavior can determine what is appropriate in any given situation. Standards of ethics should not be taken as absolutes. They seldom fit every instance of behavior, especially when you are considering what would be the greater good. What we have suggested are some general standards that will serve you well in practicing argumentation.

When we engage in argumentation to influence the belief or behavior of another, we usually find ourselves demonstrating what is possible or probable, rather than what is absolutely true in all situations (Cowan, 1964). In defining argumentation as a form of instrumental communication, we view the process as an audience-centered approach to the resolution of controversy. The goal of the practitioner of argumentation is to gain an audience's assent regarding the issue under consideration. Argumentation is not an end in itself but a means to the end that results when consensus is achieved.

LEARNING ACTIVITIES

1. Discuss the advantages and disadvantages of using argumentation as a means of influencing the belief and behavior of others. How will the advantages of argumentation improve your ability to communicate your views in a controversy? How will you overcome the limitations of argumentation?

2. We have used commercials to illustrate the use of emotional responses and to discuss some of the differences between communication that is expressive and communication that is instrumental. To study these differences, find examples of advertisements in magazines or newspapers that seek an emotional response from the reader. For each example indicate the emotional response sought. Do any of these examples also appeal to the rationality of the audience?

3. Find an example of argumentation that you perceive to be effective and respond to the following questions:
   A. Why is this an example of argumentation? How is it instrumental?
   B. What evidence do you have that the author of the argument is fulfilling the ethical responsibilities of arguing?

4. Think about your most strongly held opinions. Upon what are these based? Examine the sources of these beliefs for evidence of reasoning, emotions, prejudices, tradition, or authority figures.

5. Develop a code of ethical standards for your argumentation class. In particular, the class should determine what social codes will be appropriate. What will you consider to be ethical and unethical behaviors?

SUGGESTED SUPPLEMENTARY READINGS

Anderson, J. M., & Dovre P. J. (Eds.), (1968). *Readings in Argumentation*. Boston: Allyn & Bacon.
This collection of essays offers views on argumentation ranging from the classical to the contemporary. We recommend the sections on the ethics of controversy and argumentation in society, and Sidney Hook's essay on the ground rules for controversy in a democracy, which may be used to formulate a code of ethics for the argumentation class.

Martel, M. (1983). *Political Campaign Debates*. New York: Longman.
Argumentation as practiced in presidential debates is this book's focus, and it provides a thorough treatment of the goals and strategies used in them. The author analyzes the 1980 Reagan-Carter debate and offers practical suggestions for candidate debates on political issues.

Nilsen, T. R. (1974). *Ethics of Speech Communication* (2nd Ed.). Indianapolis: Bobbs-Merrill.
As the title suggests, the nature of ethics and the requirements of ethical communication are examined in depth. Particular emphasis is given to the speaker's obligation to offer the audience the opportunity to make an informed choice. This is an excellent work on ethics and persuasion.

Rives, S. G. (1964). Ethical Argumentation. *Journal of the American Forensic Association, 1*, 79-85.
Rives describes the relationship between ethics and argumentation and focuses on the ethical responsibilities of arguers in terms of communication behaviors that regulate argumentation. He takes the perspective that an ideal democratic society would obligate communicators to operationalize three value standards: truth, human welfare, and rationality. These standards are explained in the context of academic argumentation.

2

WHAT DO I NEED TO KNOW BEFORE I CAN BEGIN TO ARGUE?

There are three commonly observed conventions of argumentation that are useful in determining your responsibilities concerning proof and reasoning when you engage in argumentation. In both real-world and academic argumentation, those who advocate change and those who oppose it assume roles that assign certain responsibilities to each of them at the outset of the dispute. We will use the term **advocate** in argumentation to refer to the person who communicates to encourage a change in the belief or behavior of others. The term **opponent** identifies the person who acts to discourage the change supported by the advocate. This person plays the role of spokesperson for the existing beliefs and behaviors of the audience targeted for change by the advocate. Using sports as an analogy, the advocate plays offense, the opponent plays defense. The conventions of presumption, burden of proof, and prima facie case development identify the playing field. We will discuss the first two of these in this chapter, and the third in the chapter that follows.

PRESUMPTION

All argumentation takes place over a piece of figurative ground occupied by existing belief, policy, or institutions. This figurative ground represents the way things are at present. **Presumption** is the term that specifies who occupies this ground at the beginning of the controversy. Historically, the concept of presumption has reflected one of two viewpoints: artificial or natural. The concept of *artificial* presumption comes from the legal system. In the American legal system, every defendant is presumed innocent until the probability of his guilt can be demonstrated by the state, in the case of criminal law, or by the plaintiff in the case of civil law. This presumption of innocence is termed artificial because it is the result of argumentative ground having been assigned arbitrarily to one side in the dispute because of a societally accepted belief. The French system of justice, for example, proceeds from the opposite assumption: The accused is guilty until he proves the probability of his innocence.

Natural presumption derives from the observation of the natural order in the world around us. When an advocate challenges a belief or behavior that is the consequence of the existence of some institution, practice, custom, value, or interpretation of reality, presumption automatically rests with the belief or behavior being challenged simply because it currently exists. Our understanding of natural presumption is drawn from the work of Anglican Archbishop Richard Whately (1828/1963). In discussing presumption, he used the analogy of a company of soldiers inside a fortress. Change would require these troops to march forth to meet the enemy; presumption, would suggest that they remain secure within their fortress rather than venturing out onto an unknown battlefield. Since natural presumption reflects the way things are in the world around us, the natural order of things suggests that troops do not normally abandon a secure position in favor of an open field. They leave it up to the opposing force to attack their fortified position.

Pragmatically, presumption can serve as a decision rule for determining which viewpoint remains acceptable if the advocate for change fails to win the argument. Whately was particularly concerned that those who argue realize what presumption means in preparing an argumentative case. He urged that they begin by knowing where presumption lies and that in their arguments they point out whose is the burden of proving their argumentative position.

The importance of determining where presumption lies is emphasized when we consider that natural presumption resides in whatever point of view the audience presently holds. In addition to existing institutions, Whatley also identified that for which the audience holds "deference" as a source of presumption. The persons, practices, ideas, or sources of information the audience accepts can be regarded as presumptively occupying the figurative ground. A contemporary example illustrates how presumption may change depending upon the audience.

Suppose you are speaking in favor of abortion before two audiences, one composed of members of a right-to-life group and the other composed of members of the National Organization for Women (NOW)—groups holding opposing views on the subject. The right-to-life supporters will not automatically grant that the Supreme Court decision allowing abortion, *Roe* v. *Wade*, should stand until good and sufficient reasons come along to change it. They believe that good and sufficient reasons already exist. If you supported abortion, you would have to make a case for its continued existence, because natural presumption for this audience rests with those who oppose existing practice. Before the NOW audience, the situation is reversed. Since this group favors freedom of choice in the matter of abortions, natural presumption suggests it will acknowledge existing practice as acceptable until good and sufficient reasons to change it are provided.

These two audiences firmly hold diametrically opposed positions on the abortion issue and illustrate how certain aspects of natural presumption can shift given the audience. Not all audience beliefs will be as firmly held, however. The strength of any natural presumption will vary from strong to weak depending upon the degree of importance the audience attaches to the subject. You might address these same two groups on a different topic, such as Social Security benefits, and find they hold similar feelings about the existing institution of Social Security, or that if they hold different feelings they hold them less passionately.

Realizing this audience-centered aspect of presumption can be very useful in practical applications of instrumental communication. Presumption is a communication convention with implications for audience analysis. Determining an audience's beliefs allows you to survey the figurative ground over which argumentation will occur and decide what your responsibilities as an arguer will include (Matlon, 1978 and Sproule, 1976). Sproule suggests a series of questions to ask in determining natural presumption:

> The arguer is advised to ask such questions as: (1) To what groups do members of the audience belong? (2) To what sources of information (persons, books, groups) do audience members accord deference? (3) What is the popular and unpopular opinion on a particular subject? (4) What information on a subject might hold the advantage of novelty? Such queries would assist the advocate in selecting arguments and evidence best fitted to persuading persons on a given subject. (p. 128)

In addition to the view that presumption favors existing institutions and the view that presumption is found in audience attitudes, there is the view that presumption is a decision rule for determining who "wins" the argument. Usually applied in academic argumentation, the proposition for argumentation is a hypothesis to be tested by the cases for and against its acceptance (Brydon, 1983; Patterson & Zarefsky, 1983; Vasilius, 1980; Zarefsky, 1972). The testing of the hypothesis occurs as advocate and opponent argue back and forth, with an evaluation made on the strength of their arguments, the quality of their proof, and the soundness of their reasoning. Hypothesis testing is a form of artificial presumption because academic argumentation usually awards presumption to the opponent and rests on the assumption that he or she who asserts a proposition must prove it.

We may, then, view presumption from three different perspectives:

1. Presumption identifies existing beliefs, policies, practices, or institutions.
2. Presumption is determined by prevailing beliefs of the audience.
3. Presumption is a decision rule that determines what the advocate must prove in testing the proposition as a hypothesis.

Which version of presumption should you use in preparing to argue? Decide by examining the context in which argumentation will take place. In interpersonal communication and certain public speaking contexts, analyzing your audience may be the best means of determining presumption. In a context where it is obvious that there seems to be universal agreement about what beliefs, policies, practices, or institutions exist, you may immediately recognize who or what occupies the figurative ground. In an academic setting, using presumption in the form of a decision rule may be more appropriate. Whichever version of presumption you have decided best fits your communication context, you will use the convention of presumption to identify the ground over which argumentation will take place.

Presumption grants initial possession of the figurative ground to the person fulfilling the role of opponent. The opponent represents an existing belief, policy, or institution and gains a logical advantage. We assume that what exists should be maintained unless good reasons exist to change it. Presumption simply describes what exists without making any kind of judgment about its worth or effectiveness. Consider the following description:

> The existing curriculum at Northern State University involves courses which are mostly worth four credit hours, although a few one-, two-, and three-credit courses exist. Student schedules and faculty teaching loads are designed around the four-credit-hours-per-course system. Some faculty and students would like to have the system converted to a three-credit standard.

In this case, presumption states that a system of four-credit courses exists and functions at Northern State University. Presumption does not suggest this is necessarily good for learning or teaching, just that it is present. Controversy over the credit-hour system would revolve around the efforts of advocates to present a series of good reasons for changing the system and the efforts of opponents who, using the logical advantage of presumption, might argue the that present four-credit system exists and functions and may be defended on the basis of its functioning.

In argumentation the importance of the convention of presumption lies in the responsibility it places upon the advocate. Since the advocate does not have the benefit of presumption, which favors no change, he must show good and sufficient reasons why we can no longer rely on those beliefs or behaviors that are afforded presumption because they presently exist. We may summarize presumption in the following principles:

1. The term presumption describes a situation that currently exists and points out a prevailing order, that the opponent presently occupies the figurative ground over which the argument will be contested.
2. Presumption only describes. It does not judge the value or lack of value of the existing beliefs, practices, policies, or institutions presently occupying the ground.

With these principles in mind, we can move to the second convention of argumentation, which logically derives from presumption.

BURDEN OF PROOF

Presumption describes the preoccupation of ground in argumentation by the opponent; the **burden of proof** is the obligation of the advocate to contest the ground by offering arguments that are logically sufficient to challenge presumption. The advocate of change has the responsibility of proving his position. To understand fully what the burden of proof involves, begin by recalling that presumption describes what exists without passing judgment on it.

The advocate, in fulfilling the burden of proof, both passes judgment on and criticizes present belief or behavior and recommends a new belief or behavior. He begins by specifying or naming what it is that should not continue—the existing belief or behavior awarded preoccupation of the ground by presumption. To fulfill the obligation of burden of proof, the advocate must demonstrate why whatever presently occupies the disputed figurative ground should not continue to do so. The content and scope of the burden of proof is specified by the statement of the proposition argued.

The burden of proof may be thought of as the obligation of the complaining party in a dispute. In civil law, this obligation would be identified with the responsibility of the plaintiff to proceed first and make a case against the defendant, proving his complaint by a preponderance of evidence. If you were dissatisfied with an automobile you had purchased and decided to sue the dealership, as the plaintiff you would have to demonstrate through the introduction of evidence and testimony that you had been harmed or damaged in some way as a result of the dealer's actions. In criminal law, the state acts as advocate and must prove beyond reasonable doubt that the accused is guilty of the crime. This constitutes the state's burden of proof.

In a controversy, the burden of proof always falls upon the party who would lose if the complaint were rejected or if a settlement did not occur. In the case of your suing the auto dealer, as the person bringing the complaint you would lose if you could not demonstrate that you had been harmed or if you could not prove the harm was a consequence of the dealer's actions. In the example of criminal law, the presumption of innocence means that if the prosecution was unable to demonstrate the guilt of the accused at a sufficiently high level of probability, the state's case would be lost.

In some real-world applications, the requirements for the burden of proof may not always be as clear as they appear in legal argumentation. This is why audience analysis to determine presumption can be a good idea. It will help you discover exactly what your audience expects you to prove. If you were a student advocate addressing a Northern State University policy-making body made up of faculty and administrators, you might determine that their attitudes favored maintaining the four-credit-hour standard because the faculty would be expected to undertake an additional course preparation and demand a salary increase for the extra work load. You would have to show that the greater good to students, obtained from changing to a three-credit-hour standard, would justify the salary increase or the increased faculty work load.

Sometimes you have to make an educated guess regarding how much proof is sufficient to fulfill your burden to support change. An audience who already supports the change will require a simple affirmation of its beliefs, and those who oppose the change become the ones who must provide good reasons to prevent it. An uncommitted audience may be open to the change but may require substantial reasoning and information to see that change is a good idea. An unbelieving audience may resist the change no matter what proof is presented, but may sometimes be reached by your demonstrating that there are areas upon which agreement can be achieved. The latter is a common practice in labor-management negotiations and diplomatic relations. How many arguments are necessary and how much proof must support them depend upon an audience's expectations and degree of commitment.

In academic argumentation, the burden of proof is the logical opposite of presumption. The advocate has the responsibility of proving that the change being proposed is supported by good reasons. The opponent has the advantage of relying on existing belief or practice that will continue in the event the advocate fails to make a good case for change. We may summarize the burden of proof in the following principles:

1. The advocate has the responsibility to prove the argument. This is the burden of proof.
2. In fulfilling the burden of proof, present beliefs and behaviors described by presumption are judged and evaluated based on the available evidence, and an alternative pattern of thought or action is proposed.

How do you know when you have fulfilled this burden of proof? The third convention of argumentation provides the answer. But before moving on to consider it, let us conclude this chapter by discussing the place of propositions in argumentation. If the concepts of presumption and burden of proof help us begin to understand the respective roles of the advocate and opponent as they contest each other's right to possess a figurative piece of ground, the limits of that ground are specified by a proposition.

THE NATURE OF PROPOSITIONS

The **proposition** is a statement that identifies the argumentative ground and points to a change in belief or behavior. Stating the proposition identifies the limits of the topic of argument, places the burden of proof with the advocate, and gives presumption to the opponent. Since controversies commonly arise over questions of "What happened?" "What is?" "What judgment shall I make in this situation?" or "What is the best course of action to follow?" the limits of controversy must be identified so the advocate and the opponent know the bounds of the argumentative ground. The proposition serves as the starting point for argument, setting the arguers on a particular path, and restricting them to it (Sproule, 1980).

The proposition defines the locus of disagreement and whether that disagreement is over some proposed change in belief or behavior. To argue effectively, in ways that will offer sound reasons to your audience, you must state the controversy in a way that readily identifies what the argument is about. By identifying the locus of disagreement in the form of a proposition, you will be able to fulfill three objectives in beginning and successfully pursuing argumentation.

Selecting Terms for Definition

The first objective is that arguers define the terms that describe the argumentative ground. By phrasing the locus of disagreement in the form of a proposition, important words or phrases that may need definition are made more obvious to both the arguers and their audience. One question frequently arises: What do the advocate and opponent mean when they use particular words or phrases? The proposition provides a semantic framework for argument and allows the advocate and opponent to offer interpretations of the important words and phrases contained in it.

For example, let's examine a possible proposition for argumentation: The federal government should significantly strengthen the regulation of mass media in the United States. This is a proposition for what you will soon learn is called policy argumentation, but the same objective also applies to propositions for what is termed factual and value argumentation. In order for the advocate to fulfill the burden of proof, he must identify and define the terms in the proposition that the rational reader or listener must understand in order to be able to realize what sort of change he seeks. In the example, three key phrases establish the figurative ground of the argument: (1) federal government, (2) significantly strengthen the regulation of, and (3) mass media. Only by determining the meaning of these terms can the advocate determine what the proposition means and what his burden of proof includes. Specific details concerning how to identify terms requiring definition and go about defining them will be discussed in Chapter 6.

Although the opponent does not begin the process of definition, she is not obligated, in all instances, to accept the definitions provided by the advocate in his initial presentation. In some instances, an early step in the argumentative process for an opponent involves arguing about the definition of specific terms in the proposition. Hence, the proposition is an important first step in clarifying the boundaries of argumentative ground.

The advocate for our proposition concerning federal regulation of mass media, for example, might choose to define one key phrase in this way: Mass media mean films and video cassettes that depict explicit sexual acts between children under the age of twelve and adults of the opposite or same sex. The opponent may have the same uneasy feeling you just had, since she has now been cast in the role of defender of the right of pedophiles to obtain child pornography. Any artificial presumption deriving from her role as opponent is stripped away or even reversed by this definition of mass media, since it is difficult to conceive of many rational people accepting the notion that if child pornography exists, it should continue to exist in the future unless good reasons are provided to show otherwise.

Our sample proposition is one for academic argumentation, about which more will be said shortly. In this instance, we see why an opponent might contest a definition, since failure to do so would place her at an extreme disadvantage. The opponent might suggest child pornography is not included in the argumentative ground, since it does not meet commonly accepted standards of what we define as mass media. Such an argument over the way a term has been defined would ask the audience to make a decision based on determining who has the most reasonable definition of key terms in the proposition. There is no established list of rules for making such a decision, but the practices for defining terms described in Chapter 6 offer many usable rules for defining terms. One of these practices that would be appropriate in making a decision about the present example is: Common understanding of a term by most members of a society can be used to determine its definitions.

Specifying Direction of Change

The second objective in beginning argumentation, fulfilled by having a proposition, is that it identifies the alteration of belief or behavior sought by the advocate and resisted by the opponent. A proposition must specify the action to be taken or the belief to be altered. By identifying the change sought, the proposition identifies both the advocate's burden of proof and the presumption of the opponent's position against the change.

Taking our sample proposition once again, let us assume that the advocate has offered the following definitions:

- **federal government**—the Federal Communications Commission
- **significantly strengthen the regulation of**—impose a specific code of standards to govern the depiction of acts of violence
- **mass media**—all television programming broadcast by the three major networks, independent stations, and cable or pay television systems

The change sought involves increased regulation of the depiction of violence in television programming. Those of you who are reading carefully probably recognize that the way the proposition was defined directed change at both entertainment and news programming. The advocate has the burden to prove that such a change is necessary, desirable, and achievable. The opponent has the presumption of the present system of regulation by the Federal Communications Commission and the codes of standards and practices of the various broadcast companies.

Even without definitions, the proposition pointed to the kind of change the advocate is expected to support. To state that the federal government should significantly strengthen the regulation of mass media in the United States is to point the advocate in the direction of supporting greater control. The proposition identifies the agency for change which the advocate must employ—the federal government. It identifies the type of change—significantly strengthened regulation. It points to the target of change—mass media in the United States.

Change is also specified when the propositions is one of value or fact. Readers or listeners are asked to alter their beliefs regarding how something is to be valued or understood. In a value proposition such as "Preventing the sale and use of controlled substances on school property is more important than an individual student's right to privacy," the agency for change is the audience. It is asked to make a mental commitment to value safety over privacy. The advocate's burden to prove that change is necessary, desirable, and achievable involves arguing one value's supremacy over the other. In a proposition of fact such as "The use of controlled substances on school property is increasing," the audience is asked to believe the trend indicated in the proposition and the advocate's burden is to prove it is occurring. Even before definitions were supplied, these propositions set general boundaries for argument that were flexible enough to afford both advocate and opponent the opportunity for interpretation.

This characteristic, flexibility, is usually found in propositions used in academic argumentation. We can distinguish these propositions from those found in real-world contexts. In everyday experience, the world of politics, or the legal system, controversy results when a very specific end or objective is sought. Real-world controversies are usually "associated with a real or imagined threat to people's needs, values, or purposes" (Windes & Hastings, 1965, p. 36).

In the legal process, the essence of a formal proposition is usually found in the statement of charges in criminal proceedings or in the plaintiff's complaint in civil proceedings (Mills, 1968). Defendant X has violated law or statute Y. If X is the owner of an adult bookstore and if Y is designed to prevent the production, distribution, sale, or exhibition of child pornography, then argumentation between prosecutor and defense attorney is joined over whether X is guilty of violating Y. The proposition being argued is specific and leaves fewer opportunities for interpretation than the academic proposition introduced earlier.

Fewer opportunities do not mean none. While we indicated that the opponent in academic controversy might object to the definition of mass media as child pornography, her real-world counterpart, the defense attorney, might employ a similar strategy. The presumption for child pornography is as weak in the real world as it is in the academic. Recognizing this, the defense attorney may attempt to redefine the proposition and put the law, rather than her client, on trial. Where presumption is found can be broadly interpreted. Rather than focusing on the specific act of selling pornographic materials, the defense attorney might turn to the law as a source of presumption. The First Amendment to the Constitution states "Congress shall make no law" regarding a number of institutions, one of which is the press. Since there is strong presumption for this document, the defense attorney might argue that the law under which her client is charged represents a greater threat to society than do the materials he is accused of producing, distributing, selling, or exhibiting because it violates the Constitution.

The clash of values in this example, and the feelings they evoke, are typical of real-world argumentation because it produces real consequences. Disputes over pornography usually take place over the figurative ground of which value is more important: freedom of the individual or public morality. Such examples of value conflict are common in real-world argumentation and may create paradoxes such as the American Civil Liberties Union defending the right of American Nazis to march in Skokie, Illinois, where a number of Holocaust survivors live. The point of considering this value conflict is that the direction of change specified in the proposition should be as clear as possible to avoid confusion. Identification of presumption may also require a definitional process to determine exactly what argumentative ground is at stake.

In your personal experiences with argumentation, the proposition may have been a declarative statement as simple as "I think we should go to a movie tonight" or as vexing as "If you really loved me, you'd prove it." This is not always the case. In naturally occurring argumentation, propositions are not always clearly stated at the outset of the controversy. The failure to state exactly what we are arguing about probably accounts for most instances of misunderstanding that occur in interpersonal controversy. Real-world propositions need not be clearly stated in advance; when they are, however, they are narrow and open to fewer interpretations than propositions for academic argument.

Propositions for academic argumentation often seem easier to cope with than propositions for real-world argumentation because they are always clearly stated in advance. However, since academic argumentation exists solely for the purpose of developing skills and testing ideas, the disagreements are usually artificial or induced. To maintain interest in an academic exercise, it becomes necessary to have a proposition broad enough to allow interpretation and to provide sufficient intellectual challenge to the student who may have to work with it over a period of time. The seemingly unitary nature of many propositions in the real world is neither characteristic of nor desirable for propositions of academic argumentation.

In our example on regulation of mass media, controversy over what to regulate need not involve a discussion of television violence, since mass media include movies, newspapers, books, and magazines as well as television; neither is violence the only critical issue that might be considered. This is an example of a proposition that could be argued over an extended period of time, by a number of people, without becoming boring or repetitive. It shares one important characteistic, however, with real-world propositions: It points toward some alteration of belief or behavior. If it did not, there would be nothing to argue and the misunderstanding and bypassing, which occur in some real-world argumentation, might result. When the opponent in our earlier example of academic argumentation challenges the validity of the advocate's definition of mass media as child pornography, she is saying that the change in belief and behavior he supports points in a direction not reasonably suggested by the proposition agreed upon for argumentation.

What are academic argumentative propositions about? Issues of social equality, the process of government, international relations, and economics are often topics for classroom argumentation. As a result, you may find yourself learning about past, present, and future events while you are developing and refining your skills.

Identifying Key Issues

The third, and final, objective fulfilled by a specifically worded proposition is the aid it provides in the identification of key issues. In Chapter 3 we devote more specific attention to the identification of intrinsic or stock issues; at this point it is sufficient to state that issues are central questions suggested by the specific wording of a proposition and its definition by the advocate. "An issue is an inherent and vital question within a proposition: inherent because it exists inseparably and inevitably within the proposition, and vital because it is crucial or essential to the meaning of the proposition" (Mills 1968, p. 96). Issues become the contested points in argumentation, the areas of disagreement between advocate and opponent. If the proposition can be said to define the potential boundaries of argument, the issues suggested by it provide the internal structure or frame work for argumentation.

Issues grow directly from the definition of the proposition that the advocate provides, since this definition narrows and clarifies its meaning in academic argumentation. Earlier, we offered the following definitions:

- **federal government**—the Federal Communications Commission
- **significantly strengthen the regulation of**—impose a specific code of standards to govern the depiction of acts of violence
- **mass media**—all television programming broadcast by the three major networks, independent stations, and cable or pay television systems

Our broad proposition has now come to mean something very specific: The Federal Communications Commission should crack down on television violence. If the opponent accepts these definitions as reasonable, argumentation can proceed on the issues associated with the narrowed proposition. These become the advocate's burden of proof.

What might these issues be? They are questions that a reasonable person, such as our advocate or opponent, might ask before accepting the change in the Federal Communications Commission's behavior required by the narrowed proposition.

- Is violence depicted on television?
- Does something harmful occur because of the depiction of violence in television programming?
- Would there be any advantage or benefit gained by controlling the depiction of violence in television programming?
- Is the way in which the Federal Communications Commission deals with the depiction of violence in television programming insufficient at present?
- Is the Federal Communications Commission the best government agency to use to control the depiction of violence in television programming?
- What might be the consequences of having the Federal Communications Commission control the depiction of violence in television programming?

These questions represent issues that give shape and structure to the process of argumentation over the figurative ground. By locating areas of disagreement, potential and real, the arguers specify for each other, and the listener or reader, the aspects of belief or behavior over which controversy exists. Issues, which sharpen the locus of disagreement, constitute the basis for determining whether to alter or maintain current interpretations of reality.

Those of you who were reading carefully enough earlier to notice that the definition of mass media includes both entertainment and news programming probably have two questions right now. First, exactly what does the advocate mean by violence, and does the use of the term depiction mean that while television could not show the act on the screen, it could show its consequences? Good question! In your role as opponent, listener, or reader, you would probably get a sense of the answer to your question from the arguments the advocate provided in upholding his burden of proof. That might not always be the case and this points to a problem that can occur when we define a proposition. If we are not careful, all our definition accomplishes is to shift confusion from the meaning of terms in the proposition to the words and phrases we used in attempting to narrow and clarify its meaning.

Second, you might also be asking what happened to First Amendment freedoms? If the lawyer defending the pornography merchant could try to get her client off the hook by claiming the law under which he was charged was unconstitutional, couldn't the opponent in this academic controversy invoke the same defense? After all, doesn't freedom of speech give CNN the right to bring us film of the latest acts of gang violence or CBS the right to bring the series "Tour of Duty" into our living rooms? These are good questions that point to a particular feature of the academic proposition important in issue identification. We call your attention to a six-letter word in our sample proposition, *should*—a word that is common to many academic propositions.

One of the artifices of academic argumentation is that it frequently concerns itself with what ought to be rather than what will be. In a sense, we proceed from the assumption that if something should change, it can change, be it belief or behavior. We ignore the fact that in reality it might not, no matter how strong the proof or compelling the reasons. Before dismissing academic argumentation as a frivolous twentieth-century equivalent of the thirteenth-century disputation over how many angels can dance on the head of a pin and therefore dropping your argumentation course, consider the following: The suspension of disbelief involved in academic argumentation is no different than that which operates in the real world.

The government agency that passed the antismut law our hypothetical prosecutor used in attempting to bring our purveyor of child pornography to justice probably did exactly the same thing. The government representatives asked themselves whether something should be done, answered affirmatively, and passed the law. They may never have considered whether it violated the First Amendment. If they did, they decided either that it probably did not or, more probably, that it was a question for the courts. As a practitioner of argumentation in an academic context, you will find yourself doing the same thing, keeping in mind that your purpose is developing skills and testing ideas.

Since argumentation in an academic setting often involves arguing both sides of a proposition or listening to the argumentation of classmates, you may find yourself arguing or listening to arguments about something you do not really believe in. You may find yourself believing that something is so distasteful, so wrong, that it could not happen in the real world because the courts, Congress, or the public would not allow it to happen. The same features of problem consideration exist in the real world. Some group or agency concludes that "Something ought to be done," finds a course of action and undertakes it. This sometimes produces decisions that are distasteful or harmful, as was the case when officials of the Reagan administration oversaw the sale of arms to Iran to generate funds to support the Contras' guerilla war against the Sandinista government in Nicaragua in circumvention of the Boland Amendment.

The perception that something should be done, that one value is more important than another, or that we must alter our understanding of something, carries no real-world guarantees that when a change is made, it will always turn out to be the most desirable one or that it will not have some unforeseen long-term consequences. Good argumentation in any context explores the extent of desirability and searches for potential drawbacks. As you examine propositions for argumentation in your class or in other contexts, you must practice the suspension of belief or disbelief in order to consider all aspects of the implied change. In sum, when you set out to discover what belief is best or what should be done, taking care in defining terms and examining all possible issues growing out of the proposition are important, albeit time-consuming steps.

Summary of the Nature of Propositions

1. The proposition specifies the scope of the controversy, providing boundaries for argument. Defining selected terms of the proposition helps to clarify these boundaries.
2. The proposition expresses the advocate's goal, asserting the alteration in belief or behavior for which assent is sought.
3. The proposition delineates the advocate's responsibilities regarding the burden of proof and the opponent's opportunities that may result from identifying presumption, and it suggests potential issues that constitute the argumentative ground.

THE CLASSIFICATION OF PROPOSITIONS

We classify propositions according to the ends sought by their advocates, a change in either belief or behavior, and have already referred to the three types of propositions commonly argued—*fact, value,* and *policy.* These correspond to the most common sources of controversy: (1) disputes over what happened, what is happening, or what will happen; (2) disputes asserting something to be good or bad, right or wrong, effective or ineffective; and (3) disputes over what should or should not be done. Remember that academic propositions are usually broad in scope and we will be using many examples of academic propositions.

Propositions of Fact

Propositions of fact seek to alter our beliefs. They do so by asserting an appropriate way to view reality. "Illegal immigration deprives United States citizens of jobs" asserts a relationship between the presence of illegal aliens and some qualitative or quantitative harm. We may not accept the probable truth of this proposition without further explanation. Proof of the asserted relationship would require identification of those areas in which the presence of illegal aliens in the United States causes the consequence specified.

Propositions of fact are further classified in terms of the change in belief that is sought—whether it is in the past, the present, or the future.

Past Fact
* Life evolved naturally from existing conditions on Earth.
* Few American presidents have enjoyed favorable press coverage while in office.
Present Fact
* The American mass media are relatively free from government regulation.
* Trade restrictions are necessary for the protection of American industry.
Future Fact
* Computers will change the course of American education.
* Most wildlife species will cease to exist outside of zoos in the next century.

In each of these factual propositions, the controversy concerns the relationship between something and what we are asked to believe about it. To determine the truth of the relationship in the case of past or present fact propositions the process would be similar: Discover what would be required to establish the probable truth of the statement and proceed to verify it. Propositions of future fact depend upon discovering the probability that something will be the case in the future. In Chapter 4 we explore what is necessary in proving propositions of fact in more detail.

Propositions of Value

Like the proposition of fact, the proposition of value attempts to alter belief in that it deals with our subjective reactions to things and our opinion of them. The proposition of value establishes a judgmental standard or set of standards and applies them. Any attempt to demonstrate something to be good, right, or effective ultimately depends upon the criteria for goodness, rightness, or effectiveness. The advocate of a proposition of value normally applies his own criteria, especially if he believes them to be understood and accepted by either his opponent, his listener, or both. Notice the values involved in the following academic value propositions:

- The rights of endangered animal species are more important than the rights of indigenous human populations.
- American commercial broadcasters have sacrificed quality for entertainment.
- Protecting the environment is a more important goal than satisfying America's energy demands.

"This season's new television shows are the worst ever!" "Brand X popcorn is the best." These are assertions of judgment based on subjective standards of "worstness" and "bestness" that the person making them has applied. Both are propositions of value.

If the advocate's burden of proof relative to propositions of fact may be discharged by recourse to the data, then how may propositions of value be determined to be true? Once again, the concept of what is probable is important to keep in mind. Because they reflect the subjective judgments and tastes of the individuals who advance them, propositions of value can only approach the level of being probably true, but they cannot even approach this level unless we know the criteria on which they are based. Take the statement, "Brand X popcorn is best," for example. What makes something best? In the case of popcorn, is it price, nutritional value, flavor, the amount each kernel expands during popping, or the percentage of unpopped kernels?

Some of these criteria could be objectively verified, such as the percentage of unpopped kernels. We could test this standard of "bestness" as if we were trying to prove a proposition of fact. Other standards, such as flavor, are themselves judgmental. Knowing the criteria on which the judgment is made allows the listener to assess both their reasonableness as criteria and the extent to which the data show them to be probably true of the object of the value proposition. In Chapter 4, we also discuss the development of cases for value argumentation in more detail.

Propositions of Policy

Unlike fact and value propositions, which are aimed at altering our beliefs, policy propositions seek a change in behavior. They suggest that something should be done. "The Food and Drug Administration should impose tougher standards on drug labeling" is an example of a policy proposition, as was our earlier example of federal regulation of mass media. They do more than attempt to alter our beliefs about the pharmaceutical industry and mass media. If we give our assent to these propositions, we are agreeing to a change in behaviors, ours or someone else's. The policy proposition calls for action to be taken.

The policy proposition is common in both political and academic argumentation. It is characterized by the word *should*, which only suggests something ought to be done, not that it necessarily will be done. The word should requires the advocate to indicate the specific change he supports and to prove it is *necessary*, *desirable*, and *viable* in upholding his burden of proof. It may have occurred to you that the words necessary, desirable, and viable are suggestive of a set of value propositions. That is one of the secrets to successfully advocating or opposing policy propositions—sub-propositions of value, as well as fact, are frequently used in supporting them. This means that in argumentation the advocate seeking to alter behavior first establishes a rationale for altering beliefs.

Policy propositions are sometimes more complex than propositions of fact or value. Proving a change is necessary, desirable, and viable may be more time-consuming than proving the existence or worth of something, if only because demonstration of the probable truth of several value propositions is involved. Arguing a policy proposition calls for a more sophisticated and developed series of arguments. "The policy proposition involves facts and values, but extends into expediency, practicality, and action" (Mills, 1968, p. 80).

Let us examine some typical policy propositions used in academic argumentation to discover their complexity. What aspects of fact and value do you find? What actions are implied?

- The federal government should significantly strengthen the guarantee of consumer-product safety required of manufacturers.
- The federal government should control the supply and utilization of energy in the United States.
- The United States should seek restoration of normal diplomatic relations with the government of Cuba.

These topics all deal with significant and highly complex political, economic, and social issues. How might you go about demonstrating that any of the changes suggested by them are necessary, desirable, and viable? Through examination of supporting factual and judgmental propositions. These policy propositions would be accepted only if arguments concerning certain subpropositions of fact and value were accepted. Therefore, the three types of propositions are related.

For example, to demonstrate why the alteration in behavior suggested by any of the policy propositions suggested here should be accepted, the advocate's burden of proof might require demonstrating that:

- a problem exists (fact proposition)
- because of this, people are harmed (fact and value propositions)
- despite people being harmed, the means of dealing with this problem are presently either inadequate or nonexistent (value and fact propositions)

Because acceptance of the alteration of behavior suggested by the policy proposition rests on a foundation of fact and value propositions, the concept of the probable is once again pertinent. In marshaling proof and good reasons to address the rationality of listener or reader in the attempt to precipitate change, the advocate supports what he believes to be the best course of action. Chapter 5 provides a complete discussion of argumentation involving policy propositions.

Summary of the Classification of Propositions

1. Propositions of fact assert a relationship between things, or between persons and things; with the exception of propositions of future fact, the advocate's burden is to prove them to be probable by direct verification.
2. Propositions of value assert the worth or lack of worth of something; the advocate's burden is to prove them to be probable through the application of criteria developed by the individual or discovered in society.
3. Propositions of policy assert that a course of action or behavior should be taken; the advocate's burden is to prove them to be probable by establishing the probable truth of supporting subpropositions of fact and value.

With the nature and classification of types of propositions firmly in mind, we can now conclude this chapter by discussing how to phrase argumentative propositions so they properly assign presumption and the burden of proof.

PHRASING THE PROPOSITION

Phrasing propositions concerns choosing language that will properly establish the argumentative ground. The importance of wording a proposition for academic argumentation cannot be over emphasized. Clear phrasing is needed to provide a meaningful basis for the process that follows. A failure in proposition wording is an invitation to misunderstanding and poor analysis of its component issues (Zeigelmuller, Kay, & Dause, 1990).

First, the proposition should be phrased as a clear statement of the change in belief or behavior the advocate will be obligated to seek. To do otherwise confuses the assignment of presumption and the scope of the burden of proof. Consider the proposition, "Something should be done about the possibility of a nuclear war." This proposition fails to meet the first rule for phrasing a good proposition. "Something" is vague, and determining burden of proof and presumption is very difficult. "Something" could involve increasing the number of weapons to bolster the nuclear deterrent, unilaterally freezing the development and production of weapons, creating an international organization to control such weapons, establishing a regular negotiation system among nations that possess nuclear weapons, and so on. If the idea of arguing this subject is to consider the viability of a nuclear freeze, a more appropriate wording for this proposition would be "The United States should freeze the further development and production of nuclear weapons."

The advocate has the burden of proving a freeze on nuclear weapons will accomplish something positive. Presumption is also more clearly specified in the revised proposition. The opponent may expect to defend a policy of deterrence or suggest an alternative to a unilateral freeze that might achieve the same goal. Both advocate and opponent have a better understanding of the argumentative ground in this proposition. This will benefit the analysis each will undertake in preparing to argue.

A second rule to observe in phrasing a proposition is that the proposition should contain only one central idea. Having improved our sample proposition by clarifying the change it seeks, let's see what happens when more than one central idea is introduced. "The United States should freeze the further development and production of nuclear weapons and significantly strengthen conventional foreign military commitments." This is no longer a single proposition. It now contains two separate and unrelated topics. They are related only to the extent that both deal with aspects of defense policy. Further, the advocate is committed to affirm reduction in one area and expansion in another.

A proposition with more than one central idea saddles the advocate with separate burdens of proof for each idea—nuclear weapons freeze and increasing conventional military commitments—and the opponent is faced with two separate areas of presumption to defend. This introduces unnecessary complication into the argumentative process. Phrasing a proposition around one central idea facilitates and improves the process of analysis. An arguer breaks down a proposition into its component issues by looking for the questions that are central to it. If the proposition contains multiple ideas, the process of issue identification is made more difficult. For this sample proposition, both advocate and opponent may find it impossible to establish an internally consistent argumentative position because it calls for changes in two distinct areas of defense policy.

For example, one reason an advocate might present for a freeze on nuclear weapons is that such weapons increase the probability of a war. If that is a good and sufficient reason for the freeze, it may also be a good and sufficient reason not to increase conventional military commitments since, like nuclear weapons, conventional forces may contribute to the escalation of armed conflict. It is better to phrase several separate propositions than to try to cramming multiple central ideas into a single one.

A final rule for phrasing propositions is that they should be couched in neutral terms. The wording should favor neither side in the controversy. The advocate who falls prey to temptation words a proposition with emotive language. "The United States should freeze the foolish development and wasteful production of weapons of the nuclear holocaust." Such value judgments should be saved for the development of arguments about the proposition. In academic argumentation, the idea of fair wording is stressed so that neither advocate nor opponent begins with an unfair advantage (Zeigelmuller, Kay & Dause, 1990).

Summary of Rules for Phrasing Propositions

1. Propositions should be phrased to indicate the direction of change in present belief or behavior that the advocate is responsible for supporting.
2. Propositions should be phrased as a single statement containing one central idea.
3. Propositions should be phrased in neutral language so that the cause of neither advocate nor opponent is favored at the outset.

This chapter has covered two key concepts in argumentation—presumption and burden of proof. These concepts establish the figurative ground over which argumentation occurs and some of its rules. They require the advocate, as the party seeking a change in belief or behavior, to prove his case in order to overcome presumption which artificially or naturally favors no change. The playing field of argumentation is further delineated by the propositions, or topics, about which people argue. This chapter has examined the nature of propositions, discussed three types of propositions, and explained how to phrase propositions properly. The nature of the playing field is brought completely into focus by the third key concept alluded to at the beginning of this chapter—the prima facie case. The next chapter discusses this key concept; relates it to the stock issues associated with propositions of fact, value, and policy; and explains the basic structure of arguments which address the questions raised by these stock issues.

LEARNING ACTIVITIES

1. Discuss what the three different views of presumption mean to the advocate and opponent in argumentation. Should we always assign the roles before determining presumption? In which communication contexts might you use the traditional view that pre sumption rests with existing institutions? In which would it be appropriate to determine the prevailing beliefs of an audience? Should we use the idea of hypothesis testing in other than academic contexts?

2. Choose an ongoing controversy such as smokers' versus nonsmokers' rights, abortion versus right to life, environmental protection versus the need for employment. Which side in the controversy has presumption? Which has the burden of proving that change should occur?

3. Find an editorial from a current newspaper or magazine that you believe is intended to alter belief or behavior. Analyze it in terms of the following:
   A. What is the presumption the editorial is trying to overcome, and with whom or what does that presumption lie?
   B. To what extent does the author of the editorial provide sufficient reasons and proof to overcome presumption?
   C. What do you see as the relationship between presumption, burden of proof, and the implicit or explicit proposition in the editorial you selected?

4. Examine the following propositions. Identify the kinds of propositions—*fact, value,* and *policy*—represented. Be prepared to discuss how each example does or does not meet the rules for wording propositions suggested in this chapter.

Energy
   A. Domestically produced energy sources are preferable to foreign imports.
   B. By 1999, the United States will run short of fossil fuels.
   C. The federal government should implement an accelerated program of conversion to domestically produced energy.

Ecology
A. The present system of environmental protection creates toxic-waste dumps.

B. The United States should significantly improve its environmental protection policy.

C. The protection of the national environment ought to take precedence over the expansion of industrial production.

Law Enforcement
A. The judicial system should provide compensation to the victims of crimes against persons and property.

B. The victims of crimes against persons and property are seldom compensated for their losses.

C. The American judicial system unfairly favors the accused.

Foreign Policy
A. United States foreign-policy commitments overextend the federal budget.

B. United States foreign-policy commitments ought to reflect the American belief in the sanctity of human rights.

C. The United States should substantially reduce foreign aid to nations which fail to protect the rights of their citizens.

Education
A. The quality of education in American public schools ought to be the nation's first priority.

B. The education of teachers does not place sufficient emphasis on academic subjects.

C. The Department of Education should create and maintain certification standards for all public school teachers.

5. Taking the propositions in activity 4, pretend you are listening to an advocate's speech on each topic. As a member of the listening audience, identify what words or phrases in each proposition you think would need to be defined.

6. Select three topic areas you might like to investigate in greater depth in completing future assignments. Formulate specific fact, value, and policy propositions that these topic areas suggest to you.

SUGGESTED SUPPLEMENTARY READINGS

Cronkhite, G. (1966). Propositions of Past and Future Fact and Value: A Proposed Classification, *Journal of the American Forensics Association, 3*, 11-16.
   Discusses how value propositions should be analyzed to determine the arguments that will focus attention on the value, the choice of criteria, and the facts that match the value object to the criteria. This article emphasizes that the choice of arguments will be based, in part, on how much time the arguer has to develop a position and what the audience is likely to accept without much argumentation.

Golden, J. L., Berquist, G. F., & Coleman, W. E. (1989). *The Rhetoric of Western Thought* (4th Ed.). Dubuque, Iowa: Kendall/Hunt.
   This book surveys rhetorical theory from the Greeks to the present. We recommend you examine the portion of Chapter 9 relating to Richard Whatley and his development of the concepts of presumption and burden of proof. Also examine Chapter 21, "Rhetoric as a Way of Knowing: Stephen Toulmin and the Nature of Argument," which describes the philosophy behind the model and discusses the superiority of the Toulmin model as a means of generating understanding.

Mills, G. E. (1968). *Reason in Controversy* (2nd Ed.). Boston: Allyn & Bacon.
   Although many of the examples are dated, this book offers a thorough discussion of propositions, analysis to determine issues, and a discussion of traditional policy argumentation. The appendix contains texts of debates and a discussion of debating by presidential candidates.

Sproule, J. M. (1976). The Psychological Burden of Proof: On the Evolutionary Development of Richard Whatley's Theory of Presumption, *Communication Monographs, 43*, 115-29.

A review of the development of the concept of presumption in Whatley's several revisions of his *Elements of Rhetoric*. Sproule concludes that Whatley thought presumption should be determined on the basis of audience beliefs and attitudes. He suggests how arguers might use the theory of presumption as a guide to audience analysis and argues that the psychological makeup of the audience should determine the responsibilities of advocate and opponent.

Vasilius, J. Presumption, Presumption, Wherefore Art Thou Presumption? In D. Brownlee (Ed.), *Perspectives on Non-Policy Argument*, ERIC Document ED 192 382.

Originally presented at the 1980 Desert Argumentation Symposium at the University of Arizona, this paper offers ten justifications for using presumption to test hypotheses in value argumentation. Vasilius examines the problems faced by Cross-Examination Debate Association (CEDA) debaters in determining the responsibilities of advocates and opponents. She explains how employing hypothesis testing as the philosophical basis for argument resolves this problem.

3

WHAT AM I GOING TO ARGUE ABOUT?

In Chapter 2 we said argumentation takes place whenever an advocate and an opponent contest possession of a figurative piece of ground specified by a proposition of fact, value, or policy. We indicated that the opponent initially has possession of the ground because of a natural or artificial presumption that the change in belief or behavior required by the proposition is one listeners or readers will not accept on the basis of the face value of the proposition alone. The advocate has the burden of proof, the responsibility to show these listeners or readers that there are good reasons to no longer rely on presumption to guide their belief and behavior. In this chapter we will discuss the general concept of the prima facie case, its specific application to the various kinds of propositions through stock issues, and the model of argumentative structure developed by Stephen Toulmin which identifies the locus of controversy over these stock issues.

THE PRIMA FACIE CASE

To overcome the presumption that a belief or behavior should continue to exist, the advocate must present a fully developed case, one strong enough to justify a change unless successfully challenged by countering arguments. Literally, a **prima facie case** is one that "at first sight" or "on the face of it" is sufficient to justify changing belief or behavior. A prima facie case causes us to suspend our reliance on presumption as a guide for belief or behavior. This suspension of presumption will either be temporary, if valid countering arguments are provided, or permanent, if the opponent is unable to establish a reason to continue to rely on the original presumption.

Because she would lose the dispute if a prima facie case were not presented to fulfill the burden of proof and suspend presumption, the advocate normally initiates the argument by speaking or writing first. This initial presentation must be prima facie and sufficient to support her position concerning the proposition being argued. The legal system once again provides an example to clarify the concept. In order to establish the guilt of a person accused of a felony, the prosecution must present an indictment of this individual that suspends the artificial presumption of innocence. This presentation must constitute a prima facie case.

Suppose Ralph is accused of auto theft. A prima facie case would, at the very least, consist of evidence and testimony supporting the following arguments:

- An automobile was reported missing from the dealer's lot.
- Subsequent to receiving this report, the city police apprehended Ralph with the vehicle in question in his possession.
- Ralph's possession of the automobile was unlawful. He had neither purchased it nor had he received consent of any dealer representative to take it for a test drive.

Proving these three arguments would constitute a prima facie indictment of Ralph for grand theft-auto. The presumption of Ralph's innocence would be suspended until his attorney had mounted a successful defense. The defense attorney would have the responsibility of attempting to reestablish the presumption of Ralph's innocence by attacking the truth of one or more of these arguments, or by introducing argumentation demonstrating extenuating circumstances mitigating Ralph's guilt.

Since very few of you would confront the task of presenting a prima facie case on the proposition that Ralph is guilty of stealing an automobile, the question remains, how do you know when you have discharged your responsibilities as advocate regarding the burden of proof? Recall that the content and scope of the burden of proof is determined by the proposition being argued. In Chapter 1, we indicated how the Romans, in refining Greek rhetoric, developed a series of questions that were crucial in legal proceedings. These questions established the content and scope of the burden of proof for legal propositions. They are similar to the questions the prosecutor considered in preparing the case against Ralph. For fields of argument other than the law, similar sets of questions exist. They are commonly referred to as **stock issues**, the questions that listeners or readers want answered before they will accept the advocate's arguments as sufficient to warrant a change in belief or behavior. These questions focus the controversy and are naturally derived from the proposition being argued. In the last chapter we introduced several types of propositions about which people commonly argue, and there are specific stock issues that pertain to each type of proposition.

Before we move on to discuss these stock issues, two other concepts pertaining to the prima facie case in academic argumentation require discussion. In addition to being logically adequate and offering sufficient proof, the advocate's prima facie case for changing a belief or behavior must fall within the bounds of the topic of the controversy, the proposition, and must demonstrate inherency.

The advocate is responsible for developing a *topical* prima facie case. In academic argumentation, the advocate and the opponent agree to a proposition that identifies the broad, general topic to be argued. In ordinary conversations, and in some instances of real-world argumentation, it is easy to drift from topic to topic. When you want to make a specific case for or against some proposed change, that is not a desirable quality. Sticking to the topic you agreed to argue, the proposition, prevents the audience from becoming confused about the issues. If you had agreed to argue about changing Northern State University's credit-hour system, the proposition might be stated as: Northern State University should adopt the three-credit-hour course as the university standard. In providing a prima facie case, the advocate would not contest the amount a student pays per credit hour or the manner in which fees are collected, since these issues are clearly outside the bounds of the proposition. Tuition constitutes a different controversy requiring a different proposition and has as much relevance to a discussion of the credit-hour system at Northern as unpaid parking tickets would have to Ralph's guilt or innocence on the auto theft charge.

In addition to being topical, a prima facie case for a proposition of value or policy must demonstrate *inherency*. Argumentation is used to decide whether change is justified. To justify change, the advocate must examine both the deficiencies in existing beliefs or behaviors, and the reason for their existence. The concept of inherency is concerned with the relationship between problems and the circumstances that produced them (La Grave, 1975). Inherency addresses questions such as: What is the cause of the problem? Is change necessary to overcome this cause? If we do not change, will the cause disappear and the problem correct itself?

Since it is generally assumed that if a problem's cause cannot be found we cannot determine how best to remedy it, inherency is a crucial part of an advocate's prima facie case. If the advocate fails to identify a reason for a problem to exist, it will be impossible to determine if change will eliminate the problem. Inherency arguments establish the causal relationship between the absence of the change requested by the advocate and the continuation of a problem (Patterson & Zarefsky, 1983).

A problem's inherent nature is established by the presence of three elements: cause, permanence, and reform (La Grave, 1975). Cause establishes that the problem exists as a direct result of existing belief or behavior. If the cause is found in the beliefs of society, inherency is said to be "attitudinal." If the cause is found in behaviors which operationalize these beliefs, inherency is termed "structural." Permanence establishes that, without intervention, the problem will remain. Finally, reform establishes that only the change proposed by the advocate will eliminate the problem.

Attitudinal inherency results from beliefs, those opinions, feelings, or emotional reactions we have about things. To illustrate the power of belief as a cause, consider the following examples. The opinion that women are less capable of studying mathematics than men kept women from pursuing careers in many scientific fields. The feeling that college athletes are "dumb jocks" who receive preferential treatment can make them exiles in the classroom. Emotional reactions to the seeming unfairness of the tax system has led some to cheat on their taxes. Attitudes are often difficult to identify, but they play a powerful role in causing us to accept something as true or false, to value one thing over another, or to act or refuse to act in a certain way.

Structural inherency results when society adopts formal policies that operationalize a belief that is strong or widely held. Laws, institutions, and agreements form the fabric of our society. Structural inherency argues that a problem's cause is found in the behavior which formal policies require. In searching for the inherent causes of a problem, the advocate examines these policies, laws, institutions, and agreements to see if their presence or absence is what has produced the problem.

In our example of argumentation concerning Northern State University, if the principal reason we have for wanting to change Northern's credit-hour system is that the present system is too restrictive of a student's options in choosing courses or does not get maximum productivity from staff and facilities, we would be citing problems that are built-in features of the existing four-credit-hour system. Inherency in this case is structural, the problem is caused by the four-credit-hour policy. This policy has been in effect for a number of years, suggesting that the second element of inherency, permanence, is also characteristic. Faculty belief that a three-credit system would increase their work load also serves as an inherent barrier to change. If the faculty prefer the four-credit-hour system they have little or no inclination to change it; therefore, third element of inherency, reform, would be present. The problem could only be solved by implementing a change that the existing power structure is ambivalent toward putting in place.

The role of faculty attitude in preventing reform also illustrates that it is possible for structural and attitudinal inherency to be present at the same time. It is a characteristic of controversy that there may be several causes for a problem's existence. To remedy a problem, however, it is necessary to remove its prime cause. The advocate and opponent, in examining existing beliefs and behaviors, frequently disagree over whose explanation most clearly represents the probable truth. Conceptually, inherency is important in determining whether a prima facie case has been presented because it forces arguers to examine why things exist and to explore whether they will correct themselves by the natural processes of change.

We view people as simultaneously in the state of being and the process of becoming. Some change in beliefs and behaviors is expected as a natural consequence of living and experiencing new situations. The same thing can be said regarding institutions. Inherency prevents us from arguing over trivia and things which would probably happen in the normal course of events. It is pointless to argue the proposition "The next century should be called the twenty-first century." At present, nothing prevents designating the years from 2001 to 2100 the twenty-first century. Arguing about calling that period something else would be trivial unless good reasons were provided to justify some other title. If good reasons existed for such a change, they would constitute a prima facie case for something inherently precluded by present practices that are unlikely to change.

We may summarize the concept of prima facie argument with the following principles:

1. The advocate has the responsibility of presenting a prima facie case, one that at face value justifies a change in belief or behavior.
2. The form and content of the arguments offered determines the face value of an advocate's case.
3. A prima facie case must be both topical and inherent.
4. Presentation of a prima facie case causes the suspension of presumption unless it is successfully challenged.

STOCK ISSUES AND PROPOSITIONS OF FACT

The goal of the advocate of a proposition of fact is to win the listener's or reader's assent that the proposition is probably true. Successfully gaining assent is accomplished by the presentation of a total "package" of proof and reasoning perceived as valid by its receivers. The advocate must develop a prima facie case through a series of arguments that marshal sufficient support to gain possession of the contested ground, at least temporarily. The opponent responds by casting doubt on the existence of such a prima facie case. Questions of fact, value, and policy are interrelated; so the ability to argue propositions of fact successfully lays the foundation for advocating and opposing both value and policy propositions. In addition, factual argumentation is an end in itself.

You may already have had some experience in arguing factual propositions. If you have ever written a research paper or an essay in which you had to develop a point of view or take a position on a topic such as "The Vietnam War was an illegal war," "The Union blockade of Confederate ports was the decisive factor in the South's defeat," or "The Monroe Doctrine justifies U.S. intervention in Latin America," you have argued a factual proposition. The thesis sentence of the paper served as your proposition of fact and your subsequent development of ideas was intended to establish its probable truth. The research and thinking you put into the paper were designed to fit your audience, the instructor whose favorable evaluation you sought.

In the real world, we encounter argumentation over fact in several different fields. Courts of law examine past fact, what is alleged to have happened. Lawyers, judges, and juries are concerned with determining the probable truth or falsity of questions such as "Has some law been violated?" or "How should some law be interpreted in the given case?" In the field of politics, factual argumentation is involved as laws protecting or interpreting freedom of speech, press, and religion are considered. Although the main activity of legislative bodies is policy making, various agencies and committees engage in "fact-finding" investigations to determine the probability of something having been the case or to predict what will be the case in the future. Scientific disputes occur over the laws of nature—what biological specimens are, how flora and fauna are to be classified, or how life began. In the real world, factual propositions often arise subsequent to the discovery of information requiring interpretation or application.

In the context of academic argumentation, the proposition of fact also helps us to establish what was, is, or will be. To qualify as a proposition of fact, or an argument over fact, disputes must be limited to those questions that draw inferences about the past, present, and future (Ehninger & Brockriede, 1963) rather than those questions that may be resolved by consulting the appropriate source of information. "Abraham Lincoln was the first U.S. president to travel by rail" is not arguable because its probable truth can be determined by examining a book on presidential trivia (Andrew Jackson was the first president to travel by rail in 1833). "Forces of the marketplace presently determine the extent and quality of children's television" is not an arguable fact, since it can be confirmed by observation. It provides insufficient grounds for controversy, drawing no inference and not requiring argumentation to prove its probable validity. Contrast such nonarguable statements with examples of arguable propositions of fact:

- The "big bang," a massive cosmic explosion, created the universe.
- Allowing market forces to determine the extent and quality of children's television has resulted in the best children's shows being canceled.
- Granting tuition tax credits to the parents of children who attend private elementary and secondary schools will perpetuate segregation.

The discovery of issues pertinent to the presentation of a prima facie case on any of these controversies, and the decision concerning which you would use in arguing your position, are facilitated by the existence of stock issues—issues that exist in any argumentative situation. In Chapter 2, we stated that a proposition of fact infers a relationship between the subject and object in the propositional sentence. Propositions of fact are argued to determine whether this inference is probably true. The single stock issue regarding factual argumentation focuses attention on the means by which the inference may be verified and discovering if it is possible to employ these means to do so. It focuses the advocate's and opponent's attention on determining the answer to one question:

1. **Is (are) the reason(s) offered sufficient to validate the inferred relationship between the subject and the object of the proposition?**

This stock issue is generic to all propositions of fact. While the specific issues contested will vary from one proposition to another, they "fill in the blanks" provided by this stock issue. The decision regarding which specific issues to include as you fill these blanks will also be influenced by what you know about your audience and what aspect of the figurative ground you think is likely to be contested. If one issue seems most important to your audience, that should be an issue to which you devote some attention. This, in conjunction with consideration of the question raised by the stock issue, will enable you to determine the specific reasons you will have to supply. These reasons will take the form of one or more claims. Claims, the most basic element of argument, are discussed further at the end of this chapter.

STOCK ISSUES AND PROPOSITION OF VALUE

Propositions of fact attempt to determine what is most probably true of a past, present, or future relationship inferred by the proposition. Value propositions differ in that they attempt to establish what is the most acceptable application of judgment to a particular person, place, event, policy, or idea. In value argumentation, the controversy centers on which of two or more opposing evaluations is the most credible.

Values are deeply rooted mental states and are formed early in life. They predispose us to categorize something as existing somewhere along a mental continuum ranging from highly positive to highly negative. A value, which may be held by an individual or a group, may not be verbalized or discussed until it comes into conflict with some other value about which judgment is going to be made. Because no two people possess exactly the same life experiences, the potential for value conflict is present when people begin to make judgments. Lastly, values do not exist independent of each other. They exist in a hierarchy, with some values being deemed more important than others in a given set of circumstances.

Where do we find examples of value argumentation? Almost any statement, lengthy or brief, can contain a value judgment. How we describe something or someone will necessarily be colored by our feelings toward that which we have described. Throughout this textbook, both implicit and explicit claims are made about the worth of studying and practicing argumentation—they are value judgments. Value argumentation communicates our feelings about something or someone and the standards of judgment from which those feelings derive. Value propositions exist about any subject and are characterized by the use of intrinsic or extrinsic judgmental criteria.

There are some fields of endeavor that deal almost exclusively in value argumentation. Religion and philosophy are both concerned with right and wrong, moral and immoral, and ethical and unethical behavior. Both fields seek to determine standards of socially or doctrinally acceptable behavior. A theologian examines behavior in terms of whether it measures up to a moral code expressed in sacred texts. The philosopher may speculate on the existence of several alternatives for ethical and unethical behavior.

The arts—film, theater, music, sculpture, photography, painting, and dance— concern themselves, in part, with judging what is produced against a set of critical standards to determine "good art." The critics continually seek and revise these standards to keep pace with trends and changes. We rely on the opinions of the professional critic to help us determine what we will patronize and accept. You have a chance to observe how critical standards for evaluating film are developed and applied through value argumentation by watching the various movie review programs on television.

Other fields also engage in value argumentation, particularly regarding standards of ethical behavior. Medicine, law, business, education, public relations, and almost any other field you can name, are concerned with determining acceptable behaviors for their practitioners. Is prescribing a certain drug to certain categories of patients ethical? Is a certain sales technique an ethical business practice? Is a certain behavior appropriate for a professional educator? Often professional organizations draw up codes of behavior, such as the Public Relations Society of America's and the American Bar Association's codes of ethics. Such codes provoke extensive value and policy argumentation as individuals and groups seek to interpret and apply them.

The locus of value argumentation in real-world contexts is as varied as the groups and individuals who are concerned with standards of excellence and codes of conduct. In academic argumentation, you may be asked to develop argumentative cases about the quality or lack of quality of some institution or practice, the appropriateness of the actions of certain groups of people, or whether something is in the best interests of the nation in general.

The advocate's role in arguing a proposition of value is to provide good and sufficient reasons, a prima facie case, for her audience to evaluate the object of the proposition in the same way as she does. The opponent's role in value argumentation is to examine the soundness of the arguments and to examine the present value attributed to the proposition's object. Value propositions take a particular form that aids both arguers. They identify a **value object,** some idea, person, action, agency, tradition, practice, or custom that exists or is proposed, and a **value judgment**, a general evaluation—good-bad, fair-unfair, safe-harmful, effective-ineffective—to be assigned the value object. The value judgment sets forth broad criteria by which the value object is said to be measured.

In Chapter 2 we said the proposition should always be phrased in such a way that change is implied, and so that the advocate supports a change in the judgment normally assigned to the value object. This is important because in some instances, the value proposition reflects two equally prized objects and the advocate's task is to argue the primacy of one over the other:

- The freedom to publish or read anything is more important than the moral objections that its content may raise.
- A strong national defense is more important than a balanced federal budget.

Notice that both propositions could be reversed and argued from the opposite perspective. They are worded in such a way to specify the argumentative ground to be disputed by the advocate and opponent.

In other propositions, the value object and the value judgment are unitary in nature:

- The portrayal of violence on television is extremely harmful to young viewers.
- Ronald Reagan will be remembered as the greatest president of the twentieth century.

Even though only one value object and judgment are supplied in these propositions, there are still ample opportunities for disagreement.

Issue identification relative to the creation of a prima facie case for a value proposition proceeds in the same way as for a proposition of fact. Stock issues once again take the form of vital questions that must be answered if the arguer's case is to be accepted. The three stock issues that shape value advocacy and opposition are:

1. **By what value hierarchy is the object of the proposition best evaluated?**
2. **By what criteria is the value object to be located within this hierarchy?**
3. **Do indicators of the effect, extent, and inherency of the value object show that it conforms to the criteria?**

These questions help determine the nature of the dispute, the judgmental criteria to be used to resolve it, and the kinds of arguments used to measure the value object by these criteria.

STOCK ISSUES AND POLICY PROPOSITIONS

Policy propositions concern changes in behavior ranging from the passage of new legislation or the creation of new institutions to the course of action an individual should follow. Policy propositions imply that a critical decision to do something be considered. Making this decision is the result of considering the validity of a number of intermediate claims of fact and value. Your success in arguing a policy proposition rests on skills developed in learning to argue both fact and value propositions.

Value argumentation often considers ideas that lead to policy formation. The relationship between fact, value, and policy is such that policy argumentation rests on consideration of issues of fact pointing to a particular value being attained or violated by adoption of a policy, or, given certain facts and competing values, what course of action should be followed (Young, 1980). Consider your own beliefs. They are often articulated as a series of statements about what you see as desirable or undesirable about a certain course of action.

Policy argumentation contemplates a potential course of action. Where do we find examples of policy argumentation? In the field of law, we see examples of policy making as criminal codes are devised and revised, judges set penalties for those who are found guilty, and both professionals and ordinary citizens debate the merits of capital punishment or other issues involving the law and its implementation.

One of the more obvious places to see policy making and policy argumentation in action is in legislative bodies—national, state, and local. The establishment of new programs and the evaluation of existing ones takes place in city councils and commissions, in state legislative houses, and in the U.S. House of Representatives and the Senate. Your school may have a decision-making body that sets university policy. Since many policy proposals create both strong support and strong opposition, deliberations can become quite lengthy, and even fraught with emotion.

In business, management concerns itself with the creation and implementation of policy and subsequent reviews of its effectiveness. Issues related to productivity, labor relations, purchasing, sales, and public relations lead to policy development inbusiness, where the deliberative process normally includes a definition and limitation of the problem, analysis of the problem, establishment of criteria to evaluate possible solutions to the problem, and subsequent review of the efficacy of the chosen solution after it has been implemented (Koehler, Anatol, & Applbaum 1981).

In academic argumentation, policy propositions have long been used in teaching particular communication skills and in competitive debate activities. Much of academic argumentation considers proposed actions that "should" be undertaken by some agency, usually the federal government. These propositions usually involve looking at some broad change in domestic policy, such as a proposition urging greater freedom in the investigation and prosecution of crime; or in foreign policy, such as a proposition seeking to reduce foreign military commitments. You will recall that academic propositions are usually stated in such a way that they have more than one possible interpretation and can be argued by many students over the course of a semester, or even an entire year. Because of this, academic propositions offer you the chance to examine different ways of solving problems concerning the economy, welfare and human services, foreign trade deficits, and so forth.

The stock issues for policy propositions are useful in determining the requirements for a prima facie case relative to any of these topic areas. As with value propositions, three questions frame the stock issues for propositions of policy.

1. **Is there a reason for change in a manner generally suggested by the policy proposition?**
2. **Does the policy proposed resolve the reason for change?**
3. **What are the consequences of the proposed change?**

Any topic will suggest specific reasons why a change in policy or the creation of a new policy is desirable, indicate what kinds of policies are feasible, and point to possible criteria by which the merits of those policies might be determined. These stock issues not only help you discover the kinds of arguments that must be advanced for an advocate's case to be prima facie, but also demonstrate the relationship between fact, value, and policy. Notice that one possible response to the question posed in the first stock issue, "Things are bad now," takes the form of a value judgment, as does the response to the third stock issue, "Things will be better in the future." Notice that the second stock issue forces consideration of a statement of fact, "The proposed policy resolves the problem."

Statements like these are called claims. Claims are the most basic unit of argument because they identify the locus of controversy, the center of the dispute between the advocate and her opponent. The claims which an advocate initially advances constitute a prima facie case to the extent that they answer the questions posed by the stock issues for the type of proposition being argued to her listener's or reader's satisfaction. Because claims and the proof that establishes them are so central to the process of argumentation, we conclude this chapter by discussing them in the context of the Toulmin model of argument.

THE TOULMIN MODEL OF ARGUMENT

In argumentation, particularly academic argumentation, controversy over a proposition is disputed in terms of issues. Each issue defines a unit of thought related to the proposition and is represented by one or more claims. For example, earlier in your life you may have been involved in a controversy over the policy proposition, "You should eat your vegetables." A prima facie argument advocating this proposition probably included several claims: "Vegetables have vitamins and minerals." "Vitamins and minerals are vital to proper growth." "Vitamins and minerals are important to health." Whatever topic you choose to argue, your position as advocate or opponent emerges through a series of claims supported by grounds and warrant, terminology developed by British logician Stephen Toulmin (1958; and Toulmin, Rieke, & Janik, 1984) to classify the parts of an argument.

Claims

Argumentation begins when an advocate makes one or more claims. **Claims** are conclusions that do not stand alone. A claim is something with which the listener or reader can ultimately agree or disagree. In this sense, claims both begin and end the process of argumentation. Claims begin the process by showing where an arguer has taken a stand. Claims also end the process, showing what the listener or reader is expected to accept as true or probable. Disputes concerning claims center on whether they are capable of being supported by proof and reasoning, shown to be true or probable, untrue or improbable.

Thus, the arguer's task in making a claim is to present a well-defined and supported position for the listener or reader to consider. In doing this, the arguer offers not only a claim, but the grounds and warrant that support it. The relationship between them is such that an argument is the movement from grounds, accepted by the listener or reader, through warrant to claim (Brockriede & Ehninger, 1960). These three elements make up the primary triad of the parts of an argument in the Toulmin model which structures an argument in a way that corresponds to the rational processes people use in making decisions (Golden et al., 1989). Although the arguments you hear or read may not have all three elements clearly identified, the elements of the primary triad are basic to the structure of all argument. They represent the reasoning process invoked when someone makes a statement that requires support before another is willing to accept it as true or probable.

There are four categories of claims, each of which performs a different function:

- **Factual Claims**—argue what was, is, or will be
- **Definitional Claims**—argue how something is to be defined or categorized
- **Value Claims**—argue evaluation or pass judgment on something
- **Policy Claims**—argue that something should be done

Factual claims resemble propositions of fact in that they are concerned with things that can be verified. They are concerned with past, present, or future fact. The arguer asserts that something did exist, now exists, or will exist in the future and then proceeds to offer whatever proof can be discovered to demonstrate it. Theoretically, the best proof of factual claims derives from direct observation and experimentation (Ehninger, 1974). Practically, most of us have to rely on printed sources of information for material to prove our factual claims. What might you use to prove each of the following factual claims?

- Failure to resolve the hostage crisis led to President Carter's defeat in 1980.
- The U.S. is winning its war on drugs.
- A cure for cancer will be discovered by the year 2000.

The second type of claim common to argumentation is the *definitional claim.* Such claims are used when the precise definition of a term becomes a contested issue. Definitional claims are concerned with how something is to be defined, as a particular type or category of act, individual, object, or idea. The following are examples of definitional claims:

- Mass media are commonly considered to be (are recognized as) television, radio, film, magazines, newspapers, and books.
- Computer literacy is (is defined as) the basic knowledge needed to use computers.
- The U.S. invasion of Panama in 1989 was (was categorized as) a case of international aggression.

Like the value propositions they resemble, *value claims* show the arguer's evaluation or judgment. Value claims express an attitude toward something. They are identified by the use of evaluative language in the claim statement. The following are examples of value claims:

- "Return of the Jedi" has the best special effects of the three films in the Star Wars trilogy.
- The Social Security system is a poor substitute for effective retirement planning.
- Television advertising is more effective than newspaper advertising.

The *policy claim* is like the policy proposition, stating that an action should be taken, a behavior altered. Because policy claims advocate change, they always concern the future. The following are examples of policy claims:

- You should floss your teeth once a day.
- You should purchase United States savings bonds.
- You should register to vote.

Claims, regardless of type, are what arguments are about. Because they have so much in common with propositions, it is not surprising to discover that they assert relationships between people, things, and ideas or actions. For example, in advancing the claim, "The Social Security system is a poor substitute for retirement planning," the arguer seeks to relate an institution (the Social Security system) to a judgment about it (it is a poor substitute). Standing alone, this claim represents the arguer's opinion of the Social Security system. Opinion statements of this sort are usually insufficient to alter an audience's belief or behavior. More is required.

A final point about claims concerns how they are worded. Since claims frequently express complete thoughts, they have the properties of formal sentences. Claims may be phrased as simple statements, with one relationship asserted, or as complex statements, with multiple relationships asserted. All four types of claims may be phrased as simple statements:

- Personal income tax fraud is increasing. (factual claim)
- Personal income tax fraud is the willful evasion of one's obligation to pay assessed taxes on salaries and remunerations. (definitional claim)
- Personal income tax fraud is harmful to the well-being of society. (value claim)
- Tax law enforcement should be strengthened to prevent personal income tax evasion. (policy claim)

A complex claim statement differs in that it argues more than one relationship in its assertion. Compare the following examples of complex claim statements with their simple counter parts:

- Personal income tax fraud is increasing and becoming more difficult to prosecute.
- Personal income tax fraud is the willful evasion of one's assessed taxes and a violation of federal and state laws.
- Personal income tax fraud is harmful both to United States citizens and to institutions.
- Tax laws should be revised to distribute the tax burden more equitably and punish the tax evader more stringently.

Recall that in discussing propositions, we indicated it was unwise to have multiple ideas stated in a single proposition. In wording claim statements that serve as subarguments, complex statements often serve the purpose of making argumentation more economical. By offering a single claim to argue that tax fraud harms two entities, individuals and institutions, the arguer saves time and keeps related ideas together in the listener's or reader's mind. In addition, complex statements allow the arguer to set up patterns of reasoning through comparisons. "The seriousness of income tax evasion is demonstrated by the fact that tax fraud is increasing more rapidly than crimes against persons and property." The types of crime are unrelated, but the complex statement gives the audience a basis for comparison and a measure of the extent of tax fraud.

The following example demonstrates how the concept of the prima facie case comes together with the two conventions of argumentation discussed in Chapter 2 in the formulation of an argumentative message based on a series of claims. This example, which only addresses the first stock issue for a proposition of policy, also demonstrates why claims alone are inadequate, and require the support of grounds and warrant to make that message worthy of your possible assent.

Proposition:

All students at this university should take a basic speech course as a requirement for graduation.

Presumption:

The existing state of affairs is that only some students are required to take a speech course. Presumption indicates that it is not necessary for all students to take a basic speech course and that the present system of graduation requirements should continue.

Figurative Ground Contested:

Graduation requirements for students seeking undergraduate degrees.

Burden of Proof:

The advocate of the proposition to change the present graduation requirements at this university has the burden of demonstrating a reasonable case for changing the present requirements.

Prima Facie Case:

The advocate seeks the suspension of presumption by presenting arguments, which are within the bounds of the topic and are inherent, and which a reasonable person would accept at face value. For example:

Claim 1: All students need a basic speech course.

Claim 2: Only a few departments have already recognized the need for students to have a basic speech course and required it for graduation.

Claim 3: At present, having a basic speech course become a university-wide requirement for graduation is extremely unlikely.

You are probably unmoved by this message unless the proposition states something you already believe. In that case, your attitude would cause natural presumption to override the artificial presumption established by the wording of the proposition. As advocates for the proposition, we would fail to be certain that we had established a prima facie case if all we presented were a series of claims, since claims generally are not accepted at face value. However, if we also provide the grounds and warrant which support our claims, they become good reasons for a reader's assent, a prima facie case.

Claim 1: All students need a basic speech course.

Support: At present, students are required to prepare and deliver oral assignments in many nonspeech courses. In History 101, Sociology 101, and Political Science 101, all general requirements at this university, students are required to make an oral presentation. Such requirements necessitate students having some basic speaking skills.

Claim 2: Only a few departments have already recognized the need for students to have a basic speech course and required it for graduation.

Support: At present, the Departments of Business, Accounting and Finance, and Criminal Justice, have recognized this need and require their majors to take a basic speech course. This suggests that at present some departments believe such a course should be required for graduation.

Claim 3: At present, having a basic speech course become a university-wide requirement for graduation is extremely unlikely.

Support: Individual academic departments set their own requirements with the advice and consent of the academic senate. There is no sign that departments that do not presently require their majors to take a basic speech course for graduation will do so in the foreseeable future.

Grounds

Since a claim alone is insufficient to alter belief or behavior, you must consider the second major element of the Toulmin model—grounds. Grounding the claim provides the foundation on which an argument rests, the proof required for a rational person to accept the claim as true or probable. The relationship of claims to grounds is such that "the claim under discussion can be no stronger than the grounds that provide its foundation" (Toulmin et al., 1984, p. 26). **Grounding** is that element in the argument given to the listener or reader which enables him to answer questions such as "what information supported this claim" or "upon what foundation is this claim based?" Common ground, that which the audience already knows and accepts, may exist, and you may draw on it to support claims. You may also add information to it to increase the probability of the audience's accepting your claim as true. A previously established claim may sometimes be used to ground a subsequent claim, creating what is called a chain of argument.

We sometimes use the generic term *evidence* to classify all proof in the form of facts and opinions discovered through research and used to support claims. Since other parts of the Toulmin model may also use evidence, this element in the primary triad is labeled as grounds to avoid confusion. What kinds of things appear as grounds in an argument? Experimental observations, statistics, expert opinion, personal testimony, matters of common knowledge, or previously established claims make up the pool of material used as grounds in an argument. More specific information on the nature and application of evidence is provided in Chapter 7.

The field in which argumentation takes place often influences the form and substance of individual arguments that make up a particular instance of argumentation. An argumentative field may exist specific to a particular problem area, type of decision making, or value system. We have discussed law as one field of argumentation that possesses features that make it unique, such as the artificial presumption of innocence. Other examples of fields of argument include business, religion, philosophy, the arts, the humanities, science, social science, and politics. Many of these fields can be divided into subfields. Science, for example, may be divided according to specific areas of inquiry: nuclear physics, biology, geology, meteorology, astronomy, and so on. Knowing the field of argument gives you some insights into the kinds of evidence which appropriately grounds claims, and the expectations which surround the kinds of reasoning which warrant accepting claims based on such evidence.

Some aspects of argument, however, are independent of the particulars of a given field. Although a geologist and a criminal lawyer use different strategies in preparing and presenting their arguments, both need a structure to follow in building those arguments. The same is true when you begin to create your own arguments. What you are in the process of learning is a system for constructing arguments that is transportable to any field, since argumentation is based on a series of common elements.

Claims must always be supported by grounds, since claims alone are only tentative hypotheses until something supports their veracity. If we make the claim "All students need a basic speech course," you might reasonably ask, "Why do they need it?" Grounds used to support a claim are selected to provide specific information pertinent to that claim as distinct from all other possible claims. Grounds should always point toward the claim, leading the listener or reader directly toward the conclusion specified by it. It would be foolish to attempt to prove our claim by citing statistics which indicate that at present only about one student in three takes a basic speech course. The second element of the primary triad in the Toulmin model, grounds, strengthens an argument by providing the information upon which the claim is made. Consider how we supported our claim earlier:

FIGURE 3.1

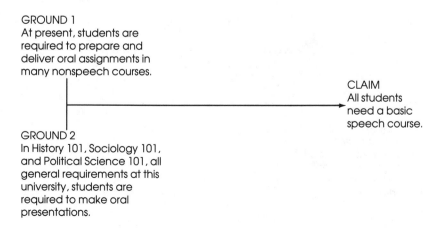

GROUND 1
At present, students are
required to prepare and
deliver oral assignments in
many nonspeech courses.

CLAIM
All students
need a basic
speech course.

GROUND 2
In History 101, Sociology 101,
and Political Science 101, all
general requirements at this
university, students are
required to make oral
presentations.

These grounds tell us that students do a fair amount of public speaking in classes required for graduation. From this it may be clear to some of our readers that our claim is valid. However, the relationship between grounds and claim is not always obvious to the listener or reader, who may ask, "Why does this mean the student must take a basic speech course?" The third element of the primary triad in the Toulmin model is needed to resolve this question.

Warrant

The third element in the primary triad is called the warrant. It shows why, if one accepts the validity of the grounds, one can also safely accept the validity of the claim. **Warrants** indicate how, given the available grounds, it reasonable for the listener or reader to make the inferential leap from them to the claim. "The assertor's task is normally to convince us not just that it was legitimate for him to adopt the initial claim for himself, but also that we should share it and so rely on it ourselves" (Toulmin et al., 1984, p. 46).

Warrants provide us with specific information about how the arguer reasons. By showing the relationship between grounds and claim, they demonstrate that making the mental leap from one to the other is rational. Warrants are found in things already accepted as true as a part of common knowledge, values, customs, and societal norms. In addition, natural laws, legal principles, statutes, rules of thumb, or mathematical formulas may establish warrants. Warrants take the form of information that shows a relationship between a claim and the grounds used to support it.

FIGURE 3.2

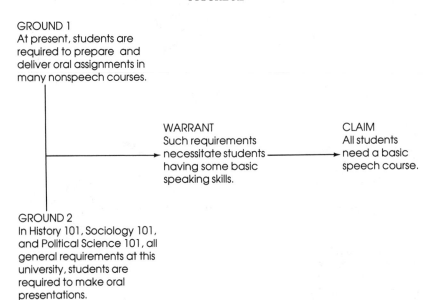

GROUND 1
At present, students are required to prepare and deliver oral assignments in many nonspeech courses.

WARRANT
Such requirements necessitate students having some basic speaking skills.

CLAIM
All students need a basic speech course.

GROUND 2
In History 101, Sociology 101, and Political Science 101, all general requirements at this university, students are required to make oral presentations.

The warrant justifies movement from the grounds to the claim. Suppose the listener or reader failed to see the connection between the requirement of giving speeches and the need to take a basic speech class, saying, in essence, "The leap I am asked to make from the grounds to the claim is unwarranted." The warrant demonstrates the logic of the connection. A rule of thumb is that if one is required to do something, being required to learn to do it properly will work to the individual's advantage.

In everyday argument, warrants are often unstated. The listener or reader must discover them. Very often, it is the warrant that defines the locus of controversy between advocate and opponent. We reason from claim to grounds or grounds to claim, and it is the warrant that specifies the reasoning. Thus, a claim stands or falls on the validity of the warrant. If you have ever confronted a claim and the grounds that purported to support it and felt, "This just doesn't make sense," it may have been because you were unable to find a warrant reasonably linking one to the other.

JEANNE: Phil really isn't a very good student.
KATHY: Why?
JEANNE: Because he's on the football team.

Kathy probably wonders, "Why does being a football player automatically make Phil a poor student?" Her question arises from the lack of a sensible warrant.

From this facetious example we can learn two things about the nature and use of warrants. First, warrants are a vital part of argumentation. If a clear link between grounds and claim is not provided, the reader's or listener's rationality may prevent acceptance of the claim. Second, the arguer should always select a warrant which the intended audience is likely to understand and accept as rational. It "makes sense" that students would learn public speaking skills in speech classes which would prove useful in their other classes. It "makes no sense" that being on the football team is a sign of poor academic achievement. The warrant is essential in argument, but it is helpful only to the extent that it is understood by the intended audience.

Summary of the Elements of the Primary Triad

1. **Claim** is a conclusion that does not stand alone but requires further proof before the audience is willing to accept it as verified.
2. **Grounds** are information of fact or opinion used to provide verification for the claim; commonly labeled *evidence*.
3. **Warrant** is the reasoning that justifies the mental leap from grounds to claim, certifying that given the grounds, the claim is true or probable.

Claim, grounds, and warrant do not always provide sufficient proof and reasoning to establish the argument. Because arguers face the need to be clear, accurate, and specific, it is some times necessary to build in additional support and qualification for the claim using the elements of the secondary triad of the Toulmin model.

Backing, Qualifier, and *Rebuttal* make up the secondary triad of elements of argument and constitute the things that show an argument's strength or force. These elements of the secondary triad need not always be used to build an effective argument, but we recommend that you use backing while you are learning argumentation skills.

Backing

The audience may require more information before they agree that, given the grounds and in light of the warrant, the claim is to be accepted. Warrants sometimes require clarification and additional information. Since "warrants are not self-validating" (Toulmin et al., 1984, p.62), the effective arguer demonstrates that the warrant supplied should be believed. **Backing** offers explicit information to establish the reliability of the warrant used in arguing the claim. "An argument will carry real weight and give its conclusions solid support only if the warrants relied on in the course of it are both sound and also to the point" (Toulmin et al., 1984, p. 63).

The type of information the arguer must use in providing backing may be either general or specific, depending on the requirements of the situation. As the warrant serves as justification for making the leap from grounds to claim, backing justifies belief in the warrant itself. Like the warrant, backing may be unstated, left to the imagination of the listener or reader. If the audience is knowledgeable on the subject being argued or familiar with the grounds used, backing, and even the warrant, may be unnecessary. However, in circumstances where the audience may not have much prior knowledge, the arguer is well advised to supply both warrant and backing to increase the believability of his position.

FIGURE 3.3

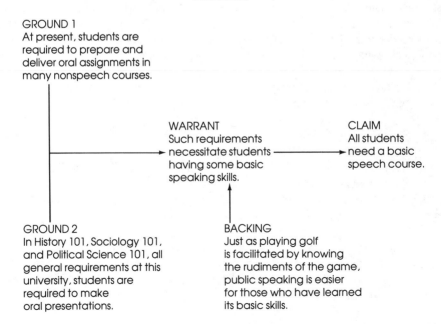

GROUND 1
At present, students are
required to prepare and
deliver oral assignments in
many nonspeech courses.

WARRANT
Such requirements
necessitate students
having some basic
speaking skills.

CLAIM
All students
need a basic
speech course.

GROUND 2
In History 101, Sociology 101,
and Political Science 101, all
general requirements at this
university, students are
required to make
oral presentations.

BACKING
Just as playing golf
is facilitated by knowing
the rudiments of the game,
public speaking is easier
for those who have learned
its basic skills.

In this example, providing both warrant and backing is not argumentative overkill. Warrant and backing help the listener or reader understand the contribution a basic speech class makes to the student's entire education. If after analyzing your audience you are undecided about whether to include warrant and backing, it is usually wisest to go ahead and include both. Claims seek to alter belief or behavior, and people are predisposed to resist change. The more proof you can provide, the greater your chances of success. Warrants and backing help an audience interpret and understand the factual basis upon which your claim rests, defining your frame of reference and instrumentally inviting them to participate in the process of argumentation.

Qualifiers

The second element of the secondary triad in the Toulmin model helps the arguer indicate the force or strength of a claim. Not all arguments have the same strength. **Qualifiers** show the degree of force the arguer believes the claim possesses. Not all claims must be qualified because, in some instances the arguer is certain of the correctness and strength of the claim. If in investigating a topic you discover exceptions or instances that disconfirm your claim, you will have to account for those exceptions in your argument. Consider the following examples of qualified and unqualified claims:

QUALIFIED: Except for those who were on the debate team in high school, all students need a basic speech course.

UNQUALIFIED: All students need a basic speech course.

The limitation of the first claim is suggested by the modal qualifier "except for those . . ." Modal qualifiers are "phrases that show what kind and degree of reliance is to be placed on the conclusions, given the arguments available to support them" (Toulmin, et al., 1984, p. 85). Modal qualifiers typically take the form of adverbs, adverbial phrases, or prepositional phrases that modify the action suggested by the claim's verb. The following are examples of frequently used qualifiers:

- presumably
- necessarily
- certainly
- perhaps
- maybe
- in certain cases
- at this point in time
- with the exception of
- in all probability

The use of such qualifying terms indicates the strength or limitation of your claim. Qualified claims provide the arguer with a means of advancing an argument in circumstances where the reliability or applicability of the claim is not absolute or universal. The arguer using qualified claims is being honest in communication, alerting the listener or reader to the fact that the claim is not valid in all instances or is not absolutely true. The use of a qualified claim does not necessarily signal that the argumentative position it supports is unsound, merely that it is not absolutely verified or verifiable.

Rebuttals

The final element of the secondary triad in the Toulmin model also provides a means of accommodating the limitations of claims. **Rebuttals** are added to claim statements that need to be limited to indicate the circumstances under which they may not be valid. Strategically, the use of a rebuttal anticipates objections to the claim and indicates the conditions under which it may not be true. Rebuttals help us avoid errors in reasoning and reflect that we are dealing with what is generally true, not absolutely true.

In our example, attachment of a rebuttal would alter the unqualified claim as follows:

- All students need a basic speech course.
- All students need a basic speech course, unless composition classes are redesigned to include instruction in public speaking skills.

You may think using qualifiers and rebuttals is not a very good idea, since they seem to diminish the strength of arguments. The use of qualifiers and rebuttals acknowledges that argumentation is not an exact science and that human affairs are seldom discussible in absolute terms. There are two circumstances in which the use of rebuttals is particularly important if you are truly interested in addressing the rationality of your listeners or readers.

The first circumstance exists when grounds, warrant, and backing support the claim only under certain conditions. This occurs in our example, calling for the qualifying statement we provided. The second circumstance occurs when grounds, warrant, and backing provide only partial support for the claim. What if History 101, Sociology 101, and Political Science 101 were not general education requirements, and fell instead into the category of classes described in the first statement of grounds? In that case, the claim would have to be restricted, so that it applied only to those students planning to take such courses rather than all students at the university.

Summary of the Elements of the Secondary Triad

1. **Backing** provides the "credentials" that help establish the legitimacy of the inferential leap from grounds to claim.
2. **Qualifiers** show the amount, or degree, of force a claim possesses.
3. **Rebuttals** limit claims, showing circumstances under which they may not be true and anticipating objections to the claim.

After hearing these arguments advocating a change in the university's general requirements for graduation, the opponent would have the opportunity to respond. He might explain why these arguments fail to justify a change in belief or behavior because of faulty support in evidence or logic. The options and obligations of the opponent will become clearer as the responsibilities of the advocate are clarified in subsequent chapters.

At this point the opponent would be well advised to ask the following questions: (1) Is presumption properly placed? (2) Is the burden of proof assumed by the advocate? (3) Is a prima facie case presented so that presumption may be assumed to be temporarily suspended? If the answer to any of these questions is no, the opponent's job is greatly simplified. The logical advantages that presumption conferred on him at the outset still remain, and the advocate has lost her opportunity to alter belief or behavior. If that is not the case, perhaps some of the strategies for opposing fact and value advocacy discussed in the next chapter would prove helpful.

LEARNING ACTIVITIES

1. Select a topic with which you are familiar. Create four arguments for that topic corresponding to the four types of claims: fact, definition, value, and policy. For each unit of argument provide and label each of the following elements: grounds, warrant, backing, and claim. When you have finished, examine your arguments. Do any of them require qualifiers or rebuttals? If so, provide and label appropriate qualifier or rebuttal statements. Concentrate on developing each part of the argument rather than on the use of evidence in establishing the grounds, warrant, and backing.
2. Find three examples of claims that use qualifiers. Develop a complete Toulmin model of each, being sure to label all parts of the argument.
3. Find three examples of claims that use rebuttals. Develop a complete Toulmin model of each, being sure to label all parts of the argument.
4. Select an argument such as an editorial, letter to the editor, or an opinion column. Complete the following:
   A. In a single sentence, state the proposition for argument.
   B. Identify the main arguments used in developing the proposition in terms of the claims advanced.
   C. Classify these claims as to type: fact, definition, value, or policy.
   D. Of the parts of argument, identify those the author uses and those left to the reader to supply.
5. Classify the following claims as to type, and identify those claims that use qualifiers and/or rebuttals. Be sure to identify that part of the claim statement which serves as qualifier or rebuttal.
   A. Argumentation is the process of arriving at conviction through the use of reason.
   B. For good performance through a severe winter, front-wheel-drive vehicles are best.
   C. Restrictions on trade and imports will not solve America's economic problems.
   D. Discretion is the better part of valor.
   E. Evolution and creation are opposing theories of the development of life on Earth.
   F. Professional sports just aren't the same now that players are paid such huge salaries.
   G. If you want to develop confidence in your ability to communicate with others, take a public speaking course.

    H. We should intervene in the affairs of Central American nations, since they are geographically close to the United States.

    I. Laughter is the best medicine.

    J. White tigers are a separate strain of Bengal tigers with recessive genetic characteristics that cause the white coat and blue eyes.

    K. In the absence of more equitable proposals, many Americans favor a policy of flat rate taxes.

    L. For those who would gain insights into the future, study the past.

6. Using the example on pages 49-50 as a model, construct an advocate's argument. Be sure to include the following:

    A. A statement of the proposition.

    B. A description of where presumption would lie.

    C. A delineation of the ground being contested.

    D. A statement of your responsibility regarding burden of proof.

    E. A prima facie case that would suspend presumption.

7. Exchange your assignment from activity 6 with a classmate. Examine the arguer's case in terms of the following:

    A. What is the locus of presumption?

    B. How does the arguer fulfill the burden of proof?

    C. In your opinion, has the arguer succeeded in creating a prima facie case?

    D. Assume that you will be the opponent for this case, indicate what you might argue in response.

SUGGESTED SUPPLEMENTARY READINGS

Ehninger, D. (1974). *Influence, Belief, and Argument.* Glenview, Ill.: Scott, Foresman.
    This book is full of excellent examples that have not become outdated. The fundamentals of argumentation are discussed in terms of the Toulmin model.

Toulmin, S., Rieke, R., & Janik, A. (1984). *An Introduction to Reasoning* (2nd Ed.). New York: MacMillan.
    For the most comprehensive discussion of the Toulmin model, turn to the source, particularly Chapters 2 through 13. This book is clear and understandable for the beginner. It also examines several fields—law, science, the arts, and management—in depth.

4

HOW ARE PROPOSITIONS OF FACT AND VALUE ARGUED?

Whether your interest in argumentation is motivated by a desire to learn to construct a sound argument or by a desire to become a more perceptive consumer of argumentation, you will discover that arguments vary considerably in form and substance. In both academics and real life, people argue about all sorts of topics: which new car to buy, which hockey player is most adept, which candidate would make a more effective president, or which law is unfair. The possibilities for subjects of argumentation are limited only by the number of topics of interest or importance that people can discover. In this chapter we will examine how arguments are developed for propositions of fact and value.

The Toulmin model provides a useful system for examining the internal structure of individual arguments. However, individual arguments are seldom sufficient to adequately advocate or oppose the central issues that define a controversy over fact, value, or policy. To develop a series of arguments adequate to the task at hand, you need to understand the three basic patterns by which claims are organized to address issues. These patterns shape argumentation for both advocates and their opponents.

SIMPLE, CHAIN, AND CLUSTER ARGUMENTS

A *simple* pattern of argument exists whenever a single claim supports an arguer's position relative to the main point being made or, in some case, the entire proposition.

Assume for a moment you are married, and have two children. While out running some errands, you see a sports car on a dealer's lot and decide you must have it. When you get home, you and your spouse argue the policy proposition: We should trade the station wagon in on a sports car. Your spouse claims owning a sports car is impractical: It has two seats (grounds 1); There are four family members (grounds 2); Family income restricts you to one car (grounds 3); Going anywhere as a family would require twice as many trips and make long family trips impossible (warrant). You didn't get your sports car, but hopefully you do get the idea behind simple patterns of argument. A simple pattern of argument is useful when a single telling point needs to be made to win the argument. However, the simple pattern also makes the job of the person you are arguing against simpler, and, if the point is not a telling one, your use of a simple pattern may give them an edge.

A *chain* of argument exists whenever a series of claims are linked together in such a way that each becomes an integral part of the next, providing grounds, warrant, or backing. Assume that when you go to work next Monday you learn you have been promoted and given a big raise. You can now afford a second car, and the dealer still has the one you want. The policy debate resumes, and your spouse changes tactics by arguing sports cars are dangerous. This argument relies on a chain of interconnected claims rather than a single one.

First, sports cars are smaller than most other cars on the road. Second, because they are smaller, they are less likely to be seen by drivers of larger cars. Third, because they are less likely to be seen, sports cars are more likely to be involved in accidents. Fourth, because they are more likely to be involved in accidents, and those accidents will involve larger cars, the sports car occupants face greater risk of injury or death, therefore making sports cars dangerous.

While it is organizationally more complex, a chain of argument is not necessarily any stronger than a simple argument. Since a chain is no stronger than its weakest link, it is not necessary to refute every argument your spouse offered to get your dream car. Arguing that a sports car's superior handling and braking increases its ability to avoid potential accidents calls the third claim in the chain into question, and possibly keeps you from having to drive to work the next day in the family station wagon.

Cluster arguments are those in which a number of claims independently point to the same conclusion. Suppose the dealer gets the car you want in a shade of red so visually arresting that even your spouse admits no one could miss seeing it as you drive down the street. The argument now shifts to the main point that sports cars are too expensive, supported by the following claims. First, the price of sports cars is higher than the price of cars in general. Second, the cost of insuring a sports car is higher than the cost of insuring a car in general because of the surcharge most insurance companies add. Third, the cost of driving a sports car is higher than the cost of most other cars because its high-performance engine requires the use of more expensive, premium fuel. Fourth, the cost of repairing a sports car is higher than the cost of repairing other cars because the parts are more expensive.

While the main point in the cluster argument is supported by four claims, as was the main point in the chain example, the cluster argument is not only organizationally complex but also stronger than simple argument. Like claims in a chain, claims in a cluster argument add up to support the main point. Unlike claims in a chain, claims in a cluster do so independently. As a result, calling the validity of any claim in a cluster into question does nothing to diminish the validity of the remaining claims. Responding to your spouse's third claim with an argument that better fuel mileage offsets the higher price of premium gas may call it into question. However, this victory does not diminish the probative force of the claims about higher purchase price, insurance premiums, of repair costs, or get you out from behind the wheel of the family station wagon.

In the argumentation that goes on in both the real and academic worlds, advocates and opponents frequently use all three patterns of argument—simple, chain, and cluster—in presenting their cases.

ADVOCATING PROPOSITIONS OF FACT

Construction of a prima facie case for a proposition of fact begins with analysis of the proposition. An advocate for the proposition "We can afford a sports car" may have discovered the locus of controversy was the implicit concern that family finances precluded the purchase of a second car. Consideration of the terms in the proposition led the advocate to decide *afford* was a term which required definition. To avoid confusion, it should be taken to mean "the ability to make payments over 60 months," not the ability to pay cash for the car.

Chapter 3 outlined the responsibilities of the advocate in constructing a prima facie case: Specify the belief to be changed, interpret the proposition in a topical manner, and present arguments adequate to satisfy the requirements of the stock issue. For a proposition of fact, this means providing a satisfactory answer to the question "Is (are) the reason(s) offered sufficient to validate the inferred relationship between the subject and the object of the proposition?" With this in mind the advocate was ready to begin constructing her case.

How does the advocate determine the inferred relationship? Interpretation of the proposition combines aspects of the definition of the key term "afford" with the issues isolated as the locus of controversy. Combining the definition of terms with the key issues of family finances, the advocate could state, "While we would be unable to purchase a sports car for cash, the state of family finances is such that we would be able to make a down payment of $5000 and monthly payments of $400 for 60 months." Identifying the inference is a way of making a broadly worded proposition more specific.

Building the Prima Facie Case

A prima facie case supporting the advocate's inference would have to answer two questions to determine the nature and strength of presumption: What is currently believed about the inference? What change in belief is sought? *The advocate must consider the audience being addressed relative to the proof needed to convince them of the probable truth of the inference.* Whether our hypothetical family is well informed and has very specific opinions about the subject or is relatively uninformed with few if any opinions makes a difference in how the advocate's case will be argued. An advocate in academic argumentation may analyze her audience to determine their beliefs, but she should treat presumption as a decision rule and view the proposition as a hypothesis that must be tested by demonstrating the inference about it is probably true.

Preempting Opposing Arguments

Finally, the advocate is well advised to take a moment to *consider the proposition from the opponent's perspective.* What is the opponent likely to argue, and where are points of clash likely to occur? Is your spouse likely to raise questions about the family's ability to afford insurance, maintenance, and operation? If so, consider including **preemptive arguments** in your case, arguments that respond to the probable objections of your opponent in advance of their being raised. Prudent use of preemptive arguments keeps the discussion focused on the proposition and keeps presumption and burden of proof where they belong.

However, the advocate who chooses to preempt an opponent's arguments must avoid excess, preempting everything but the kitchen sink, and creating a series of what might be unrelated arguments. Kitchen sink preempts are also a bad rhetorical strategy because they run the risk of weakening rather than strengthening the advocate's position in the minds of the audience. They create the impression that the advocate's position is weak if she can find so many objections to it herself.

Summary of Fact Advocacy

1. What is the inference identified in the proposition of fact?
   A. Is the inference about past, present, or future fact?
   B. What is the nature of probable truth concerning this proposition and how should it be argued?
2. What does the stock issue lead you to discover about this proposition of fact?
   A. What reasoning pattern is sufficient to establish the key issues?
   B. Is sufficient proof available to support this reasoning pattern?
   C. What will audience expectations be in regard to proof and reasoning? Should warrant and backing be included in establishing the pattern of reasoning?
3. Have the requirements of a prima facie case been satisfied?
   A. Are terms defined where necessary for clarity?
   B. Is the interpretation of the proposition topical?
   C. Does the development of issues provide good and sufficient reasons for accepting the advocate's inference?
4. Should preemptive arguments be used?
   A. Is the opponent likely to be skeptical of the advocate's interpretation of the issues?
   B. Will preemptive arguments focus argumentation or create confusion?

OPPOSING PROPOSITIONS OF FACT

Whether the proposition is one of fact, value, or policy, both advocate and opponent are obligated to follow certain rules. The advocate has the burden of proof and must develop claims that uphold it, the opponent initially possesses presumption. He may choose to question the validity of the advocate's allegations concerning fact in a number of ways. Determining exactly what to argue as an opponent is a matter of using the resources gained while analyzing the proposition and paying careful attention to what the advocate has argued.

The opponent begins construction of his case by examining the inference made by the advocate in interpreting the proposition. The inference established her unique way of describing the relationship between the subject and the object of the proposition. The opponent's task is to determine what strategies to employ in disputing the probable truth of the advocate's inference.

Evaluating the Inference

The opponent's first strategic decision is to determine whether to accept the advocate's inference as topical. The inference grows out of the advocate's definition of terms and issues discovered while analyzing the proposition. While the opponent is not obligated to dispute the manner in which the advocate has defined terms, it may be advantageous to do so. If the advocate has defined terms in such a way that the inference represents an unreasonable interpretation of the proposition, the opponent may wish to argue for a different definition of terms. The opponent should consider whether the advocate has developed a topical prima facie case.

The advocate defined *afford* solely in the context of the down payment and monthly payments. The opponent could argue that such a definition was unreasonably restrictive, especially if the advocate did not preempt arguments on the cost of insurance, maintenance, and operation. In this instance, the first element in the opponent's case would be an overview suggesting how the relationship between the subject and the object of the proposition is best understood, and why this interpretation was more reasonable than the advocate's.

Using Presumption to Dispute the Inference

Recall that presumption may be considered from a number of different perspectives. It may represent the audience's current beliefs, the sources of information to whom they defer in matters of judgment, or the view that the proposition is a hypothesis to be tested. Presumption lies with the opponent at the outset of argumentation because he nominally represents the interpretation of fact the advocate wishes to change. The opponent's second strategic decision concerns how, or if, presumption will be used.

The opponent has the option of using presumption to argue in favor of existing beliefs. If the audience was previously skeptical of the affordability of sports cars, the opponent could offer arguments that suggest their previous interpretation of fact was a correct one. This may be a weak strategic position for the opponent. If the advocate has presented a prima facie case, the presumption of previously existing beliefs the opponent is celebrating has been at best suspended, or at worst reversed.

A stronger strategic position is created when the opponent contrasts the presumption against the advocate's inference to the arguments offered on its behalf. Recall that arguments establish the probability of a claim being true, and in many cases cannot reach a level of absolute certainty. If presumption was being used as a decision rule, the opponent would be arguing that the advocate's interpretation of the proposition should be rejected as a hypothesis because the probability of its being "true" is unacceptably low.

Refuting by Denial and Extenuation

Having examined the advocate's inference to assess its topicality, and arguments in light of presumption, the third strategic decision that the opponent makes concerns how to respond to the remaining arguments. The opponent must determine whether the strategies of denial and extenuation can be used to refute these arguments. The opponent makes this decision after examining how well the advocate's arguments satisfy the requirements of the stock issue for factual argumentation.

First, the advocate will have selected a particular pattern of reasoning to use in constructing arguments substantiating the proposition. The opponent should make sure that this pattern is sufficient to demonstrate the probable truth of the inference made about the proposition. Second, the opponent may elect to challenge the sufficiency of the proof offered by the advocate. In essence, this strategy asserts that while the advocate's claims themselves would be sufficient to establish the probability of the inference, those claims are not grounded in proof and reasoning sufficient to warrant assent. The two strategies commonly used by opponents to refute the advocate's arguments are denial and extenuation.

In employing a strategy of **denial**, the opponent does not argue that the advocate has knowingly engaged in distortion or deception but that the arguments offered are nonetheless fallacious because the advocate has:

1. misanalyzed the situation, and the analysis provided by the opponent is proper;
2. overlooked certain important facts, which the opponent provides along with an explanation of the significance of their having been overlooked;
3. given undue significance to certain facts, and the opponent explains why they lack significance; or
4. drawn unwarranted conclusions from the proof, and the opponent provides the proper conclusion.

Those who disputed the conclusions of the Warren Commission, that Lee Harvey Oswald, acting alone, assassinated President Kennedy, based their arguments on the strategy of denial. Oswald was not that good a marksman, the rifle he was alleged to have used could not be fired rapidly enough to inflict all the wounds, evidence suggested that the shots came from more than one direction, and so on.

Denial is a form of refutation in which the opponent argues that the advocate has either failed to determine what proof would be sufficient to establish the inferred relationship or has failed to provide sufficient proof to establish it.

Extenuation is the other strategy commonly used to oppose the advocate of a proposition of fact. Arguments of extenuation focus on the circumstances surrounding the facts about which the inference is to be made. In this type of refutation, the opponent argues that the relationship inferred by the advocate is based on a limited understanding of the circumstances surrounding those facts, and that a more complete understanding of those circumstances would lead to a different inference. Extenuating or unusual circumstances warrant a conclusion other than the one normally drawn when these facts are present. The defense team for John Hinkley, Jr. may have conceded that he fired the shots that hit President Reagan, but it did not concede the criminality of the act. Extenuating circumstances, in this case insanity, lead to another inference—a proposition of fact advanced by the nominal opponent. John Hinkley, Jr. was not guilty of shooting the President of the United States by reason of insanity.

Responding to Preemptive Arguments

The final strategic choice the opponent must make concerns what to do if the advocate presents preemptive arguments. Is the opponent obligated to respond to them? No. The opponent has as much right to determine a strategy and select the arguments he will advance in refutation of the proposition as the advocate has in advancing the proposition itself. The opponent must examine the advocate's preempts carefully. Although they may represent a sincere and ethical attempt to keep argumentation focused, they may be nothing more than a collection of straw-man arguments cynically and unethically introduced to gain an advantage.

Summary of Fact Opposition

1. Will the advocate's definition of terms be challenged or accepted?
   A. Does the advocate's definition of terms stay within the bounds of the proposition's figurative ground?
   B. What definition of terms does the opponent offer, and why is it a more reasonable interpretation of the proposition?
2. Will the opponent support presumption?
   A. Are there existing interpretations of fact that the advocate has overlooked that the opponent wishes to argue?
   B. What is the level of probability that the advocate's arguments are true? Is that level of probability greater than the level of probability associated with presumption?
3. How will the advocate's argumentation on stock issue be opposed?
   A. Will denial arguments be used to argue that the advocate has misanalyzed the situation, overlooked important facts, given undue significance to certain facts, or drawn unwarranted conclusions?

B. Will extenuation arguments be used to argue that special conditions or circumstances result in interpretations of fact other than those made by the advocate.

4. If the advocate has presented preemptive arguments, how will they be addressed?

    A. Are such arguments truly representative of the opponent's point of view or are they straw-man arguments?

    B. Do preemptive arguments reveal flaws in the advocate's interpretation of the proposition?

Propositions of fact attempt to establish what has been, is, or will be. The means by which they are argued by advocates and opponents have applicability to value and policy propositions as well. The stock issue suggests a series of questions about the proposition that must be answered before listeners or readers feel their assent to the proposition is warranted. An understanding of the manner in which propositions of fact are advocated and opposed provides important insights into the argumentation of propositions of value. To gain greater insight into how value argument works, let us dispense with the hypothetical dispute about sports cars, and examine an example of real-world value advocacy.

VALUE ADVOCACY IN ACTION

Mrs. Susan Baker of the Parents Music Resource Center (PMRC) was the first witness to testify during the Hearing on Contents of Music and the Lyrics of Records conducted by the Senate Committee on Commerce, Science, and Transportation. Her statement, part of which is reproduced here, opened debate on a proposition of value which was never explicitly stated: "A system for rating the content of record albums, similar to that used to rate movies, poses less of a threat to society than the message contained in the lyrics of rock music." As you read her testimony, try to identify the claims Mrs. Baker makes and decide whether you think her grounds and warrant are sufficient, identify her use of patterns of argument, and look for the preemptive argument in her case.

> The Parents Music Resource Center was organized in May of this year by mothers of young children who are very concerned by the growing trend in music toward lyrics that are sexually explicit, excessively violent, or glorify the use of drugs and alcohol.
>
> Our primary purpose is to educate and inform parents about this alarming trend as well as to ask the industry to exercise self-restraint.
>
> It is no secret that today's rock music is a very important part of adolescence and teenagers' lives. It always has been, and we don't question their right to have their own music. We think that is important. They use it to identify and give expression to their feelings, their problems, their joys, sorrows, loves, and values. It wakes them up in the morning and it is in the background as they get dressed for school. It is played on the bus. It is listened to in the cafeteria during lunch. It is played as they do their homework.

They even watch it on MTV now. It is danced to at parties, and puts them to sleep at night.

Because anything that we are exposed to that much has some influence on us, we believe that the music industry has a special responsibility as the message of songs goes from the suggestive to the blatantly explicit.

As Ellen Goodman stated in a recent column, rock ratings:

The outrageous edge of rock and roll has shifted its focus from Elvis's pelvis to the saw protruding from Blackie Lawless's codpiece on a WASP album. Rock lyrics have turned from "I can't get no satisfaction" to "I am going to force you at gunpoint to eat me alive."

The material we are concerned about cannot be compared with Louie Louie, Cole Porter, Billy Holliday, et cetera. Cole Porter's "the birds do it, the bees do it," can hardly be compared with WASP, "I f-u-c-k like a beast." There is a new element of vulgarity and violence toward women that is unprecedented.

While a few outrageous recordings have always existed in the past, the proliferation of songs glorifying rape, sadomasochism, incest, the occult, and suicide by a growing number of bands illustrates this escalating trend that is alarming.

Some have suggested that the records in question are only a minute element in this music. However, these records are not few, and have sold millions of copies, like Prince's "Darling Nikki," about masturbation, sold over 10 million copies, Judas Priest, the one about forced oral sex at gunpoint, has sold over 2 million copies. Quiet Riot, "Metal Health," has songs about explicit sex, over 5 million copies. Motley Crue, "Shout at the Devil," which contains violence and brutality to women, over 2 million copies.

Some say there is no cause for concern. We believe there is. Teen pregnancies and teenage suicide rates are at epidemic proportions today. The Noedecker Report states that in the United States of America we have the highest teen pregnancy rate of any developed country; 96 out of 1,000 teenage girls become pregnant.

Rape is up 7 percent in the latest statistics, and the suicide rates of youth between 16 and 24 have gone up 300 percent in the last three decades while the adult level has remained the same.

There certainly are many causes for these ills in our society, but it is our contention that the pervasive messages aimed at children which promote and glorify suicide, rape, sadomasochism, and so on, have to be numbered among the contributing factors.

Some rock artists actually seem to encourage teen suicide. Ozzie Osbourne sings "Suicide Solution." Blue Oyster Cult sings "Don't Fear the Reaper." AC/DC sings "Shoot to Thrill." Just last week in Centerpoint, a small Texas town, a young man took his life while listening to the music of AC/DC. He was not the first. . .

Today parents have no way of knowing the content of music products that their children are buying. While some album covers are sexually explicit or depict violence, many others give no clue as to the content. One of the top 10 today is Morris Day and the Time, "Jungle Love." If you go to buy the album "Ice Cream Castles" to get "Jungle Love," you also get, "If the Kid Can't Make You Come, Nobody Can," a sexually explicit song.

The pleasant cover picture of the members of the band gives no hint that it contains material that is not appropriate for young consumers.

Our children are faced with so many choices today. What is available to them through the media is historically unique. The Robert Johnson survey on teen environment states that young people themselves often feel that they have: One, too many choices to make; two, too few structured means for arriving at decisions; and three, too little help to get there. (Record Labeling, 1985, pp. 11-12)

ADVOCATING PROPOSITIONS OF VALUE

We must begin discussion of value argumentation by indicating the range of meanings applied to the term. Consider how a number of scholars have tried to fix the meaning of something that is a psychological and sociological process:

> Values are intangibles...things of the mind that have to do with the vision people have of "the good life" for themselves and their fellows. (Rescher, 1969, p. 4).

> A value is a general conception of what is a good end-state or a good mode of behavior. (Rieke & Sillars, 1984, p. 125)

> A *value* is an enduring belief that a specific mode of conduct or end-state of existence is personally or socially preferable to an opposite or converse mode of conduct or end-state of existence. A *value system* is an enduring organization of beliefs concerning preferable modes of conduct or end-states of existence along a continuum of relative importance. (Rokeach, 1973, p. 5)

> Values may be defined as concepts that express what people believe is right or wrong, important or unimportant, wise or foolish, good or bad, just or unjust, great or mean, beautiful or ugly, and true or false, and that, therefore underlie all choices. (Walter & Scott, 1984, p. 224)

From these definitions, we can begin to perceive what the arguer grapples with in a controversy involving values. In value propositions, controversy exists over opposing evaluations of a person, object, event, or idea. The purpose of argumentation is to decide how we should judge something—a political candidate, a product, a federal program, an artistic performance, or a moral standard. As can be seen in the preceding example, advocacy of a value proposition rests on a series of fact and value claims. Construction of a prima facie case for value advocacy is a four- step process that begins by defining key terms and proceeds through consideration of the competing values within a hierarchy, to criteria identification, and ends with the application of the criteria to the value object.

Define the Value Object

Defining the value object is the first step in the process. In some instances, the value object may be instantly recognizable and may not require lengthy definition. If the advocate was arguing that rock music has had great impact on young people, she might not feel compelled to provide an extensive technical definitions of rock in order to clarify the nature of the value object. Such is not always the case. If the value proposition involves an assessment of the impact of a particular type of rock music, it would be necessary to specify what is included in the category. That definition should clarify the value object's meaning for the audience.

Identify the Hierarchy

Value hierarchy identification is the second step for the advocate. The advocate identifies a particular value standard that serves as a potential source of criteria for judging the value object, and elevates it to a point of preeminence in the hierarchy of competing societal values. The advocate has a range of fields of argument—legal, moral, ethical, political, economic, scientific—from which to choose in establishing a hierarchy. The value hierarchy created will be drawn from the field most appropriate to her approach to arguing the proposition. In the example you have just read, the field chosen is political and the value of public safety is elevated to its pinnacle.

Value argumentation attempts to resolve questions regarding an object's appropriate place in the value hierarchy. The political field has placed "Don't restrict free speech" relatively high in its value hierarchy. This value ordering was translated into law and policy, and created the circumstances that Mrs. Baker decries. In working out the hierarchy of values in a particular field, the advocate starts with the notion of what standards are appropriate and suggests why a particular value should be considered ahead of all others.

The advocate's responsibilities are to identify the field from which value standards are drawn and to locate the value object in a value hierarchy. The appropriateness of the advocate's repositioning of the value object within the hierarchy can be verified by arguments which (1) prove the superiority of the advocate's interpretation of the value object relative to all other possible interpretations, (2) offer the testimony of "admirable people" who support valuing the object of the proposition in this way, and (3) identify signs demonstrating that this interpretation best fits the existing societal value hierarchy.

Conflicting values are framed by value propositions, and value argumentation is aimed at resolving this conflict. The advocate attempts to resolve the conflict in her favor by creating a decision rule: (1) proving the advocate's value maximizes another agreed-upon value, (2) proving the advocate's value subsumes opposing values, (3) proving the advocate's value has more desirable consequences, or (4) arguing from definition in which the advocate's value is the defining property of the opposing value, (Zarefsky, 1976). This initiates argumentation on the first stock issue: "By what value hierarchy is the object of the proposition best evaluated."

Specify the Criteria

Statement of the criteria for evaluation is the third step in value advocacy. Description of the criteria for evaluation occurs first as the advocate states what criteria will be used. Because the criteria defining values lie at the heart of argumentation over these propositions, the two approaches that can be taken in identifying and applying them need to be considered, *criteria discovery* and *criteria development*.

Criteria discovery uses an existing framework of values—one already under-stood, and generally accepted—as a standard by which phenomena may be evaluated. These criteria may be set forth in a general statement, but because they are so commonly accepted, advocate and opponent focus all argumentation on the ap-propriateness of judging the value object as a member of the class of phenomena to which this evaluation is commonly applied. Consider the general outline of advocacy using criteria discovery:

Value Proposition:

Drug XYZ is an effective treatment for cancer.

Criteria as Discovered from the Medical Field:

The effectiveness of a drug rests on its ability to cure, contain, or prevent a disease, without producing adverse side effects.

Inference Relative to the Object of the Proposition:

If drug XYZ can safely cure and contain cancer without producing adverse side effects, it can be considered an effective treatment.

Claims:

Drug XYZ can cure cancer.
Drug XYZ can contain cancer.
Drug XYZ has no adverse side effects.

In this instance, the decision to adopt discovered criteria is reasonable. Most listeners and readers would consider a substance with purported medicinal properties to be effective if it had curative powers. Three criteria, the ability to cure cancer, the ability to contain cancer, and the absence of adverse side effects, are applied.

Criteria development is used in situations where the advocate finds the criteria by which value may be determined either do not exist or are not commonly understood and, therefore, require explanation. This approach may also be used in situations where the criteria may be understood but are not readily accepted and, therefore, require substantiation. If upon analyzing the proposition the advocate decides to combine value standards from different fields or to use a relatively unknown value standard, criteria development will be the best approach. In criteria development, the locus of controversy may include the stock issues of hierarchy and criteria as well as the issue of whether or not the value object is appropriately measured by them. A prima facie case is established only if proof and reasoning relevant to all three stock issues of value are presented.

In arguing value propositions, a reasonable question to ask is "Should I use discovered criteria or should I develop them?" Sometimes, a controversy over values has its genesis in a misunderstanding of the value term. A "good" sandwich may be tasty to you, economical to me, and nutritious to someone else. For this reason, criteria development may be the best approach because it has the potential of better assuring clarity of focus in argumentation rather than assuming it will occur naturally. By identifying and defining specific criteria to measure values, the advocate is less likely to find her arguments dismissed out of hand because they were misunderstood.

However, the advocate must exercise good judgment. Remember that argumentation is an instrumental process and you should consider the audience as well as your opponent. If the advocate and her audience share an understanding of the criteria that define a particular value at the outset, it is a waste of time and an insult to the audience's intelligence to use anything but a criteria discovery approach.

The advocate then establishes the necessary and sufficient characteristics of these criteria. For example, in the case arguing that drug XYZ is an effective treatment for cancer, the necessary characteristics were (1) that it could cure cancer, (2) that it could contain cancer, and (3) that it did not have seriously harmful side effects. Notice that these conditions individually are insufficient to warrant acceptance of the proposition. A drug that merely has no seriously harmful side effects is not acceptable as criteria for that drug's use. It must also possess some other properties. The criteria advanced by the advocate must include all necessary and sufficient properties of the value object being argued. How believable would argumentation have been concerning rock's potential adverse impact if the only evaluative criteria had been the presence of objectionable material in song lyrics? While the presence of such material is certainly a necessary condition for adverse impact, it alone would have been insufficient to demonstrate such impact actually took place.

In some instances, value advocacy involves consideration of two other issues relevant to the criteria. If the connection between the criteria and the value object is not readily apparent, the advocate must establish the relevance. For example, if she had wanted to evaluate rock music using other criteria, Mrs. Baker might have had to explain their relevance. If she combined criteria from more than one field, but the proposition seemed to lie in only one, she would have had to explain their pertinence to the field of the proposition. Consider a more transparent example. Although questions of abortion, euthanasia, and genetic engineering lie in a scientific-medical field, the criteria you use to evaluate them could come from legal, ethical, or moral hierarchies. As an advocate, you would have to explain how criteria from these fields are pertinent to the medical-scientific aspects of the quality of human life.

Measure the Object

Measuring the value object with the criteria for value judgment is the fourth step in value advocacy. Three subissues must be addressed as the advocate confronts the third stock issue of value argumentation: "Do indicators of the effect, extent, and inherency of the value object show that it conforms to the criteria?" The amount of proof and the number of arguments used in establishing effect, extent, and inherency are matters of choice, but all three subissues must be discussed for value advocacy to be prima facie.

By **effect** we mean what the value object is purported to do. Arguments of effect result from analysis of the immediate causes of a controversy. For example, as a value object, rock music might be said to make its listeners more sexually active. This effect can be judged depending on what the evidence suggests.

Extent relates to the severity or frequency with which the effect occurs. Does the object of the proposition do what it is purported to do with serious consequences or regularity? Arguments of extent also result from investigation of the immediate controversy; they show how significant or consequential the value object's effect is. For example, if only a very small portion of young people listen to rock music, or if only a few of them become sexually agitated, the severity or potency of the effect may be insignificant or inconsequential. Although an effect may exist, if it doesn't have some significance, it may not be worth the audience's concern. Effect and extent arguments are both necessary elements of value advocacy. If a value object is shown to exist extensively, but not have much effect on society, concern may not be justified. Equally, if the effect of the value object is very serious but does not extend to a significant number of individuals, concern may not be justified.

Inherency pertains to causation. Are the effect and its extent the result of something intrinsic to the value object? In value argumentation, inherency often results from societal attitudes toward the value object. For example, if record companies do not feel young people are influenced by what they hear, this attitude would cause a lack of concern about the content of rock records. Inherency arguments examine attitudes to determine what might produce these attitudes and the identified effects. Keep in mind that causality is often the consequence of complex, interrelated factors, so inherency arguments have to consider the possibility of multiple causes. Mrs. Baker suggests inherency is also structural, because present packaging and the lack of a rating system preclude adequate parental supervision.

Effect, extent, and inherency arguments must be present for a case to be prima facie. This is only logical. If the extent of the effect is not inherent to the fundamental nature of the value object, then measurement of the value object by the criteria is invalid. Inherency arguments prove that the effect and extent attributed to a value object are central to the value system of society or some elements of it. The most carefully constructed arguments about the effect of rock music and the extent to which it harms young listeners will not warrant a change in the audience's evaluation of the music industry if the most probable reason for the existence of the effect and its extent can't be given. After examining the following summary, decide for yourself whether Mrs. Baker's case was prima facie.

Summary of Value Advocacy Strategies

1. Define the terms of the proposition's value object.
2. Place the value object in the appropriate field and state the value hierarchy of the field in which the value object is now placed.
3. State the criteria for evaluation.
   A. Have the characteristics of the criteria been defined or described?
   B. Are the criteria identified as necessary and/or sufficient to warrant acceptance?
   C. Has the relevance of the criteria to the value object been established?

    D. Are the criteria consistent with placement of the value object in a given field?

4. Measure the value object against the value judgment criteria, demonstrating that the value object fits the criteria on the basis of the following:

    A. What element of the society is influenced by the value object? (arguments on effect)

    B. To what degree or in what amount does the effect occur? (arguments on extent)

    C. What is the cause that produces the effect and extent of the value object? (arguments on inherency)

VALUE OPPOSITION IN ACTION

The following is part of the statement made by Stanley M. Gortikov, president of the Recording Industry Association of America (RIAA), Inc. in response to earlier testimony before the Senate Committee on Commerce, Science, and Transportation. Mr. Gortikov's testimony did not immediately follow Mrs. Baker's, coming instead several hours later. Thus, we have created something of an artificial debate between the two of them, although the PMRC's concerns were well known to the RIAA. As you read what Mr. Gortikov had to say, identify the points of clash between his position and Mrs. Baker's, examine how he handles her preemptive arguments, and decide whether his opposition to what she had to say restored presumption to the music business.

> In this hearing today you have heard some understandable protests by the PMRC. We plan to act upon these concerns seriously. However, I also must spotlight five equally important truths that are essentially ignored by the PMRC in its media pronouncements, but hopefully which will be recognized by this committee.
>
> The first relates to unfairness. The sheer number of offensive recordings is minute compared with the total mass of recordings released by the industry. Yet the narrow targeting of the PMRC unfairly characterizes all artists and all companies as universal practitioners of evil.
>
> Second, positives. Whereas some lyrics may be objectionable, the mass of lyrics reflects pure entertainment or socially positive attitudes and practices. If recordings do in fact affect young minds, as maintained by the PMRC, then the heavy thrust of our industry's input is positive, not negative.
>
> Other forces. The PMRC, and therefore this committee, is focusing solely on rock music. But why is only rock music unfairly singled out for the scrutiny of the PMRC and the U.S. Senate while all other explicit negative influences on younger children go untargeted? What about movies and magazine ads, prime time television, soap operas, books, cable programs? If there is to be a negative review of negative forces in the environment of younger children, let it be a review of all such forces, not one which focuses on rock music alone. If the PMRC somehow were to be able to purify all music according to its own standards, who is going to purify the remainder of their children's world?

Fourth, behavior. The PMRC concentrates on modes of human behavior that it finds objectionable, but those realities are not invented by record companies, songwriters or performers. Adults in the society, some of them parents, are the real initiators of those extremes. Recorded music reflects rather than introduces society's values and the realities of human conduct, both good and bad.

And last, in respect to rights, although in this forum we address the rights of parents and younger children, we cannot submerge the rights of others. We are on delicate ground here in respect to censorship and the first amendment. We must not trample the rights of parents and other adults whose standards do not coincide with those of the PMRC or any other group. Further, recording artists and songwriters have their own rights and freedoms of expression and even have contractual protections that legally must be respected. We must assure that the noble intentions of the PMRC do not somehow get translated into a dilution of the rights and freedoms of others.

Those five realities which I have just articulated merit the consideration of this committee, too. And as to the PMRC, I am getting a little apprehensive about its motives and fervor.
. . .

The PMRC now seems committed to impose its will on an entire creative community and on broadcasters, on record retailers, and thus on all who buy and hear recorded music.
. . .

The members of the PMRC are parents. I and many of my colleagues are parents, too. The PMRC has no monopoly on love and concern for kids. Child supervision is my personal parental responsibility, and degrees of control versus freedom are mine alone to set. I certainly would not be content to assign any part of my responsibility to some outside surrogate, like a record company, a radio station, a censorship panel, a government body, or a parent organization.

"Censorship" can take subtle forms and need not be confined to a deliberate surgical excising of dirty words. Censorship, in one of its manifestations, can be the stifling of the creative act—an insidious filtering out of creative energy—a homogenizing of creative output.

Some musical content may be considered offensive. We offend some people some of the time. Down through the ages, there always has been shocks in popular music—even from prime shockers like Cole Porter, Elvis Presley, and the Beatles. I cannot recall, however, definitive damage to children from any one of them. We here today, in fact, are ourselves some of those "victimized" children.

Some of our music, then, may cause one to wince. That wincing, the fleeting moments of discomfort, are the occasional prices one pays to get access to basic creative energy, to the talent pool, to the resources of excitement from which music and all art forms flow. One risks strangling those precious energies by rules and criteria and panels and coalitions and inquiries and even inscriptions. (Record Labeling, 1985, pp. 96-98)

OPPOSING PROPOSITIONS OF VALUE

The analysis of the proposition and search for issues are just as important for the opponent as they are for the advocate. To gain any advantage from presumption, the opponent must be aware of how the value object is presently viewed in its field in particular and by society in general. The opponent should investigate every possible aspect of the value object—how it is regarded in its field, what opinions have formed about it, what value standards are used to judge it, and what controversies exist concerning it. On the basis of this analysis, the opponent chooses his strategies for refuting the advocate's case.

Establish Strategy

We shall conclude this chapter by cataloging the opponent's options for responding. Since any individual response will be tailored to fit the strengths and weaknesses of the advocate and opponent's respective position, some of these techniques may not have been included in Mr. Gortikov's arguments. The opponent normally begins with an overview of the value proposition reflecting the position he will take in presenting arguments refuting the advocate's case. This is sometimes referred to as a philosophy, and it expresses the essence of the opponent's perspective on the controversy and includes a preview of his strategy. It tells the listener or reader that he will defend present values, present alternative values, or demonstrate the weakness of proof and reasoning in specific areas of the advocate's arguments; in short, it elucidates whatever strategy is chosen. The purpose is to clarify where the opponent stands on the proposition's value object.

Examine Definitions and Hierarchy

Since the first step in advocacy was to define the value object, that may be the opponent's next area of concern. Has the value object been properly defined? Does the opponent agree with the method of definition used by the advocate? If he thinks that the value object should include elements the advocate has failed to consider, or exclude elements she has included, the first point of clash with the advocate will be over how to define the value object.

The opponent's next step is to make use of the stock issues of value argumentation. Recall that the first stock issue asks by what value hierarchy the value object is best understood. There are two questions the opponent should ask in preparing arguments about this issue. First, is the hierarchy the advocate has chosen really valued by society as the advocate suggests? The opponent may attempt to demonstrate that society or those in the field of the proposition do not accept the validity of the value hierarchy the advocate has identified. Second, has the advocate identified a value hierarchy appropriate to better understanding of the value object? Does he see other more appropriate value hierarchies that the advocate has failed to recognize? Does the advocate provide an adequate justification for her choice of a value hierarchy? Should the hierarchy be determined by some other standard?

In terms of the example of value advocacy provided earlier in this chapter, the advocate's choice of hierarchy and criteria restricted her opponent's options. That does not mean that he has no choices. He still could choose to dispute the value that she has placed at the pinnacle of the hierarchy, which he did, substituting creativity or freedom of thought and expression. This illustrates one of the fundamental differences between fact and value argumentation. While it would have been inappropriate for the opponent to respond to the advocate of fact by saying "Yes, we can afford a sports car, but sports cars are very dangerous," the opponent in value argumentation could propose an alternative candidate for the pinnacle of the hierarchy.

The reason for the difference is that agreeing to argue a proposition of fact commits both advocate and opponent to contest its figurative ground. Relative safety is a different proposition, albeit a value proposition, that concerns an entirely separate ground. Agreeing to argue a value proposition commits advocate and opponent to an exploration of how something should be judged, with at least part of the figurative ground covering the decision as to what constitutes the most appropriate basis for judgment.

Challenge Criteria

The opponent's next concern is with the appropriateness of the criteria used in measuring the value object in terms of its effect, extent, and inherency. Has the advocate established unique criteria for a value object for which other more commonly understood or accepted criteria exist? The opponent may choose to argue that the value criteria are inappropriate to the value object because these criteria are too unusual or more appropriate to measuring some other object. He would then provide arguments establishing that better criteria exist, criteria that are more appropriate to the value object, or more widely recognized by experts in the field or society, or that the advocate has misinterpreted the value in question.

Refute Measurement

Finally, the opponent will turn to the third stock issue to determine if the value object is appropriately measured by the value criteria. With the concepts of effect, extent, and inherency clearly in mind, the opponent considers strategies for opposition. First, remembering that the advocate must establish a prima facie case, the opponent asks himself, "Have effect, extent, and inherency been argued by the advocate?" If one or more have not, a prima facie case has not been established. He should begin refutation, by pointing this out. Second, since arguments of effect, extent, and inherency are advanced as claims, they require supporting proof and reasoning. The opponent should examine the advocate's support for claims, asking, "Does the proof and reasoning offered by the advocate meet the tests established to determine its validity?" If it does not, the existence of a prima facie case would be in serious doubt.

If after analyzing the advocate's case construction strategy, the opponent decides that the value criteria are fairly drawn, he must concentrate refutation on the goodness of fit between the criteria and the value object in the proposition. Since we have already discussed the use of the strategies of denial and extenuation against claims used to support propositions of fact, we shall not repeat that discussion here, but careful reading of Mr. Gortikov's testimony reveals his use of both.

In employing denial and extenuation to oppose the value advocate, the opponent searches for proof and reasoning to ground (1) arguments stating that the effect suggested by the advocate occurs only in an exceptional case or that extenuating circumstances produce the effect, (2) arguments denying that the value object's influence is as extensive as the advocate suggests, (3) arguments showing that only a small segment of those who place value on this object are influenced, (4) arguments showing that prominent sources in the field do not consider the effect or the extent to be of great importance, (5) arguments showing that either the effect or the extent is a temporary phenomenon brought about by the unusual circumstances, and (6) arguments challenging inherency by demonstrating that the value in question is either not central to the society or is subject to change over time.

Summary of Value Opposition Strategies

1. Give a statement of the opponent's philosophy that overviews the stand to be taken against the advocate's case.
2. Challenge or accept the advocate's definition of the value object.
3. Consider what criteria should be used to measure the value object.
   A. Is the asserted value as good as the advocate claims?
      1) Does society recognize it as good?
      2) Do experts in the field recognize it as good?
   B. Have the value criteria been correctly identified?
      1) Are there other values involved in the standard used?
      2) Does the advocate provide adequate justification for the value criteria selected?
      3) Is there a better standard by which to evaluate the value object?
4. Evaluate how appropriately the value object has been measured by the value criteria.
   A. Does the value object fit the stated criteria?
   B. Is the effect of the value object created by an exceptional case or extenuating circumstances?
   C. Is the extent temporary, insignificant, or improperly measured?
   D. Is the value inherent in the value hierarchy of society or the field of the value proposition? Is there some alternate causality?

Propositions of value attempt to establish how something or someone ought to be judged. They are argued by determining the criteria or standards by which the evaluation ought to be made and then determining the goodness of fit between the object being evaluated and these criteria. Advocates of value propositions must be sure their argumentation considers effect, extent, and inherency, regardless of whether they proceed by means of criteria discovery or criteria development. The opponent, besides employing techniques applicable to arguing propositions of fact, may also use the strategies of proposing different criteria and charging improper classification. Understanding how propositions of both fact and value are argued provides important insight into the next chapter's subject—how policy propositions are argued.

LEARNING ACTIVITIES

1. Examine the text of a landmark Supreme Court decision such as Marbury v Madison (1803), Brown v the Board of Education of Topeka (1954), or Roe v Wade (1973). What issues seemed most important in the court's decision? What interpretations of law were made in deciding the case? What factual inferences form the bases of the decision?

2. How would you discover probable truth for the following propositions?
   A. One of the two major political parties will nominate a woman for the presidency by the end of this century.
   B. The international monetary system will collapse under the weight of third-world loan defaults.
   C. Nuclear arms will be brought under international control.
   D. Computer literacy will soon be a requirement for graduation at most four-year colleges and universities.
   E. The number of narrow-cast services on cable television will continue to expand.

3. Read Ramona Parish's essay, "Messages from a Welfare Mom," in *Newsweek*, May 23, 1988, p. 10. The author argues the factual proposition: Living on welfare destroys an individual's dignity. What is the inferred fact? What is done to prove the probability of the alleged fact? Is the argumentation sufficient to warrant your assent? Why or why not?

4. Read the essay, "The Elderly Aren't Needy," by Robert J. Samuelson, in *Newsweek*, March 21, 1988, p. 68. The author uses the strategies of opposition in refuting the belief that most elderly Americans live in poverty. What strategies of opposition are used? How does the author support his claims? Do you find his argumentation convincing? Why or why not?

5. Discuss each of the following value propositions in terms of the value(s) to be supported by the advocate, the field(s) from which value criteria could be taken, and the specific judgmental criteria that might be used in measuring the value object.
   A. Students will benefit from classical literature studies in grades 6 through 12.
   B. For most people, buying a home computer is a waste of money.
   C. The rights of endangered species ought to take precedence over the rights of indigenous human populations.
   D. Humanitarian rather than geopolitical objectives ought to govern foreign policy decisions.

6. Read the essay "Confessions of a Teacher," by Michael Shenefelt in *Newsweek*, March 5, 1990, pp. 10-11. Analyze the case using the stock issues of value argument. Which advocacy responsibilities does Professor Shenefelt fulfill? Are there any that he omits? What are the value object, hierarchy, and criteria?

SUGGESTED SUPPLEMENTARY READINGS

Church, R. T., & Buckley, D. C. (1983). Argumentation and Debating Propositions of Value: A Bibliography. *Journal of the American Forensic Association, 19,* 239-50.
A comprehensive bibliography on value argumentation covering the work published in the field of speech and related disciplines.

Naisbitt, J. (1982). *Megatrends.* New York: Warner Books.
Naisbitt predicts change based on social, economic, technical, and political shifts, and he identifies ten ways in which society will change between now and the end of this century. Among the areas of interest is how technology will influence what is valued. This is a very readable book and an excellent example of argumentation of future fact.

Rieke, R. D., & Sillars, M. O. (1984). *Argumentation and the Decision Making Process.* Glenview, Ill.: Scott, Foresman and Co.

Chapter 6 discusses the American value system and argues that understanding such systems are necessary if we are to understand how decisions are made. The book represents an audience-centered approach to the study of argumentation, and the authors suggest means of discovering your audience's values.

Sproule, J. M. (1980). *Argument: Language and Its Influence.* New York: McGraw-Hill.

This is a book for the more advanced student, but it provides extensive discussion of argumentation in the larger context of persuasion. Of particular interest here is Chapter 4, "Descriptions: Arguments That Draw Issues of Fact," in which Sproule considers the use of examples, statistics, and testimony as the basis for grounding factual arguments. The chapter features an interesting extended example of argumentation on the existence of UFOs.

Warnick, B. (1981). Arguing Value Propositions. *Journal of the American Forensic Association, 18,* 109-19.

The author examines the basic issues found in value propositions. She suggests that to be prima facie, the advocate's case must establish a set of values that, when applied to the value object, are shown to be more fundamental than those presently associated with the value object. As a result, analysis of value propositions must be centered on how the audience or society views that which is evaluated. An outline of the steps to follow in analyzing a value proposition is provided.

Young, M. J. The Use of Evidence in Value Argument. In J. Rhodes & S. Newell (Eds.), *Proceedings of the Summer Conference on Argumentation.* ERIC Document ED 181 503.

A very good discussion of what is necessary to ground value arguments. In particular, the concepts of *harm* and *significance* are discussed as value judgments intrinsic to policy argumentation.

5

HOW ARE PROPOSITIONS OF POLICY ARGUED?

Those who successfully advocate and oppose propositions of policy employ their understanding of how fact and value are argued. They also may benefit from the fact that the field of speech communication has historically devoted a great deal of critical attention to the unique requirements of policy argumentation. Intercollegiate debate has served as an academic context for testing ideas as well as a crucible for examining the means by which those ideas may best be tested. As a result, a considerable body of knowledge has emerged relative to how propositions of policy, and more recently value, are argued. While Appendix A discusses intercollegiate debate in more detail, the ideas discussed in this chapter apply many of the concepts developed in contest debating to policy argumentation in general.

ADVOCATING POLICY PROPOSITIONS

Creation of a prima facie case for a policy proposition begins with the advocate's identification of a disparity between things as they exist now, or are likely to exist in the future, and how they would be under a more ideal system (Sproule, 1980). For example, suppose a group of people were endangering public safety, and the societal response was inadequate to prevent them from continuing to do this. Many people believe this is what is actually happening in the case of drunk drivers, and that a disparity exists between the way things are and the way things ought to be. The analysis of stock issues in a policy proposition leads to discovering the existence of this disparity. The first stock issue asks what unresolved problems exist or will exist in the future: *Is there a reason for change in the manner generally suggested by the policy proposition?*

Advocacy of the First Stock Issue

Answering this question is important because, if no reason for change exists, change is unwarranted. If someone walks up to you and asks to borrow ten dollars, they are advocating the policy proposition, "You should give me ten dollars." Your probable response will either be "no," because they've given you no reason to warrant action on your part, or "why?" because you would like to know their reason. Inquiry into the reason for change involves consideration of what the advocate perceives the disparity between actual and ideal to be.

The advocate's response normally takes the form of a value claim, and four subissues must be advanced to win assent. These subissues provide the answers to questions customarily asked to determine whether a reason for change exists:

1. What is the nature of the disparity?
2. How extensive is the disparity?
3. Does the disparity cause harm to something or someone?
4. Is the disparity inherent in the present nature of things?

Advocacy of the first stock issue, reason for change, makes the listener or reader aware of an unresolved problem now, or in the future, which is a consequence of the way things are at present.

Identify the Disparity   The first subissue, the nature of the disparity, requires the advocate to substantiate at least one definitional claim, that something which presently exists can be defined or classified as representing a disparity of a certain type. Because there is a natural resistance to change, people will usually be unresponsive unless the disparity is a serious one. "Accidents caused by drunk drivers kill innocent victims." The seriousness of the disparity is suggested in the definitional claim and further supported by arguments on the next two subissues, extent and effect. This should sound familiar since it is basic value argumentation. The advocate may discover that more than one disparity must be identified to produce a case that is compelling or prima facie. "Accidents caused by drunk drivers kill and injure innocent victims, and increase the cost of auto insurance for us all." Although this may make the advocate's case complex, the use of cluster arguments would be no more complex than when a number of different ways of measuring the extent of a single effect are argued.

Quantify the Disparity   The second subissue explains or quantifies the extensiveness of the disparity, alleging the magnitude of this present or future problem. If the extent of the problem is demonstrable in quantitative terms, the advocate will advance and substantiate a factual claim. If the question is addressable only qualita-tively, the claim will be definitional—that the disparity is to be classified as being of a certain qualitative type, widespread or all-encompassing for example.

Characterize the Consequences

Characterize the Consequences   The third subissue concerns the ef-fects, or consequences, of the disparity. A value claim is presented, suggesting that the consequences are in some way harmful to those experiencing the disparity. Why is this important? We could probably prove that every person reading this book is not presently a student at the University of Tokyo, a disparity that is extensive; but unless we could demonstrate that as a result you are being hurt, our advocacy of the policy proposition "You should transfer to the University of Tokyo" would be unwarranted. Thus, the advocate uses the third subissue to examine the consequences of the present or future disparity. These consequences are evaluated in negative terms by first establishing the criteria for harm and then demonstrating the goodness of fit between those criteria and the present disparity.

Establish Inherency   The final subissue used in developing argumentation on the first stock, reason for change, concerns itself with inherency. You might review the discussion of inherency in Chapter 3. In policy propositions, inherency is argued to determine the cause of the serious, extensive, and harmful disparity. Blame for the existence of the disparity is placed at the doorstep of things as they are now—existing laws, institutions, or beliefs. A factual claim is used to establish the causal relationship between that which exists and the disparity. The demonstration of inherency is critical. Subscribing to the philosophy of "If it ain't broke don't fix it," the advocate's readers or listeners will be unwilling to change something that is apparently innocent of having caused the problem for which a remedy is sought.

If the reason for change rests on the hypothesis that some more desirable future state will not be achieved because of things as they are now, the advocate must demonstrate that this state will probably not be reached because of the way things are now. People tend to give existing laws, institutions, or beliefs the benefit of the doubt, assuming they are likely to change naturally in ways that result in a future that is better than our past or present. The advocate must preclude this kind of thinking by demonstrating that existing barriers render the more desirable future state she supports, unavailable by any means other than those she will propose.

Having successfully upheld the burden of proof with regard to the first stock issue, reason for change, the advocate must now propose a way to remedy the disparity. The remedy is a new policy by which a preferred state, one in which the disparity would cease to exist, is reached. *Does the proposed policy resolve the reason for change?*

Advocacy of the Second Stock Issue

Assuming change is warranted because the advocate has proven the existence of a problem, she must provide the solution to win assent. This solution, or proposed policy, should explain exactly what is to be done, and it should include the following elements:

1. **Change**—What behaviors are to be enacted that are not presently being enacted? What will be done differently?
2. **Mechanism**—On whose authority will these behaviors be undertaken? Will a new law be passed, a new agency or institution created, or will individuals do this on their own?
3. **Financing**— If the change or mechanism incurs any costs, how much will they be, and how will they be paid?
4. **Enforcement**—Unless everyone is willing to go along with the change, how will violations be detected? Who will be responsible for this detection, and how will violators be dealt with? What means are used to assure compliance?

Unless a separate definition of the key terms in the proposition is provided, the advocate's proposal serves as an operational definition of the meaning of the proposition.

Suppose the advocate has suggested that present laws regarding drunk drivers should be changed because of the number of deaths and injuries attributable to them. The proposal for change might include the following:

> The federal government will remove the requirement of probable cause and mandate that law enforcement officers randomly stop one vehicle per shift and administer a test of sobriety to the driver. Drivers with blood alcohol levels above the legal limit shall be subject to license revocation for one year. Persons caught driving during the period of revocation will receive a one-year jail sentence. Since this proposal involves the addition of no new manpower or facilities, it is essentially a free solution to the problem.

All four elements a policy proposal should have are contained in this example. After its details are spelled out, the advocate will be obliged to demonstrate how the reason for change has been satisfied. This involves considering the third stock issue: *What are the consequences of the proposed policy?*

Advocacy of the Third Stock Issue

At the very least, we expect solutions to work, to solve the problems that called them into being. If, in addition to this workability, other good things happen coincidentally, we are very pleased. The advocate guides the listener or reader through the consequences of the proposed policy by considering four questions:

1. How does the proposed policy address the disparity?
2. How does the proposed policy overcome its inherency?
3. How workable is the proposed policy?
4. What are the subsidiary effects of the proposed policy?

These four questions represent the subissues the advocate must develop in support of the third stock issue of policy argumentation, the consequence of change.

Demonstrate Solvency   The first question pertains to the concept sometimes referred to as solvency. Does the proposed policy address the disparity in such a way that it eliminates or substantially minimizes it? Does the proposed policy get us to, or at least nearer to, the more ideal state the advocate seeks? The proposed solution to the problem created by drunk drivers rests on the laws of probability. If 10 percent of the people who are driving could not pass a sobriety test, then 10 percent of the random stops should result in arrests and convictions. The penalties are hoped to be severe enough to deter people from driving while intoxicated or to incapacitate them if they were not deterred but were caught. The advocate of this policy would have to offer proof and reasoning in support of these claims alleging the solvency of the proposal.

Overcome Inherency   The second subissue is important. If existing institutions cannot address the reason for change because of inherent barriers, the advocate must demonstrate how her proposal is not hamstrung by these same barriers. Normally, the mechanism section of the policy proposal will fiat the necessary change. If the barrier was structural—for example, the present requirement of having probable cause before stopping a driver and administering a sobriety test—the advocate would argue that her proposal removed or altered it in such a way that it no longer constitutes an impediment. If inherency was a consequence of something's absence at present—for example the lack of a federal mandate and determinant sentencing for drunk drivers—the advocate must show how her proposal fills these gaps. If inherency resulted from attitudes, the advocate must be able to prove these same attitudes will not undermine the solvency of the proposal, or provide some means to change them. For example, if inherency was due to police attitudes—they feel that catching murderers, rapists, and thieves is more important than stopping someone who may have had too much to drink—the advocate would be in serious trouble because those charged with enforcing her proposal would not attach much importance to the task.

Establish Workability   The third subissue turns attention to the fundamental nature of the proposal itself and analyzes its workability. A proposal may solve problems and overcome inherent barriers but be totally unrealistic and unworkable. To suggest that the most effective solution to the problem of drunk driving would be to prohibit the manufacture and sale of alcoholic beverages may be true but unworkable. The nation tried that particular policy for moral reasons in the past and discovered that most Americans not only did not favor it, but willfully violated it. The advocate must develop and use criteria of effectiveness to argue the proposed policy is more workable than that which it replaces.

Identify Subsidiary Effects   The fourth subissue, identifying the subsidiary effects of the proposed policy, allows the advocate to conclude discussion of the consequences of change by pointing to whatever desirable side effects occur as a result of assent to her proposal. Do the members of her audience get something for nothing? The advocate of tougher action against drunk drivers could claim they might. While her reason for change concerns deaths and injuries attributable to those who drive while intoxicated, a problem the proposed policy is thought to remedy, a subsidiary effect of the policy might be lower insurance premiums for everyone.

To be considered a subsidiary effect, something must be an inherent consequence of the success of the proposed policy, over and above remedying the disparity that motivated its being proposed. Subsidiary effects are like fringe benefits, they are nice to have but they are not always available. Therefore, the absence of subsidiary effects does *not* render an advocate's case non-prima facie. Nor do subsidiary effects constitute a warrant for change in themselves. If a reason for change does not exist, or if the proposal for change fails to remedy the problem it is intended to resolve, the advocate's cause is lost even if her proposal produces some pleasant side effects.

Patterns of Organization

Before we turn to an example of policy advocacy, some comments about patterns of organization are in order. While we have labeled the stock issues first, second, and third, the logic of the advocate's approach should dictate the order in which they are presented. The overall pattern presented here reflects traditional organization, known as need-plan-advantage. It is used when the reason for change involves righting past wrongs and showing the subsidiary benefits of the proposed policy. For this type of advocacy, the order in which the stock issues have been discussed in this chapter is most appropriate.

However, if the reason for change relates to the attainment of a more desirable future state, then the means to attain that state, the second stock issue, should be discussed first. This is called comparative advantage structure. It compares the advocate's proposed policy to existing policy and argues that the advocate's proposal is more advantageous. It is used when serious present problems under the stock issue of reason for change cannot be discovered or are not widely accepted. It is also used when there is almost universal agreement that a reason for change exists, but controversy surrounds the question of the best future course of action. This is often the case in legislative debate. Argumentation compares the proposed solution to existing policy. The second and third stock issues, the proposed change and the consequences of change, provide the focus for argumentation.

Although there is no rule regarding how many advantages are necessary to warrant a change, the advantages must be demonstrated to result from the new policy and their value must by qualitatively or quantitatively measurable. The same is true of advantages claimed in the traditional need-plan-advantage case. The organization of comparative advantage advocacy begins with the presentation of the policy proposal that specifies change, mechanism, financing, and enforcement. The advocate then indicates one or more advantages to be achieved by adopting this proposal. Each advantage should be unique. Only the proposed policy, when compared to existing policy, is capable of achieving it. In addition to demonstrating uniqueness, the advocate establishes a quantitative and/or qualitative measure of each advantage's value to society.

A third type of organization exists for policy advocacy that uses many of the features of value argumentation. Goals-criteria advocacy begins by examining what society values and the goals it has set to achieve these values. If full employment is a goal of society stemming from our valuation of the work ethic, a proposal to achieve full employment might be advocated on the basis that it better achieves the goal and, therefore, more fully realizes the relevant value. Criteria are used in the same manner as in value argumentation. The proposed policy is then examined in terms of value criteria that measure its ability to obtain the desired goal.

The advocate's presentation may be organized in accordance with different philosophies—traditional, comparative advantage, or goals-criteria—but arguments will still address the same stock issues. As you read through the following example of policy advocacy, decide which pattern of organization the advocate is using.

POLICY ADVOCACY IN ACTION

On June 20, 1984, California Representative Norman Y. Mineta testified before the Subcommittee on Administrative Law and Government Relations of the House Committee on the Judiciary. The Subcommittee was holding hearings on a series of bills dealing with the relocation of Japanese-Americans and Aleut Indians during World War II. Representative Mineta's speech, excerpted below, advocated the policy proposition: "The subcommittee should recommend passage of H.R. 4110 to the House of Representatives."

> Congress, with the assistance of this subcommittee, enacted in 1980 Public Law 96-317, creating a special Commission on Wartime Relocation and Internment of Civilians. That Commission was to study the internment during World War II of Americans of Japanese ancestry and of Aleut islanders and to "recommend appropriate remedies."
>
> I believe that Commission's work was exhaustive and complete. Its report, "Personal Justice Denied," is the definitive study of the internment. . .
>
> That report showed conclusively that Americans of Japanese ancestry were law-abiding, loyal Americans, who posed absolutely no threat to the peace and security of this Nation, and wanted nothing more than the opportunity to share in the liberty and defense of this Nation. Moreover, the Commission concluded that the internment constituted a "grave personal injustice" that violated our most basic norms of constitutional due process.
>
> After the Commission issued its report and recommendations last year, a group of Members of both bodies met and decided to draft legislation that implemented all of the Commission's findings, "alpha to omega," as one of us said. That is now the bill before us, H.R. 4110.
>
> H.R. 4110 contains an explicit legislative finding accepting the Commission's findings as accurate and complete. The legislation also includes the five specific recommenda-

tions proposed by the Commission as remedies for the historic damage to civil liberties caused by the internment. These five remedies in the bill are:

First, a formal apology by the Government for the internment. As title I of the bill states, "On behalf of the Nation, the Congress apologizes."

Second, a request that the President offer pardons to those few dozen individuals who were convicted of violating the internment and associated laws and directives because of their refusal to accept racially discriminatory treatment.

Third, a request that the administration review "with liberality" applications for administrative relief such as changing dishonorable discharges to an honorable status. Several thousand young men were summarily thrown out of the Armed Forces in 1942 solely because of their Japanese ancestry. No new statutory authority is created here.

Fourth, the creation of a trust fund to finance educational, social and humanitarian programs designed to foster knowledge and concern for civil liberties. This fund would have $1.5 billion appropriated by Congress and would exist only until those funds were spent. The fund would be managed by a nine-member board of directors.

And fifth, the payment out of that trust fund of $20,000 to each of the estimated 60,000 survivors of the internment camps. The $20,000 figure was set by the Commission.

Although the loss of property and income from the internment is estimated at perhaps as high as $6.2 billion in comparable current dollars, these payments are intended, in my mind, not as compensation for lost property but as liquidating damages resulting from the profound abridgement of basic constitutional rights.

Now, I share the belief of many that these payments are an essential element of the legislative package, and that any step short of compensation would be an empty gesture. Similar recommendations are included for the few hundred Aleuts who were interned.

The case for this legislation is based on the conclusion that the internment was caused not by any military or security necessity, but by prejudice, ignorance, fear, and greed.

Moreover the internment constitutes one of the most significant and one of the most indefensible abridgements of civil rights in our history. I realize that people of good faith may well disagree on the appropriate remedy for the damage left by the internment. But surely the internment itself is nothing more than a shameful and dishonorable episode that is a blot on our Nation's record until erased with this legislation. . .

Mr. Chairman, on behalf of all Americans of Japanese ancestry who were interned, I ask and entreat this subcommittee to give us back our honor. Give us back the dignity and the pride that this Government so unnecessarily took from us in 1942. Every citizen of this land will benefit from our rededication today to equal justice.

I realize that some who were involved in the original decision to intern us are still defending their actions. I suppose if I had made as big a mistake as they did, I would also be reluctant to admit it. I do not think they were evil men, but they were caught up in a web of racism and fear that blinded them to the truth and set them on their foolish course.

Their blindness was monumental. Gen. John L. DeWitt, head of the Western Defense Command and a key figure in the internment, actually managed, in speaking of the fact that no disloyal acts had been committed by Americans of Japanese ancestry, to say "The very fact that no sabotage has taken place to date is a disturbing and confirming indication that such action will be taken." So much for the principle of "innocent until proven guilty."

But I come back to our premise. As the Commission report made plain, we were not traitors, we were farmers, we were business men, we were homemakers and teachers. We were not secret agents. Nearly 25,000 of us were 14 years old or younger. Nearly 6,000 were born in camp. And 1,862 internees died while in camp, a figure which does not include people like my father-in-law, Saijiro Hinoki, an immigrant who owned a dry cleaning store in Colusa, CA and was a member of the local Rotary Club as early as 1937.

The FBI arrested Mr. Hinoki early in 1942 without charges, and for 2 months told his family nothing about where he was or why he was being held. Finally, the family was told he had been sent to a detention camp in Bismarck, ND. Those who knew him—because I never met him—said Mr. Hinoki never regained his lost will to live. He died a few years after leaving camp.

I firmly believe, as the Commission found, that there was no reason to distrust the Americans of Japanese ancestry. But even if there had been reasons to suspect the loyalty of some individuals, which I stoutly deny, what excuse is that to lock up 120,000 innocent and loyal Americans without a trial, without regard to the Constitution?

We did not lock up German-Americans. We did not lock up Italian-Americans. Nor did we even seriously consider locking up Americans of Japanese ancestry on Hawaii, where the military dangers were the greatest.

Why is it that we just happened to lock up an ethnic group subject to decades of blatant and cruel discrimination? Because this was the group that popular opinion—and, indeed, the entire California delegation at that time— demanded to have locked up.

Mr. Chairman, I could speak on this subject for quite a while, but my time is limited and you have been very generous with me. I could tell you about some of loyal and brave men that I know, men who left the internment camps to fight bravely to defend this Nation, and who rescued the lost battalion of the 36th Texas Arrowhead Division. I could tell you of the old women torn from their homes of decades and forced to live in cold, spartan barracks, only to oblige the prejudice of greedy neighbors.

I could tell you of communities such as my hometown of San Jose, which stood by us and welcomed us home, and the many towns unlike San Jose, which, reeking with prejudice and fear, fought to prevent former internees from returning to their homes.

But let me tell you about my family. My father was not a traitor. He came to this country in 1902 and he loved this country. He sold insurance from a small office in our home on North 5th Street in San Jose, CA. My mother was not a secret agent. She kept house and raised her children to be what she was, a loyal American. Who amongst us was the security risk? Was it my sister Aya, or perhaps Etsu, or Helen? Or was it my brother Al, a sophomore pre-med student at San Jose State, who is now an M.D. in San Jose? Or maybe I was the one, a boy of 10 1/2 who this powerful Nation felt was so dangerous that I needed to be locked up without a trial, kept behind barbed wire, and guarded by troops in high guard towers armed with machine guns. . .

What was it I had done that made me so terrifying to the Government? Murderers, arsonists, and even assassins and spies get trials. But not young boys raised in San Jose who happened to have odd-sounding last names. Is that what this country is about?

Chiseled in the marble over the Supreme Court it does not say "equal justice under law except when things get sticky." It says "equal justice." That is what we ask for, Mr. Chairman, no more, no less. We have waited 42 years. The time has come.

So I ask on behalf of the 60,000 internees who have died with their honor clouded, I ask on behalf of the 60,000 still alive and seeking justice, I ask on behalf of all Americans who believe that our Constitution really does mean what it says, that we are created equal.

I ask that we act with firmness and speed. (Japanese-American and Aleutian Wartime Relocation, 1984, pp. 73-76)

If you concluded that the advocate followed a need-plan- advantage pattern of organization, you were right. Did you feel his case was prima facie? You may want to review it using the following summary of the stock issues of policy advocacy. Remember, since this example is drawn from a legislative debate, many of the details relative to the second stock issue were contained in the bill being debated. In order to be prima facie, the advocate's case must include arguments that address the following questions:

Summary of Policy Advocacy

1. Is there a reason to change in the manner generally suggested by the policy proposition?
   A. What is the nature of the disparity?
   B. How extensive is the disparity?
   C. Does the disparity cause harm to something or someone?
   D. Is the disparity inherent in the present nature of things?
2. Does the policy proposed resolve the reason for change?
   A. What will be done differently?
   B. Who will be responsible for doing it?
   C. What will it cost, and how will costs be paid?
   D. What means are used to assure compliance?
3. What are the consequences of the proposed change?
   A. How does the proposed policy address the disparity?
   B. How does the proposed policy overcome its inherency?
   C. How workable is the proposed policy?
   D. What are the subsidiary effects of the proposed policy?

OPPOSING POLICY PROPOSITIONS

The opponent of the policy advocate attempts to demonstrate that good and sufficient reasons exist to consider the proposed policy unacceptable. Remember that the advocate must develop arguments in support of three stock issues. Although the second one many become essentially noncontestable as soon as a proposal for change is advanced, the advocate must win the two remaining stock issues. There must be a reason for change and the consequences of the proposed policy must be such that, at a minimum, the reason for change is remedied. Must the opponent also win both these issues in order to defeat the advocate? No! In fact, the opponent doesn't even have to contest both! Thus, the first strategic choice the opponent makes concerns whether to argue one or both of the remaining stock issues. One seems clearly winnable and the other not, he may choose to attack only where he has the advantage, focusing audience attention on that portion of the contested ground where his arguments are strongest.

Why is this strategic choice possible? A prima facie case is one that can be taken at face value, meaning that the reason for change, the proposed change, and the proposed change's ability to resolve the reason for change must be present in the advocate's case before it can be termed prima facie. If the opponent can successfully attack the advocate's position on the first or last of these stock issues, the case is no longer prima facie. It no longer offers good and sufficient reasons for a listener's or reader's assent. As a rule, the advocate's position will not be so clearly deficient in its development of the three stock issues to make this decision an easy one. Therefore, the opponent usually attacks on both fronts, and determines the real strengths and weaknesses of the advocate's case based on the arguments used to defend it.

Establish Strategy

The opponent's case usually begins with an overview of his rationale for rejection. What will he defend? What will he oppose? How does he wish the listener or reader to view the proposed policy? The opponent examines the advocate's case, identifies the central idea behind the proposed change, and asks the following questions. Does the reason for change contain assumptions that are unwarranted because they have not been fully proven? Are there implied values the reader or listener is asked to accept without explanation? What is the advocate's burden of proof and has it been met? In addition to determining whether the advocate has fulfilled the responsibility of the burden of proof, the opponent assesses the evidence and reasoning contained in individual arguments, applying tests of evidence to the proof grounding and backing claims, and examining the reasoning for fallacies. You will learn how to do these things yourself in Chapters 7, 8, and 9.

Examine Definitions

The opponent also determines whether to contest the advocate's definition of terms. If the proposition has been defined operationally, refutation of the ability of the proposal to do what the advocate claims it will do is equivalent to contesting the definition of terms. But if the advocate chose to define the subject of the proposition independently, the opponent applies the same tests employed in opposing fact and value propositions—has the advocate excluded something important or included too much?

Refute the Reason for Change

Opposing argumentation on the first stock issue uses the strategies discussed in Chapter 4, since the stock issue of reason for change is advanced by fact and value arguments. The opponent may use arguments that deny that the disparity exists or that it is not as great as the advocate suggests. The opponent may use arguments that deny the harmfulness of the disparity or attempt to prove the harm is insignificant. He may also argue that extenuating circumstances, which are only temporary, explain the existence of the disparity.

Challenge Inherency In regard to reason for change, the opponent may offer arguments showing that the disparity is not inherent to society, its institutions, or their policies. In arguing inherency, the advocate wants the reader or listener to believe that what presently exists causes the problem and, by implication, that the only remedy lies beyond the reach of existing laws, institutions, or patterns of belief. If this were absolutely true, society would be locked in place, totally incapable of change. In reality, that which exists at present is, to a certain degree, in a state of flux and in the process of becoming something else. The opponent may capitalize on this, denying the inherency of the reason for change on the basis of society's self-correcting abilities. This is normally referred to as a **minor repairs** argument.

The philosophy of minor repairs does not give the opponent license to claim whatever he wishes. Whatever minor repairs are suggested to that which exists must meet certain tests. First, *minor repairs must be attainable within the foreseeable future.* To assert that someday the state of the art in automotive safety technology will be such that people will no longer be killed or injured in an accident, thus rendering unnecessary an advocate's proposal to crack down on drunk drivers, stretches both an audience's credulity and the limits of the foreseeable future beyond their breaking points.

Second, *a minor repair must be attainable without benefit of a structural or attitudinal change*—it must be a natural consequence of that which presently exists. To argue that states could decide to suspend probable cause without the federal mandate provided by the advocate would violate this second standard. However, arguing that there is a current trend toward tougher sentences for those convicted of drunk driving, which causes many to think twice before driving while intoxicated, and that this trend will continue into the future, conforms to the second standard.

Third, *minor repairs are subject to the same standards of proof*, insofar as their solvency, inherency, and workability are concerned, as the policy proposed by the advocate. Fourth, and finally, *minor repairs should not themselves be interpretable as a legitimate part of the policy proposition.* If the proposition calls for the prevention of drunk driving, the opponent could not propose as a minor repair the installation of ignition interlock devices, which prevent intoxicated drivers from starting their cars. While the suggestion differs from the specific interpretation of the proposition presented by the advocate, it still constitutes "advocacy" of the proposition's intent. Because it also constitutes a structural change in the way society attempts to control drunk driving, it is neither a defense of present policy nor a reasonable interpretation of what present policy is in the process of becoming.

Refute the Consequences of Change

Question Solvency   Opposing argumentation on the third stock issue requires creativity, along with a firm belief in the principle "Whatever can go wrong, will go wrong." What might preclude solvency? Almost anything or anyone, whose actions are necessary to remedy a problem, has the potential to interfere. In the drunk-driving example, suppose the accuracy of some devices used to determine blood alcohol content could be shown to be questionable. The advocate's proposal provides no funding to purchase the right kind of equipment. As a result, a police department with the wrong kind of equipment could find all the cases it brings to court being dismissed. In addition, if most police cars are not sent into the field with testing equipment because of the expense, how are the officers to make their daily determinations of sobriety?

Identify Barriers   What might preclude inherency being overcome? While the proposal will normally fiat a means to overcome present barriers, two things must be remembered. First, attitudes cannot be legislated. Second, people resist change, especially when they are not sure that a change is in their best interests. This leads the opponent to an analysis of what are commonly called **circumvention arguments**. How might circumvention occur in the present example? Police are only human. Some of them may even have a drink from time to time. One of the current impediments in convicting drunk drivers is the "There but for the grace of God go I" syndrome. Enforcement relies on the police, and if they suffer from the aforementioned syndrome, they may choose to let marginal cases go or only stop those whose driving indicates they are obviously intoxicated, those for whom they would have had probable cause under the old system anyway.

Dispute Workability   What renders a proposal unworkable? If the means by which it operates are so slow, so inconvenient, or so time-consuming that the cost of making a proposal work outweighs the benefits gained when it does, we deem it unworkable. Simple proposals are rarely all that simple. The efforts expended by those who make the system work should not be excessive. In the drunk-driving case, for example, requiring the police to spend time either waiting by the roadside for the car with the test equipment to arrive or driving around late at night on deserted streets looking for a car to stop suggests a relatively high proportion of wasted effort.

Present Disadvantages   Up to this point we have said nothing about the fourth subissue, subsidiary effects. Proposals are like pebbles tossed into ponds, they make waves. Sometimes these waves are small, but usually one or more may be of epic proportions. The opponent should look for these, since they constitute the *disadvantages* to the advocate's proposal. Development of arguments of this kind rest on performing a "worst case" analysis of a situation in which the consequences of the proposal are portrayed to be as bad, or worse, than the problem the proposal was intended to remedy.

What would be a worst case situation in the proposal we have been discussing? A person who would not fail the sobriety test, but who has had a drink, is driving home. A police car pulls up behind him and turns on the red light. The person panics and flees, resulting in a high speed chase in a congested area. Or, more likely, a person who has lost his license but has continued to drive is the driver in our worst case. Although he has not had a drink, he knows he will be arrested for driving without a license. The result is the same and the consequence is at least as potentially serious as the problem the policy was designed to remedy.

How are disadvantage arguments developed? The opponent begins by assuming the policy will do exactly what the advocate says it will. This means that solvency, inherency, and workability are, partially or wholly, granted to the advocate. The argument is then developed in the same manner that an argument advocating a value proposal would be. The opponent establishes criteria for evaluating the advocate's proposal as if it were in existence, and then demonstrates the goodness of fit between these criteria and the proposal. This also means that he assumes a burden of proof similar to that of the advocate of a value proposition.

A final note concerning disadvantage arguments. Opponents must resist arguing disadvantages indiscriminantly. To be effective, disadvantages must possess *uniqueness*; they must occur only in the presence of, and as a consequence of, the advocate's proposal. If the same disadvantage would occur as a result of a minor repair the opponent has suggested, or would occur even without the repair as a consequence of that which presently exists, its impact in dissuading the reader or listener is diminished.

If the opponent has to concede so much, and be so careful, in arguing a disadvantage, why bother? Because disadvantages are the potential "service aces" of argumentation. The opponent can concede everything, the stock issues of reason for change and the ability of the proposed change to remedy the problem; but if the audience can be convinced that a single disadvantage, or series of disadvantages, to the advocate's proposal represents a greater harm to society than the one the proposal remedies, their assent can be won.

Consider the relationship between the pharmaceutical industry and the Food and Drug Administration as a real-world example of the power of disadvantages in determining the outcome of argumentation. A drug company makes a product intended to produce certain health-improving effects. Assume the drug produces these effects, along with some dangerous side effects. If it determines that these side effects are so harmful and extensive that they outweigh the benefits the drug produces, the Food and Drug Administration would not allow the company to market the product, or would force it to take the product off the market if they were discovered later.

The burdens placed on the advocate seem so great, and the opponent may defeat a policy proposal with one telling disadvantage, so why bother to argue? Why risk advocacy? The advocate actually has a number of natural advantages, not the least of which is the ability to define the nature of the ground over which argumentation is joined. The policy advocate makes the best possible case for a proposal's adoption.

However, if the good to be achieved would be outweighed by the greater evils that would occur, rational decision making suggests that the reader or listener ought to reject it.

Offering Counterproposals

One final strategy the opponent may elect to employ is to accept as valid the advocate's reason for change and offer a **counterproposal**, an equally acceptable alternative. This strategy is seldom used in academic argumentation but is quite common in real-world contexts. In law making, business, and family decision-making situations, all parties may agree a problem exists which must be solved, but they may disagree over which policy would represent the best solution. In the legislative context, this often results in an amendment to a proposal being suggested.

When you examine the sample of Policy Opposition in Action, you may get the sense that the opponent would be happy if one part of the advocate's proposal was withdrawn. However, the opponent in academic argumentation normally does not follow this strategy. Opponents usually seek rejection of the advocate's case as a whole. In academic argumentation, the requirement that the proposal must be non-topical applies to counterproposals and minor repairs alike. In addition, the counterproposal in academic argument must be competitive, which means that its adoption must preclude the ability to also adopt the advocate's proposal. The audience is asked to choose between two mutually exclusive proposals. If the opponent chooses to use a counterproposal, he assumes the same burden of proof as an advocate and uses the subissues of the second and third stock issues in his argumentation to demonstrate the superiority of his proposal.

Patterns of Organization

Opponents typically follow the pattern of organization provided by the advocate, arguing first things first and proceeding to subsequent arguments in an order that juxtaposes each with the advocate's argument it addresses. This helps listeners and readers clearly understand the points of clash and disagreement. While the opponent has a number of strategic options available, all of these options can never be used simultaneously. The following example reflects one set of choices the opponent might make in constructing a case. Notice the manner of its organization.

POLICY OPPOSITION IN ACTION

On the day following Representative Mineta's advocacy on behalf of H.R. 4110, Representative Dan Lungren, also of California, testified in opposition to one of the five recommendations in the bill. Portions of his presentation before the Subcommittee on Administrative Law and Government Relation of the House Committee on the Judiciary are excerpted below.

Last year, as this subcommittee knows, the Commission, by an 8 to 1 vote, recommended that the U. S. Government pay $1.5 billion "to provide a one-time per capita compensatory payment of $20,000 to each of the approximately 60,000 surviving persons excluded from their places of residence."

As the Vice Chairman and the only member of the Commission actively serving in the Congress, I was the sole dissenter on the issue of individual monetary reparations. Having chosen to dissent, some might conclude that I in some way find fault with the basic conclusions of the Commission on Wartime Relocation and Internment of Civilians. Let me hasten to make clear that I do not. . .

However, with the benefit of the Commission report, Congress now is being asked to decide which of the Commission's recommendations, if any, to accept. H.R. 4110, the Civil Liberties Act of 1983, the bill before this very distinguished subcommittee, is the legislative form of the Commission's recommendations. It is my opinion that the Congress should reject the proposals for individual monetary redress. There are five reasons for my dissent and I would like to take this opportunity to elaborate them.

First, I strongly disagree with those who suggest that in order for any action, Government or private, to be sincere, it must be translated into the coin of the realm. Should the Congress accept the Commission's suggestion of $20,000 per internee, the total appropriation would be nearly $1.5 billion.

It seems to me that raises several serious questions which Congress must confront. Do we truly believe that nothing can be sincere and credible unless it involves something of a monetary nature? Have we reached such a state in our society that unless money is attached nothing can be a genuine expression of concern or action? H.R. 4110, as written, will not make more credible and sincere any declaration of concern by the United States over violations of human rights committed by other nations.

Mr. Chairman, as I have looked at the legislative history of the Commission upon which I served, it was very clear that in order to gain passage of the legislation creating that Commission there was not to be an implicit understanding that the Commission, first and foremost, was to come up with some sort of monetary redress. There was never any suggestion whatsoever that, absent the finding, the Commission would not be successful, and even the most ardent proponents of the legislation creating the Commission took pains in the debate in both the House and Senate to suggest that would not be the case.

Therefore, I find it rather difficult to accept an argument that is now being made, that unless you have those funds attached to anything, what we do is meaningless. That was not the basis upon which the legislation was drafted; it was not the basis upon which the legislation was argued; frankly, it was not the basis upon which the legislation was passed in either the House or the Senate.

Second, Mr. Chairman, I believe it is degrading to those who were interned to place a flat dollar amount on their experience. How can one accurately make evaluation on time spent in wrongful detention? In 1979, Judge William Marutani, a fellow Commissioner, writing in the Pacific Citizen, said this:

"I find it personally insulting as an American that my freedom, my liberty, my dignity, can be bought. Such a paltry sum—" and they were discussing $25,000 at the time. Dr. Ken Masugi, a resident fellow at Clairmont Institute and whose parents were relocated, testified before a Senate subcommittee, noting that: "any legislation stemming from the report and recommendations will be far more likely to promote racism and bigotry than to dampen those evils." He was talking about monetary redress.

In the words of the Commission report, "Personal Justice Denied," some find such an attempt, in itself, a means of minimizing the enormity of these events in a constitutional republic. History cannot be undone. Anything we do now must inevitably be an expression of regret and an affirmation of our better values as a nation, not an accounting which balances or erases the events of the war.

Third, Mr. Chairman, I am concerned that monetary redress has been mistaken as the major focus of the Commission. This is probably my prime point. It would be a grave failing to interpret the primary objective and findings of the Commission to be merely a determination as to what financial reparations should be. During the Commission deliberations, all of us as Commissioners feared that the recommendations would overshadow the historical report. In fact, it was because of this concern that the Commission deliberately released the historical findings in February 1983 before we even voted on the issue of reparations. In fact, the final recommendations were not released until June 1983, nearly 5 months later than the Commission report.

In our historical report, "Personal Justice Denied," the Commission has been able to achieve what I believe was its main purpose—to educate the American people about the internment which occurred. Many people today are not even aware of the magnitude and extent of the internment. . .

A fourth major objection I have against individual monetary compensation is that the Commission's recommendations may establish a precedent to pay money for the redress of other long-past injustices. Carried to its logical extension, such a principle of restitution could have untold consequences. For instance, should the Chinese be repaid for their underpaid role in helping the railroads open the American West? Should the people of German ancestry be compensated for being denied rights in World War I? Should we pay monetary redress for the abhorrent practice of slavery or the inhumane treatment of Indians 100 years ago? Do we, then, as a nation, want to set a precedent that places a price tag on the loss of individual freedom? And I ask this question: Does it make sense for a present guiltless and uninformed generation to pay reparations for the decisions made by leaders who are all long ago removed from the scene?

I understand the argument that some say: "Look, if this were a court situation and a grievance has been made against you, you have a right to compensation." We can go back in the arguments and suggest that even though we say this is wrong, in hindsight, in fact the Supreme Court told us at the time that it was a proper thing to do. If this were a regular case, you can't get compensation later on for having followed what was considered constitutional at that time.

But, in addition, if some suggest that monetary redress is a way of deterring future action—and if it were, I think we should seriously consider it. But I have to ask this question: Does this deter a similar type of mistaken action in the future by telling public officials that may make those decisions: "If you make a mistake, 40 years later, after nearly all of you are dead, and two generations have grown up in this country, they will be required to pay for the mistakes you made." Where's the deterrent there? I mean, there is no deterrent there. I think we ought to recognize that as one element in making our decision.

Fifth, given the reality of the budget situation confronting the Federal Government, I am concerned that the Commission recommendations may be seen as an empty gesture, unfairly raising the hopes of those affected. I don't believe the Congress is of a mindset to commit funds of the magnitude that we have recommended. The comment attributed to Senator Daniel Inouye of Hawaii some time ago, that $25,000 is not enough and $3 billion is too much, he was suggesting in the first instance that it is not enough for those interned, and in the second instance it is too much for the U.S. Treasury.

Congress has had to deal with tough issues of restoring solvency to the Social Security System, and this has required reductions of prospective increased benefits from the System. Similar difficult decisions have been made by Congress in regard to a whole host of other domestic programs. When this request for individual funds of reparations is placed against those of Social Security recipients, food stamps, and nutrition programs, senior citizen housing, and national defense needs, within the context of an already hemorrhaging Federal deficit, my question is—does it stand up? I think these are important questions we have to ask.

As I point out, I was the only still-serving Member of Congress to serve on the Commission. I felt that I had a perspective that may be different than the other members of the Commission because I had the perspective of a Member of Congress who will have to make the decision as to whether payments would be made. I think that one thing that we have to understand in the Congress, one thing we oftentimes fail to understand, is that when we make an appropriation, we're not taking it out of your pocket, or my pocket, or some large tree full of money in this place we call Washington, DC; we are basically saying to American citizens that what we are doing here is so right and so proper, that we're going to take money out of their pockets, take it to the Government, and transfer it to somebody else's pockets. We do that on a daily basis. But I don't think we ever truly understand that in many, many circumstances. I think you have to gauge this, as we should gauge other legislation, in that context. (Japanese-American and Aleutian Wartime Relocation, 1984, pp. 84-87)

The examples of policy advocacy and opposition were specifically chosen to allow us to demonstrate argumentation on the third stock issue, and to reemphasize the importance of the stock issues to both advocates and opponents as they analyze propositions and construct their cases. If the advocate's reason for change was not so strong, the opponent might have had less to say about the third stock issue and more about the first. Before summarizing the things the opponent of a proposition of policy should ask himself, let us comment on one argument offered by Representative Lungren which illustrates an important difference between real-world and academic argumentation.

In his fifth argument, Mr. Lungren raises the question of whether Congress would appropriate the money, a legitimate concern in the legislative context. In academic argumentation, his concern would have been termed a *should-would* argument and dismissed. In this context, it is the advocate's responsibility only to show something should be done, not to prove that it will be. This is not unreasonable, since those who argue in the academic context have no ability to compel others to act outside that context. Furthermore, in establishing inherency, the academic advocate actually proves those in the appropriate context are unlikely to take the action being proposed.

Before you dismiss Mr. Lungren's last argument entirely, consider its basis and how easily it could be turned into a disadvantage. His concern was that the money for H.R. 4110 would have to come at the expense of other programs which he suggests are more deserving. Quantifying the adverse impact on the programs, and comparing it to the benefits derived from H.R. 4110 would change his should-would argument into a disadvantage.

Summary of Policy Opposition

1. Is the advocate's case prima facie, and does it fulfill the burden of proof?
   A. Has the advocate failed to provide a rationale for change?
   B. Has the advocate failed to provide a specific proposal for change?
   C. Has the advocate failed to consider the consequences of change?
2. Will the opponent choose to argue both the first and third stock issues or only one of them?
3. What is the philosophy on which opposition rests?
   A. What will the opponent defend?
   B. How does the opponent wish the audience to view the proposed change?
4. Will the opponent accept the advocate's definition of terms?
   A. Has the advocate "broken faith" with the audience by distorting the meaning of the proposition?
   B. Has the advocate improperly included or excluded things in defining terms?
5. How will the reason for change be opposed?
   A. Is the disparity as great as the advocate has alleged? (challenges to extent arguments)
   B. Is the disparity as severe as the advocate has alleged? (challenges to effect arguments)
   C. Are there extenuating circumstances that produce the disparity? (challenges to inherency arguments)
   D. Are there other possible causes for the alleged disparity? (challenges to inherency arguments)
6. Will existing institutions ameliorate the disparity?
   A. Will the normal pattern of societal change resolve the disparity given time?
   B. Short of the change called for by the advocate, what minor repairs are available to remedy the disparity?
7. What are the deficiencies in the proposed solution?
   A. Is the solution capable of solving the problem?
   B. Are conditions necessary for the solution to work at present or will something preclude the proposal's ability to solve the problem? Can the proposal be circumvented?
   C. Is the solution workable?
8. What are the consequences of the proposed solution?
   A. Will the proposal bring about the advantages claimed by the advocate?
   B. Will the proposal cause disadvantages, or greater evils?
   C. Are these disadvantages unique to the advocate's proposal?
9. Will a counterproposal be offered?
   A. Is it an equally acceptable alternative to the advocate's proposal?

B. Is it nontopical and competitive with the advocate's proposal?

As you have probably concluded, the range of potential issues may vary greatly with propositions from different fields of argument. The number of potential reasons for change might not be as extensive for some topics as for others. The range of potential new policies may be vast or narrow depending upon the topic area. Some proposed policies may cause more problems than they solve, or they may accrue benefits in a number of different areas. However, regardless of the field of the proposition, the stock issues common to all policy propositions can be used to identify general areas of concern you should analyze. Your analysis will help you prepare to argue effectively as either an advocate or an opponent of change. In Chapter 6, the process of analysis is discussed as it applies to propositions of fact, value, and policy.

LEARNING ACTIVITIES

1. In class, present a brief description of a topic you believe suitable for policy argumentation. Lead your classmates in a discussion of which approach to case construction for policy advocacy (traditional, comparative advantage, or goals-criteria) would be most feasible for the topic you described.
2. From the *Congressional Record*, choose a recent example of a legislative debate that addressed some disparity. In a written or oral report, discuss the argumentation. How were the issues of reason for change, proposal for change, and consequences of change handled by both advocates and opponents?
3. Identify the disparity implied in each of the following policy propositions. In small groups, brainstorm possible fact and value arguments that could be used in developing the advocate's case, and proposals to achieve the change. Now discuss the arguments you would use in opposing the cases just brainstormed.
   A. Puerto Rico should be granted statehood.
   B. The federal government should institute a national sales tax.
   C. The ability to pass a nationally standardized proficiency test of basic skills should be a requirement for high school graduation.
   D. Private ownership of firearms should be more rigorously controlled.
   E. The United States should significantly decrease its foreign military commitments.
4. Identify one or more problems at your school that seem to create a disparity. Analyze this disparity in terms of its nature, extent, harm, and inherency. Suggest proposals to solve the disparity. How would each proposal solve the disparity? What advantages does each proposal have?
5. Take on the role of opponent for the policy proposals constructed in No.4. What would be a strategy of opposition? What minor repairs might be made to remedy the disparity? What would be the consequences of adopting the changes suggested?

SUGGESTED SUPPLEMENTARY READINGS

Chesebro, J. W. (1971). Beyond the Orthodox: The Criteria Case. *Journal of the American Forensic Association, 7*, 208-215.

Chesebro discusses the requirements and strategies of the goals- criteria case. He provides a rationale for using this approach to policy argumentation, suggesting it embodies value principles that are necessary conditions for policy formation. The article contains an excellent discussion of the standards of proof such a case must meet in order to be prima facie, along with a description of the pattern of case construction.

Patterson, J. W., & Zarefsky, D. (1983) *Contemporary Debate*. Boston: Houghton-Mifflin.

This book's focus is policy argumentation, its emphasis is competitive debate, and it probably represents the state of that art. Chapters 7 through 13 are devoted to the theory and practice of affirmative and negative case building, refutation, cross-examination, and judging. This book is a good resource for the nondebater who is interested in learning more about policy argumentation.

Smith, C. R., & Hunsaker, D. M. (1972). *The Bases of Argument*. Indianapolis: Bobbs-Merrill.

This book presents a broad view of the use of argument in every day situations, although it is primarily concerned with policy propositions. We especially recommend Chapters 8 and 9 for their discussion of the strategy of refutation and attack, and the options available to arguers.

6

HOW DO I ANALYZE PROPOSITIONS?

In this chapter we begin consideration of the process you should follow in putting together an argumentative "package" in advocacy of, and opposition to, a proposition. Up to this point, we have focused on the elements contained in an argument, how arguments are combined to address the questions posed by the stock issues of fact, value, and policy, and the basic strategies available to advocates and opponents of change. In the remaining chapters, we will help you put this all together as you author your own argumentative messages. This process is called **case development,** and it begins with analysis of the proposition.

The process of analysis is similar for propositions of fact, value, and policy. The ultimate goal of the process is to discover the **actual issues** you will argue as an advocate or an opponent of the change suggested by the proposition. While stock issues are generic and can be determined by properly identifying the type of proposition you are arguing, actual issues are the questions central to the specific controversy identified by the wording of the proposition you are preparing to argue. Actual issues are found through a four-step process of analysis: (1) locating the immediate cause of the controversy, (2) investigating the history of the topic, (3) determining which terms require definition and defining them, and (4) determining the actual issues in the controversy.

LOCATING THE IMMEDIATE CAUSE

The causes of controversy are usually significant events, occurrences, or circumstances in the present or near past. To find them, arguers must ask themselves why the controversy over a question of fact is important at this time. The Supreme Court's affirmation of a woman's constitutional right to end her pregnancy, or its rejection of challenges to capital punishment statutes, may be the immediate cause of arguments over when life begins and when the state has the right to end it. A significant, usually harmful event will often be the immediate cause of a controversy over fact.

Analyzing the immediate controversy helps you discover why a proposition of fact is sufficiently important to justify argumentation. You will find indications of your proposition's importance by studying recent history. Is the controversy in the news? What are opinion leaders saying about it? Are there presently laws or programs that concern it? When you discover what is being said about the proposition, examine the consequences that are attached to a given interpretation of fact. Is a serious problem evident in relationship to your proposition? Immediate controversies point to causes and their effects that are sometimes deemed to be negative, indicating that an interpretation of facts can have value implications.

In value propositions, the controversy exists over opposing evaluations of a person, object, event, or idea. The purpose of argumentation is to decide how we should judge something—a political candidate, a product, a federal program, an artistic performance, or a moral standard. Advocacy of and opposition to a value proposition rest on a series of fact and value claims.

When we argue value propositions, we are arguing both the criteria on which judgment should be based and the extent to which the object of the proposition conforms to these criteria. In order to achieve this, we have to discover as much as possible about the value object and the value judgment. Thorough analysis of the field specified by the proposition will help you discover this information.

In value argumentation, analyzing the immediate cause of the controversy seeks to discover why the value object and the proposed value judgment are salient at this time. Is something happening that causes concern? What explains the need for society to reorder its value structure? How is the value object presently seen? What status is it accorded in society? What criteria are used to evaluate it?

Immediate controversy analysis is necessary to help you discover the values presently in conflict. If the question is one of privacy versus public safety, do societal attitudes seem to favor safety at the expense of privacy or vice versa? What are our nation's lawmakers and opinion leaders saying about how the object of the proposition ought to be valued? Do these authorities offer standards by which the value object may be judged?

These present judgments are frequently made on the basis of longstanding values. Historical American value systems are of particular importance to your analysis of a value proposition. There are certain dominant patterns of valuing that can help you identify societal value hierarchies that may apply to the present controversy. Rieke and Sillars (1984) offer the following examples of dominant value patterns in the American society:

- *Puritan Work Ethic*—obligations to God and society to work hard at one's job or profession.
- *Enlightenment Value System*—belief that reason must be free and the role of the government is to protect individual rights.
- *Progressive Value System*—belief that movement of a society should always be forward, ever-increasing development and productivity
- *Transcendental Value System*—belief that self knowledge is best, the individual should turn inward for the meaning of life.
- *Personal Success Value System*—belief that one's individual achievements are what is most important.
- *Collectivist Value System*—belief that society's excesses must be controlled through law and order, the importance of teamwork in accomplishing goals.

Search the field of your proposition. Has there been an important discovery that has led to a value controversy? Has a significant event taken place that has focused national or international attention on the value object? For example, has it been determined that a person responsible for causing a serious industrial accident was using marijuana or cocaine on the job? If so, the public outcry for drug testing has not only precipitated a value controversy over the right to privacy, but also suggests that the public believes that collectivist values should take precedence over enlightenment values. This would constitute the public's value hierarchy, and it would be as much a part of the immediate cause of the controversy as the accident which sparked the public debate. Analysis requires you to discover the probable cause of the immediate controversy over the value object and judgment. The key questions are: Why has this judgment of the value object emerged at this time? What standards of judgment are attached to it?

Policy argumentation focuses on an action to be taken, and the analysis of policy propositions often works backward to discover reasons, in the form of facts and values, justifying that course of action (Dudczak, 1983). In policy argumentation, the change in policy suggested by the proposition is the contested ground. You will want to discover what reasons exist for making this change and what specific details might be included in such a policy. You will also want to know as much as possible about why such a change would be potentially beneficial or harmful. As you analyze the immediate cause of the controversy for a policy proposition, you must remember that aspects of both fact and value will be present in it.

Policy argumentation often originates when some person or group of persons believes a problem exists. Immediate controversies stem from events that suggest the nature of the problem. You should look for significant, harmful events and explanations of why these events occurred. The analysis of immediate controversies is important to your development of inherency arguments for the policy proposition. Inherency arguments show the causal relationship between the absence of the policy change suggested by the proposition and the continuation of the immediate problem you have discovered (Patterson & Zarefsky, 1983). Immediate controversies also raise the question of whether similar events, occurrences, or circumstances have occurred in the past. Analysis of propositions proceeds by investigating this question next.

INVESTIGATING HISTORICAL BACKGROUND

Investigating the contemporary and historical background provides the arguer with information pertinent to the proposition of fact, value, or policy. Even in instances where the immediate cause of a controversy over fact is obvious, discovery of historical episodes of dissatisfaction over the same questions provides important insight, especially if the investigation of historical background includes a thorough examination of past efforts to understand a body of factual information relevant to the controversy.

If you were involved in arguing the proposition, "Violence portrayed on television causes violence in the schools, the community, and the home," your background investigation might include examining social science research on the causes of violent behavior in children. You would discover that efforts to understand the impact of seeing violent entertainment on the receiver did not begin with the advent of television. Earlier in this century, educators, parents, and ministers were concerned about the effects of movies and comic books on children. You may find other historical connections to the present controversy, since the issue of violence is not a new one. Considering the proposition of fact in its historical context is important because such propositions are often argued on the basis of trends growing out of past experience and extending into the future; an understanding of past beliefs about fact can be used to argue their propensity to continue in the future.

Because values are for the most part slow to change, you must examine the background of a proposition of value extensively to identify shifts. Advocates and opponents must study the artifacts that reflect the society's structure and values (Warnick, 1981). Artifacts include such documents as the Constitution, Supreme Court and other decisions interpreting the Constitution, the Declaration of Independence, and laws. If, for example, you are engaged in an argument about abortion, artifacts might include the Supreme Court decision in Roe versus Wade and the Bible. The artifacts germane to the value object and judgment may vary considerably with the topic, but some, such as the Constitution, are basic to most controversies.

You may also find relevant artifacts in a particular field of argument. Does the proposition suggest a field such as science, politics, economics, or law? Does the proposition suggest a particular ethical system or code of conduct such as an economic system, the Judeo-Christian moral code, a political system, or a professional code of conduct? The importance of placing the proposition in its appropriate field is that the field may suggest criteria appropriate to judging the value object.

If you discover that values have changed over time, the ability to understand how change occurred may be essential if you are going to be able to explain why this change creates a value hierarchy that is either appropriate or inappropriate in the face of the immediate concern. Nicholas Rescher's (1969) discussion of the process by which values change suggests that values are seldom accepted or abandoned absolutely, except in the rare circumstances of religious or ideological conversions. Instead, values are changed through processes of redistribution, emphasis or deemphasis, rescaling, redeployment, restandardization, and retargeting.

When **value redistribution** occurs, society adopts the value of a minority group that has successfully promoted a different way of attributing importance to that value. In the past two decades, some insurance companies have promoted "women's work," or "housework," as being equally valuable as the work of wage earners and, therefore, worthy of insurance coverage against the possibility that the homemaker might die or become incapacitated. This places a new connotation on the value of housework by putting it in an insurable category of labor.

Environmental change can cause **value emphasis** or **deemphasis**. Some deeply entrenched value, perhaps one that is not even openly stated, is suddenly threatened by a change in the physiological or psychological environment and takes on a different level of importance relative to other values. In the analysis of a value topic, emphasis or deemphasis may be part of what has produced the immediate controversy. A toxic waste accident can suddenly make the protection of the community or the right to feel secure in your own home seem extremely important, while 500 miles away people in an area of high unemployment are excited about the jobs that will be created by the opening of a toxic waste dump outside their city limits.

You may be familiar with the phrases "standard of living" and "quality of life"; both refer to a system of defining that which is attained. One way in which values change is through a **value restandardization.** Societal goals in particular are subject to social, economic, and technological change. John Naisbett's book *Megatrends* (1982) suggests ten areas that will produce change, among them technological innovations that will in turn change what we view as a good life. In the past, a good job was a white-collar position in an air-conditioned office. In the future, the good job will be the one that allows you to work at home, linked to the office by your home computer. "Telecommuting" will restandardize quality-of-life values.

All of us have goals that operationalize enduring values. Since a goal does not always help us to maximize attainment of a particular value, we find ourselves engaging in **value implementation retargeting.** In this case, the value itself has not undergone a change; what has changed is the manner in which we pursue the value. Most people in our society place good health high in their value hierarchies. Government and private medical plans reflect the value we place on good health. This value has not changed substantially, but the manner in which it is pursued has. Instead of focusing on the treatment of disease, medical care has shifted toward the prevention of disease—the "wellness" concept.

Above all, in examining the historical background of your topic, search for previously predominating societal values and identify conflicts among them. Such conflicts may be current or long-standing. Sproule (1980) identifies certain values that frequently appear in juxtaposition with each other—freedom, equality, morality, safety, and privacy.

We can determine criteria for standards of value through an investigation of historical background. The examination of common sources of value is a good starting point, followed by careful consideration of the field in which the value proposition might exist. Some useful questions that can help to find value criteria include the following: What are cultural values or norms that pertain to the value object? What are the particular standards of value that have been historically established for this value object? Why is this particular value object perceived as it is?

Learning the history of your policy proposition can also be useful in developing arguments. The notion of the "history" of a proposed change should be given a very liberal definition. History may be the last two years, or the last two hundred, depending upon the specific proposition. Your research may be restricted solely to the field of your proposition, or it may require you to look at other fields as well. For example, if you are arguing a policy proposition on controlling military spending, examining past efforts to solve the problems of the high cost of equipment maintenance might include examining the system by which military contracts for replacement parts are let to vendors and the history of those companies that win these contracts. The investigation might also include researching how the private sector deals with the same problem. How do civilian airlines cope with the high cost of replacement parts? Your investigation of the topic's historical background could even stretch beyond the field of aviation to include an evaluation of how other government agencies that use technologically sophisticated equipment obtain replacement parts. What you learn might suggest possible solutions to the immediate problem, and their workability and disadvantages.

In particular, you should examine earlier attempts to institute a policy of this sort—attempts that seem identical or that embody the same principles as your policy proposition. Examine the field of your proposition to discover whether they succeeded or failed, and whether legislation is presently pending in regard to the policy. For example, if your policy proposition concerns a balanced federal budget, investigate U.S. history for instances when the budget was in balance. How was balance achieved, and what caused the budget to go out of balance? What attempts were subsequently made to balance the budget? Why did they fail? What was said about them?

You must learn the history of the controversy. You want to know if the presence or absence of a policy has created dissatisfaction in the past. Because policy making is usually consistent with the traditions of a society, you must examine society's value hierarchies and predispositions toward the topic. Policies are typically consistent with past action, so if an action has been deemed inappropriate in the past, it may still be regarded in this way. If you know a policy has not been regarded as appropriate but is the course of action you wish to advocate, you will have just succeeded in discovering an inherent barrier to change: attitudes.

Finding the immediate causes and exploring the historical background of the controversy provide you with a frame of reference from which to argue a proposition of fact, value, or policy. These two steps in the process of analysis also give you some clues to your audience's understanding of your proposition. To add additional focus to their interpretation of the proposition, the third step in the process of analysis requires you to define its terms.

DEFINING THE KEY TERMS

Recall that it is the advocate who initiates argumentation and has the responsibility of providing the initial definition of terms. Since both arguers' task is to locate the issues in the proposition, definitions can be used to identify and clarify key concepts for advocate and opponent. Select the terms in your proposition of fact that you believe need clarification and formulate definitions.

Since the definition of terms in the proposition may become a contested part of an advocate's argumentation, it is advisable for both advocate and opponent to be well versed in the process of definition. Note that disputes over definitions may arise regarding terms in a given issue as well as the terms of the proposition. The following discussion of the process of definition is intended to help you in creating decision rules for defining the terms of propositions of value and policy as well as fact. Arguers are obligated to make clear exactly what is meant when a particular word or phrase is used. To that end, we provide some general rules for defining terms, categories of terms that require definition, and suggestions for how to go about the process of definition.

Rules of Definition

The Inclusionary Rule Phrase definitions in such a way that they include everything that appropriately falls under the term. Recall the policy proposition in Chapter 2: The federal government should significantly strengthen the regulation of mass media in the United States. We indicated the term *mass media* has the potential for including more than just television. If the advocate defined mass media as television, the definition would automatically rule out argumentation over books, newspapers, radio, or magazines. You must take care not to narrow the proposition so sharply that an important issue is ruled out by the definition of the term. If both advocate and opponent agree that television is a suitable definition of mass media, there is no problem. However, the advocate should be prepared to defend this definition of mass media if it is questioned.

The Exclusionary Rule Phrase definitions in such a way as to exclude those things not appropriate to the term (just the opposite of the inclusionary rule). Your definition should not be so broad as to include things that do not properly fall into the category of the term. For instance, defining *mass media* as "all communication" would include communication between individuals, types of communication not aimed at a mass audience. Notice the problem in the following example. To define what it means to be *human* as "being a tool-using and tool-making animal" results in the inclusion of species of primates in the category *human*. Chimpanzees use objects as projectiles to be thrown or clubs to be swung and have been observed making tools to facilitate the harvesting of termites.

The Adaptation Rule Phrase definitions so that the meaning is appropriate to the context of the argument. Consider the needs of the audience before whom the argument is to be presented. While it may be perfectly legitimate to define the Federal Communications Commission using the names of its members, it may not be appropriate to use such a definition if you are arguing about things it ought to regulate. Likewise, mass media might be defined in terms of technical specifications for the transmission of television and radio signals, but such a definition may not be appropriate to an argument whose figurative ground involves significantly strengthening federal regulation.

The Neutrality Rule   Phrase definitions in such a way as to avoid unnecessary emotionality in the language chosen. It is inappropriate to use loaded language in defining terms. It would be inappropriate to define the *Federal Communication Commission* as "a group of near sighted reactionaries more concerned with protecting network profits than promoting the public good" or to define a *teachers' union* as "an organization of socialist radicals undermining the quality of education." Definitions should be descriptive of the term defined, not of your feelings about it. In the context of arguing the actual issues, you will have ample opportunity to make those feelings understood and appreciated by your listeners or readers.

The Specificity Rule   Phrase definitions so that the term itself is not a part of the definition. It may be true that "a rose is a rose is a rose," but to define a term using the term itself does not give the audience a clearer picture of its meaning. For example, what do you learn from the following definition? "The Federal Communications Commission is that commission in Washington, D.C., concerned with communications." Included in the need to be specific is the need to provide noncircular definitions. While it may be true that having money means not being poor, it scarcely improves our understanding to define *wealth* as "the absence of poverty" and *poverty* as "the absence of wealth."

The Clarity Rule   Phrase definitions so that the definition will be understood more readily than the term it defines. To define *federal government* as "that central government, commonly known as the United States government, to which the fifty states have agreed to subordinate certain powers as specified in the United States Constitution," is unnecessary and fails to improve our understanding of the argumentative ground. Although the preceding is an extreme example, the problem of cloudy definitions is common, particularly on technical topics. Try to avoid using the jargon of a field in defining terms whenever possible.

Terms Needing Definition

Five categories of terms usually require definition if understanding, necessary for effective argumentation, is to be achieved. Since you are defining terms both for your opponent and for your audience, the needs of each must be considered. When you perceive a term to be equivocal, vague, technical, new, or coined, it should be defined.

Equivocal terms have two or more equally correct meanings. Many common words in the English language have more than one standard meaning. Providing an opportunity for prayer in the public schools is an ongoing controversy. Some schools provide a period of silent meditation. *Meditation* has become an equivocal term in the controversy surrounding public school prayer. Those schools using meditation have defined it as inner prayer, quiet reflection, or silent communion. However, for many people the term conjures up images of Eastern religions or transcendental meditation. Both are legitimate interpretations of the term; for argumentation on the acceptability of school prayer to proceed, however, those arguing its value must agree on the meaning of meditation, lest they find themselves going off in distinctly different directions. You cannot always rely on context to help establish the intended boundary for an equivocal term. Care must be exercised in making clear the meaning you intend.

Vague terms have shades of meaning; they lack clear-cut definitions, so that each listener or reader is free to supply a meaning. Consider *freedom of speech*, which can have as many meanings as there are political views. Some terms, such as "democracy" can be both equivocal and vague. There are different versions of democracy such as a "democratic people's republic," and a "Jeffersonian democracy." At the same time, what constitutes the American version of democracy is subject to a great deal of interpretation. What does the term "good" or "inferior" mean to you? Value terms, terms of ideology and attitudes, are often vague. Because the term's meaning is open to so many interpretations, it must be defined clearly if the proposition's figurative ground is to make collective sense to the advocate, the opponent, and the audience.

Technical terms are jargon or specialized words belonging to a particular field or profession. Since many controversies involve the use of scientific or technical terminology, exact definition of terms such as "bioeugenics" is necessary if intelligent argument is to occur. Terms with a limited or specialized meaning should not be left undefined, since the reader or listener may not know their meaning but may supply one anyway. This is especially important when concepts are discussed in terms of their acronyms. An HMO is a health maintenance organization, a form of PPGP, prepaid group practice, not to be confused with HBO, a premium cable television service, or PPG, the Pittsburgh Plate Glass Company.

New terms are brand new additions to the language, words or phrases that do not exist in the common vocabulary. Sometimes these terms are foreign words, adopted because they better express the concept the speaker or writer had in mind. When American managers talk about the need for "perestroika on the shop floor," they are adopting a Russian word favored by Mikhail Gorbachev (1989) in discussing "the demand to pool efforts and improve practical work in every sphere or *perestroika*...dedicated, creative, efficient work fully implementing every workers knowledge and abilities" (p.6). Sometimes new terms are not foreign. *Word processing, microprocessor,* and *microchip* are terms that entered the language during the computer revolution. The broadcasting industry has also added new terms to our vocabulary in the past few years—*satellite feed, ground link,* and *the dish.* Other examples of new terms in use are cultural *literacy, numeracy,* and *the nontraditional student.*

Coined terms are those invented when a convenient term does not already exist. Many coined terms are shorthand expressions for complex ideas. *Technophobia* and *kidvid* are verbal shorthand for *fear of technology* and *children's television programming.* Coined terms are also created to describe current developments in an evocative manner. *Petrodollars, the electronic church, user friendly, telectorate* (half television viewer and half voter), and *greenmailing* (the attempt to take over a company by buying enough stock to control it) are contemporary examples. Coined terms can become standard English; consider that "television" was a coined term at one time

How to Define Terms

Terms may be defined by using a **synonym** for the term, a more familiar word similar in both denotative and connotative meaning. This is how standard dictionaries typically define terms. For example, to be *nugatory* means to be "worthless or ineffectual." To provide a more specific definition for *reproduction,* in an argument about videotape recorders, you might use its synonyms: *copies, prints,* or *representations.*

Terms may be defined by the **function** an object, instrument, or organization performs. Some terms make more sense when described in terms of what they do. If you choose to define functionally, be sure that the explanation clarifies rather than obfuscates. To define *radial valve gear* as "a gear employing a combination of two right-angle motions for the purpose of cutting off the steam supply to the cylinder at an early stage in the piston's stroke" is to define both functionally and unclearly. People unfamiliar with steam locomotives will associate the word gear with the things in their car's transmission or their wrist watch, but there are no gears as such in the valve gear of a steam locomotive.

Terms may be defined by using **examples.** A common technique, employed in this and other textbooks, is to explain something by providing examples. This is the strategy used here. When you define by example you attempt to clarify meaning by naming concrete, representative instances of the term. Suppose we were arguing the proposition: *"Social science* is the most important general requirement for graduation." If we do not know to what extent our audience shares our definition of *social science* we might define by example: "By social science, I mean the study of history, sociology, anthropology, political science, or economics."

Terms may be defined by referring to **authoritative definitions**. In a sense, your dictionary serves as an authority for the definition of words, but caution must be exercised in using standard dictionaries. The dictionary merely provides you with a list of all the ways in which users of words commonly define them. To discover just how equivocal many English words can be, consult an unabridged dictionary. Because specificity is a goal in defining, it is frequently useful to turn to a specialized dictionary for a definition, an encyclopedia particular to a field, or a recognized expert in the field. Medical dictionaries, or legal dictionaries such as *Black's Law Dictionary*, or an encyclopedia such as *The Encyclopedia of Social Science* can provide definitions when the precise meaning of a term in the clinical, jurisprudential, or sociological sense is required. It is also possible to derive an authoritative definition by turning to a respected source: "As explained by the chief justice, judicial review involves the Supreme Court's right to review any law passed by Congress in terms of its constitutionality."

Terms may be defined **operationally.** When we seek to clarify the meaning of a term by explaining it as the consequence of a single step, or series of steps, we employ an operational definition. Your stock broker tells you that "Net income on this investment should be fifteen cents per share." You look puzzled and say, "I was sure that stock would pay more." Realizing you do not understand *net income* she defines it operationally: "If you take the total amount of income paid as dividends on the stock and deduct the amount paid in taxes and brokerage fees, the resulting figure will be the *net income* on the investment." In arguing policy propositions, operational definitions are used when the new policy the reader or listener is asked to support is specified.

Terms may also be defined **behaviorally**. To define something that cannot be experienced directly, we may sometimes clarify the term by describing the behaviors commonly associated with it. It may be difficult to define *staff burnout* but relatively easy to describe the kinds of behavior associated with burnout cases: apathy toward change, absenteeism, and mistakes on the job. Behavioral definitions can be particularly useful in describing a theory or phenomenon such as intelligence. *Superior intellectual* ability may be defined in terms of a specified level of performance on the verbal and mathematical sections of the Scholastic Achievement Test.

Finally, terms may be defined by **negation**. This type of definition indicates what the term does not mean. There are some terms whose definitions are best arrived at through negation. For example, someone who is single is "not married"; someone who is insolvent is "not able to meet his financial obligations." Sometimes definition by negation is the best way to define a term: "A full-time undergraduate student is any individual enrolled for not less than twelve semester hours who has not previously received a baccalaureate degree from an accredited college or university."

Since the arguer's task is to locate the issues in a controversy over fact, value, or policy, knowing the definitions being used to limit the controversy will assist both advocate and opponent in developing their arguments. Remember that in the case of propositions of value, both the value object and judgment may require definition. In particular, value judgments often have connotative implications; they must be defined to provide the criteria by which they are to be validated. *Desirable, effective, beneficial, injurious, disadvantageous,* or *harmful,* for example, must be defined. The criteria specified identify for the reader or listener the standard of judgment to be applied to the value object. What must occur for us to deem an effect serious or adverse? What renders a policy beneficial? Criteria specify the attributes which something must possess to be evaluated in a certain way, and they serve to clarify the nature of the figurative ground over which arguments concerning propositions of value take place.

Value-laden terms should be defined in such a way that they suggest a series of statements capable of being supported with proof and reasoning. If you are arguing about the effectiveness of U.S. foreign policy, ideally your criteria would set observable standards by which effectiveness could be determined. Some possible criteria might be these: (1) An effective foreign policy keeps us out of wars, (2) An effective foreign policy makes us more friends than enemies, (3) An effective foreign policy encourages the development of democratic institutions in other nations, and (4) An effective foreign policy treats all nations equally.

The definition of terms in a value proposition is of special importance, since the way you define value terms shapes the argumentative ground. In addition to setting the criteria for judging the value object, how you define terms will shape the issues of your value argumentation.

The advocate in policy argumentation must also decide what portions of the proposition require definition. Since the most identifiable characteristic of a policy proposition is that it points toward a change in behavior, a new course of action, defining that course of action is one of the advocate's responsibilities in case construction. If the advocate fails to define what is meant by this specified course of action, asking listeners or readers to change their behavior will not only be unwarranted but also impossible because they will not know what they are being asked to do. We usually do not change our behaviors when we are unsure what the change involves. Equally, decision-implementing bodies are unlikely to change if the details of the decision are unclear. As we pointed out in Chapter 5, the advocate's proposal typically specifies change, mechanism, financing, and enforcement.

There are many legitimate methods for defining the terms of a policy proposition, and the advocate has choices to make regarding which other terms require extensive definition. Whether to define more than the proposed action is one of those choices. In some propositions the subject—the agency that will undertake change or that will undergo change—may be clearly stated: "The International Olympic Committee should hold all future Summer Olympics in Greece." In other examples the subject is not as clearly identified: "The federal government should issue identity cards to all persons residing in the United States." Since there are many branches and agencies of the federal government that could be used to implement such a program—the Federal Bureau of Investigation, the Internal Revenue Service, the Bureau of Immigration and Naturalization, for example—the advocate would probably have to define what is meant by the subject of the proposition.

The terms of the proposition may be defined individually, taking the subject of the proposition and the course of action as separate terms, or the entire proposition may be defined operationally—the meaning of the proposition is to be taken as engaging in this specific course of action. If you perceive an operational definition to be your best strategy, it is particularly important that your investigation of historical background includes examination of any similar courses of action tried in the past. If you are defining key terms individually, use the methods for defining terms discussed earlier. In either case, the definition of terms of the operational plan of action would be one of the first elements to be presented in the advocate's case.

DETERMINING THE ISSUES

Thus far in the process of analysis you will have discovered the immediate cause of the controversy, examined its historical background, and defined key terms in the proposition. This will have provided you with the necessary information to determine what is potentially arguable in the controversy. Not all the potential issues you uncover may ultimately be used in the preparation and presentation of your case for or against a proposition. The issues that finally decide the controversy are those that are actually contested, for which the advocate or her opponent provides more convincing reasoning and proof.

The advocate's selection of actual issues in a proposition of fact will be determined by two factors: what constitutes her burden of proof in establishing a prima facie case for proposition of fact, and what can be demonstrated to be most probably true with the available resources of proof and reasoning. The opponent's selection of actual issues are constrained by both the proposition of fact and the choices the advocate makes, since the opponent must try to refute the advocate's position through tactics of denial and extenuation.

For advocates and opponents arguing propositions of value, once the appropriate value hierarchy and criteria for judging values have been discovered by examining the present controversy and its historical background and articulated through a definition of terms, the central issue of value argumentation becomes, "Does the value object meet the criteria for evaluation? If only a single criterion has been advanced, it is obviously deemed sufficient to allow a proper evaluation to be made. If multiple criteria are advanced, is it necessary for the value object to meet them all in order to be judged in the manner described by the proposition of value. If this is not the case, the criteria can be applied independently, and demonstrating that the value object meets any one of them would be sufficient to warrant the judgment specified by the proposition. Determining whether these criteria are independently sufficient, or necessary in toto, may be a part of, or the sole locus of, the dispute between the advocate and opponent of change.

The decision to employ single or multiple criteria, which are either necessary or sufficient, is one of the strategic choices the advocate makes in deciding how best to advance the value proposition. These choices reflect the advocate's consideration of the information the reader or listener may legitimately require in order to assent to the value proposition. As is the case with propositions of fact, claims in support of value propositions must be worded so that argumentation focuses on the stock issues of value. In analyzing the value proposition's topic area, look for resources that will provide support for these claims. Arguing the value proposition is then accomplished through the use of factual claims with their attendant proof and reasoning.

As was the case with fact, the choices available to the opponent of the proposition of value are constrained by his available resources and the advocate's choices. The uncertainty that this creates for the opponent of value change, and for that matter opponents of fact and policy, is partially offset by the asset of presumption. It is further offset by the fact that the opponent can anticipate what the advocate is most likely to argue, based on his analysis of the proposition, his knowledge of the stock issues the advocate must address, and his understanding of the social forces the advocate can attempt to stimulate in encouraging change.

Advocates and opponents should pay particular attention to Nicholas Rescher's (1969) discussion of shifting societal values in terms of those factors that bring about change: changes of information; ideological and political change; erosion of values through boredom, disillusionment, and reaction; and changes in the operating environment of a society.

The value system of a society can change when **new information** is introduced. Consider the impact that the discovery of antibiotics or vaccines against polio and measles had on health, or the way in which the development of the birth control pill influenced moral standards. Many of today's changes are brought about by scientific discovery. One of the great unanswered questions, which may produce a significant value change if it can be resolved, is the determination of the point at which life begins. While it has sometimes been said that there is nothing new under the sun, new discoveries about old things happen with some regularity. As you seek to change an audience's value hierarchy, your analysis should consider new discoveries in the field of your subject as a potential source of actual issues.

A second way in which society is altered is through **political and ideological change.** These can be revolutionary changes as occurred in Eastern Europe in 1989 and 1990. In that situation, both political and ideological changes took place as communist governments were overthrown and attempts at democracy were begun. Such change is not necessarily abrupt; "it can take the gradualistic form of conditioning, advertising, propaganda, and promotion" (Rescher, 1969, p. 117). For instance, consider the ways in which television commercials and programs articulate what is to be valued. Advocates and opponents of propositions of value should consider the ways in which political and environmental change helps or hinders not only their cause but each other's.

The third way in which societal values change is through their **erosion**, which occurs when large numbers of people resist acting in accordance with a value. This happened during the 1960s when thousands of young men refused registration for the military draft. Erosion can also occur as a society experiences gradual change over time and, as a result, a value loses much of its importance. In an age when leisure pursuits are strongly encouraged and widely "sold" by the mass media, the value of work and the Puritan work ethic have less importance. Society may also become disillusioned with a value. In the early part of this century, sobriety was so highly valued that in 1920 a constitutional amendment prohibiting the manufacture and sale of alcoholic beverages was adopted. Disillusionment over the Eighteenth Amendment was such that it was repealed by the Twenty-First Amendment just thirteen years later. While this example shows how values influence policy, remember that it was the process of erosion that precipitated value change in this instance and that this process might serve as a criteria for judging the value object in argumentation: Present attitudes toward sexuality render existing standards for judging the appropriateness of song lyrics obsolete.

The final way in which value changes occur is through a **change in the operating environment** of the society, the "whole range of social, cultural, demographic, economic, and technological factors that comprise the way of life in that society" (Rescher, 1969, p. 117). Some of the demographic changes that have influenced society in recent years include the entry of more women into the workplace and the coming of age of the "baby boom" generation. These are the same people who will cause another change at the beginning of the next century as they reach retirement age. Among the technological changes that have brought about value changes are the widespread availability of television, the development and spread of nuclear weapons, and the increasing use of robots in the workplace.

It is in this last category of value change that you will most frequently find material relevant to value argumentation, although advocates and opponents of value propositions are advised not to dismiss the other factors discussed without first examining them. Social, cultural, demographic, economic, and technological factors that influence values also cause them to come into conflict with one another. Two important values may have to be placed in a hierarchical relationship to resolve this conflict, as is the case in the controversy over whether a clean environment or a healthy economy should be our priority. Value conflict forces a reconfiguring of the value hierarchies, the task of the arguer in a value proposition. Through the process of argumentation, you engage your listeners or readers in an examination of the relative merits of retaining old values versus the costs of changing value structures, the utility of maintaining or changing a particular value system.

Determining the actual issues to be argued for and against a proposition of policy proceeds in much the same way as it does for fact and value. One matches what can be proven from an investigation of the immediate situation and its historical development against the imperatives of what must be proven under the stock issues of policy for the advocate's case to be prima facie. If the advocate has defined the proposition operationally, the requirements of the second stock issue will have been satisfied and she needs only to justify a reason for this change and explain its consequences. Since policy propositions rest on foundation of fact and value, everything discussed so far in regard to determining the actual issues is available for the advocate to use.

If it appears that movement from fact, through value, to policy exponentially increases the complexity of argumentation and options available to advocates and opponents of change, that is because appearances in this case are not deceiving. Not only are the issues more numerous and the strategies more intricate, you will recall that, insofar as academic argumentation is concerned, policy propositions are worded in such a way that they afford the advocates of change a wide latitude in interpretation. Thus, the constraints on issue selection by the opponents of change, and the uncertainty of what actual issues the advocate will argue, appear to be compounded by policy propositions. While this is true, the opponent's plight is not hopeless. Presumption is on his side, and since the advocate's burden of proof is more complex, there are more opportunities for her to make a mistake.

The opponent has two other things to keep in mind in analyzing the proposition. First, defeating the advocate on only one of the stock issues is all that is needed to prevail. This means a series of generic arguments can be developed that would apply to a number of different interpretations of the proposition. If the proposition is likely to require the advocate to urge adoption of an expensive program, the opponent could develop a generic argument about the undesirability of either raising taxes or diverting funds from existing programs. The opponent would still be required to apply this and other arguments to the advocate's specific case, but he has something to argue no matter how far fetched the advocate's interpretation of the proposition seems. If it is too farfetched, the opponent's second alternative for coping with the uncertainty of his position is engaged.

In academic argumentation, defining the proposed action so that it conforms to the wording of the proposition is known as *being topical,* one of the advocate's responsibilities. For those of you learning the techniques of policy argumentation this is a matter of some concern, as well as a question of ethics and good faith between you and your audience. By agreeing to argue a certain proposition, it becomes a matter of trust that you will indeed argue it. If you have consented to argue the advocate's side of the question "Should the federal government be required to operate on a balanced budget? you break faith with your audience when you twist the proposition by arguing in support of a nuclear freeze that would reduce international tension and the probability of a nuclear confrontation, and "Oh, by the way," balance the budget by reducing defense spending. The opponent analyzing the proposition of policy can at least expect the advocate's case to be topical, and can achieve the winning position by proving it is not.

The process of analysis is the same for propositions of fact, value, or policy, although the breadth and depth of analysis changes. Advocates and opponents of change should examine the immediate cause and historical background of the controversy which brought the proposition they are about to argue into a position of prominence. After defining those terms which require definition, they should then decide which actual issues they will argue in presenting their case for or against change. These issues are established by the demands imposed by the stock issues of fact, value, and policy, and the resources of proof and reasoning which both parties to the dispute bring to it. The next step you should take in preparing to advocate or oppose change is a step in the direction of the library. The next chapter, which discusses the types and tests of evidence, as well as how to locate evidence, will help you make this trip profitable.

LEARNING ACTIVITIES

1. Examine the propositions listed below and determine which terms in each proposition should be defined. Formulate your own definitions of these words or phrases. Be sure to include: What type of problem word or phrase is it? What rule of definition does your definition satisfy? What type of definition have you provided?
   A. The federal government should provide a program of comprehensive health care for all United States citizens.
   B. The American education system has failed in its mission to educate students.
   C. All military intervention into the affairs of other nations in the western hemisphere should be prohibited.

D. Political action committees undermine the democratic process.

E. The federal government should require more stringent labeling of all processed foods.

F. The further exploration of space should be a priority in the 1990s.

G. A national program for recycling should be enacted.

H. First Amendment protection should not be used to justify government subsidies of pornographic art works.

2. Select one of the propositions listed above for issue analysis. What is the immediate cause of the controversy in the proposition? What are some important elements in the history of the topic? What are the actual issues that might be argued by the advocate? By the opponent?

3. Read the essay, "Looking for Good Guys," by James Moore in *Newsweek*, February 15, 1988, p. 10. What is the proposition he is arguing? What issues of the controversy over gun control does Moore address?

4. Read the essay, "The Way We Diaper," by Robert J. Samuelson in *Newsweek*, March 19, 1990. What is the proposition he is arguing? What value hierarchy does he place the "disposable diaper" in? What issues does he find in the controversy over disposable products?

5. Phrase your own proposition of fact, value, or policy. What terms require definition? What type of definition should you provide? What is the immediate controversy in your proposition's topic area? What issues may be argued by advocates? By opponents?

6. John Naisbett's *Megatrends* (1982) hypothesizes ten directions in which the United States seems to be moving. Choose one of these trends, or the trend assigned by your instructor, and make a presentation to the class in which you explain the trend in terms of a value hierarchy it suggests. What values are implied by the trend? What degree of importance does society presently attach to these values? How will the future affect the present hierarchy of these values?

SUGGESTED SUPPLEMENTARY READINGS

Church, R.T. & Wilbanks, C. (1986). *Values and Policies in Controversy*. Scottsdale, AZ: Gorrsuch-Scarisbrick.

This is a traditional debate textbook that casts argumentation in terms of competitive intercollegiate debate. For an alternate explanation of issue discovery, we recommend Chapter 4, "Discovering Issues." The authors discuss fact and value propositions in terms of the sentence structure of the proposition, the use of qualifiers, and restrictions of time and place. Analysis of policy propositions is discussed in terms of systems analysis.

7

HOW DO I PROVE MY ARGUMENT?

In some situations, proving your arguments will be a matter of drawing on your own knowledge or that of your audience. In most situations, you will need to research the topic thoroughly. You will need evidence, the term commonly used to describe the grounds for an argumentative claim or the information that backs its warrant. In this chapter, we are concerned with the discovery of evidence and the assessment of its quality in a larger sense. By definition, **evidence** is information taken from material of fact or opinion and used to establish the probable truth of a claim.

The kinds of information necessary to establish the grounds, or back the warrant in your argument, are determined by your analysis of the issues in your proposition. The standards to apply in determining the quantity and quality of proof required result from analyzing the prior knowledge and beliefs of your audience, and from applying accepted tests of evidence. Since proof is the foundation of argument, you will need to learn how to discover and apply it. This chapter concerns types of evidence, standards for evaluating its quality, and techniques for finding it.

TYPES OF EVIDENCE

As our definition of evidence suggests, there are two general classes of evidence, *fact* and *opinion.* Equally, there are two sources of evidence, your own observations and the recorded observations of others. The most reliable source of evidence is personal observation and experimentation. Consider the experience of buying a new car. "Which car should I buy?" can be considered as a question that may ultimately lead to argumentation on a policy proposition.

That proposition might be argued through a number of fact and value claims about the quantifiable performance and qualitative evaluations of a series of automobiles. The most reliable evidence would be obtained through your own road tests of these vehicles. However, even in something as personal as buying a new car, personal tests and observations are not always feasible or desirable. You may not have the time or ability to conduct as sophisticated a series of tests as those reported in *Car and Driver* or *Motor Trend*. Beyond saving time, reliance on printed sources relieves you of the need to be an expert in a number of fields. Additionally, in argumentation it is often advantageous to be able to add the credibility of expert opinion or research to your own ideas. By using published facts and the opinions of sources "in the know," you strengthen your argument and increase the credibility of its rational appeal.

Evidence of Fact

Facts are those things that can be verified as true or false. By verification we mean observation, either our own or that of someone whose ability to make such an observation we respect. Factual evidence is information obtained from direct or indirect observation. **Factual evidence** describes or reports what exists—events, objects, places, persons, phenomena. Factual evidence does not attempt to explain or evaluate, it merely reports what was observed. Direct factual evidence is observed by the arguer. Indirect factual evidence is obtained from the reported observations of external sources. In both academic and real-world argumentation, indirect evidence is used more frequently than direct evidence. Because we live in an age of relatively easy access to a variety of printed resources, using evidence obtained from the research of others has almost as much validity as evidence obtained through our own observations.

Examples and illustrations report or describe events and phenomena; they tell us what may be observed in a given situation. This type of evidence may be a brief statement or a detailed description. Compare the following:

> Some rock artists actually seem to encourage teen suicide. Ozzie Osbourne sings "Suicide Solution." Blue Oyster Cult sings "Don't Fear the Reaper." AC/DC sings "Shoot to Thrill." Just last week in Centerpoint, a small Texas town, a young man took his life while listening to the music of AC/DC. He was not the first... (Record Labeling, 1985, p. 12)

> [And] 1,862 internees died while in camp, a figure which does not include people like my father-in-law, Saijiro Hinoki, an immigrant who owned a dry cleaning store in Colusa, CA and was a member of the local Rotary Club as early as 1937.

> The FBI arrested Mr. Hinoki early in 1942 without charges, and for 2 months told his family nothing about where he was or why he was being held. Finally, the family was told he had been sent to a detention camp in Bismarck, ND. Those who knew him—because I never met him—said Mr. Hinoki never regained his lost will to live. He died a

few years after leaving camp. (Japanese-American and Aleutian Wartime Relocation, 1984, p. 75)

These two reports differ in both subject matter and degree of detail. The discussion of rock music and suicide lists a series of brief specific instances. It amounts to a series of examples. The more detailed account of the experience of one internee is longer and more informative. It possesses the characteristics of an illustration.

Statistics present descriptive and inferential information about people, events, or phenomena numerically. While an example often describes people, events, or phenomena in isolation, statistics can place such information in context. This gives the reader or listener a sense of the significance of that which is described. Compare the following statistical evidence to the series of examples just offered. While details, artists' names, and album or song titles are mentioned, the extent of the situation is conveyed by the raw numbers.

> Prince's "Darling Nikki," about masturbation, sold over 10 million copies, Judas Priest, the one about forced oral sex at gunpoint, has sold over 2 million copies. Quiet Riot, "Metal Health," has songs about explicit sex, over 5 million copies. Motley Crue, "Shout at the Devil," which contains violence and brutality to women, over 2 million copies. (Record Labeling, 1985, p. 11)

This is an example of a *descriptive statistic,* one in which the entire population of people, events, or phenomena of a particular kind are observed. The researchers looked at record sales and reported what they found. Descriptive statistics can be reported in any number of ways. Averages or percentages are sometimes used to reduce raw numbers to more manageable form, and provide standards for comparing one group of people, events, or phenomena to another. The following example of statistical evidence employs both ratios and percentages.

> The Noedecker Report states that in the United States of America we have the highest teen pregnancy rate of any developed country; 96 out of 1,000 teenage girls become pregnant.
>
> Rape is up 7 percent in the latest statistics, and the suicide rates of youth between 16 and 24 have gone up 300 percent in the last three decades while the adult level has remained the same. (Record Labeling, 1985, p. 11)

Besides demonstrating the use of ratios and percentages, this example also demonstrates something that is important to remember when statistical information is used: For statistics to have meaning, they must be interpretable. The advocate aids our ability to interpret these numbers by including comparison groups—other developed countries and adults—for her listeners to use as benchmarks. What we do not know from the advocate's presentation is precisely how the estimate of "96 out of 1000 teenage girls become pregnant" was made. Is this statistic descriptive or inferential?

An *inferential statistic,* is one in which data concerning a portion or sample of the entire population of people, events, or phenomena of a particular kind are observed, and the researcher infers that what is true of the sample is true of the population from which it was drawn. The way in which the data are reported suggests that the researchers may have looked at public health data on the total number of reported teen pregnancies in developed countries and computed the average number of pregnancies per 1000 teenage girls. However, this data could also report the results obtained from asking 1000 teenage girls in each developed country whether they had ever been pregnant. If that were the case, the statistics would be inferential rather than descriptive.

Regardless of whether statistical information is descriptive or inferential, it can be misleading when a source reports results as an *average* since that term may refer to the mean, median, or mode of a set of data. The mean is the arithmetic average of a set of numbers, the median is the middle score in that set, and the mode is the score that occurs most frequently. Given these data—98, 57, 23, 11, and 11—a source could report the average to be 40 (the mean), 23 (the median), or 11 (the mode). Be sure you understand what kind of statistics your sources are using to avoid misleading your audience.

Artifacts are actual exhibits of objects, audiotapes or videotapes, or photographs presented for verification by the audience. If you have ever watched a courtroom drama on television, you are familiar with the use of artifacts as evidence. In a courtroom, artifacts or exhibits constitute "real" evidence as distinguished from the testimony provided by witnesses. The use of artifacts as evidence enhances argumentation on certain topics. Consider how much easier it is to argue the merits of rock music if you have actual songs for your audience to hear or album covers for them to see, which is something the members of the PMRC did during the hearings.

Premises are factual evidence accepted because they reflect human belief or experience. There are some statements, which may technically be considered claims, that are so widely believed to be true that they are accepted as fact without further verification (Ehninger, 1974; Jensen, 1981; Ziegelmuller, Kay & Dause, 1990). A premise is accepted because there are so many previously recorded or reported instances of its being true. Like other types of factual evidence, premises are discovered through observation or through consulting printed sources of information and opinion (Ziegelmuller, Kay & Dause, 1990).

Laws of nature, such as "Water seeks its own lowest level," and rules of thumb, such as "Better late than never," tend to be accepted. Because premises are predictions or projections based on experience, they can be verified like facts of other kinds. In theory, an audience could suspend belief until a premise is verified. In real-world argument, premises are used as proof to save time and effort and are seldom verified. When you can predict which premises an audience will accept, it becomes unnecessary to verify them. To do otherwise might insult the intelligence of your audience. Nevertheless, persons learning argumentation should verify premises by providing the warrant and its backing. Even those experienced in argumentation follow this suggestion. As Representative Mineta noted, "Chiseled in the marble over the Supreme

Court it does not say 'equal justice under law except when things get sticky.' It says 'equal justice.'" (Japanese-American and Aleutian Wartime Relocation, 1984, p. 76)

Many premises are the product of, or are tested by, the scientific method. When we encounter a problem, perhaps our car won't start one morning, we attempt to explain it. Our explanation takes the form of a hypothesis, a guess about what might be the source of the problem. "My car won't start because the battery is dead." The hypothesis states the dependency of one thing, our car's ability to start, on the variability or independence of another, the level of charge in the battery. We would test our hypothesis that the battery is dead by seeing if the lights, radio, or horn will work. If they work, this informal measure of the charge in our battery suggests our hypothesis is false, and we would test other explanations such as blown fuses, loose wiring, or a defective starter. What you have just done is roughly equivalent to what researchers in the physical and social sciences do in laboratory and field settings. Published reports of their findings can be used to support your claims.

Scientific evidence reports the results of controlled experiments on the inferred effect of one variable on another. For example, a researcher might feel that hearing sexually explicit lyrics stimulates sexual urges in teenagers. The first variable, lyrics, is called the independent variable. Changes in it are hypothesized to produce changes in the second variable, urges, which is the dependent variable. A third class of variables, nuisance variables, include those things that could minimize or maximize the predicted effect. For example, the attractiveness of the person with whom one listens to music might alter the urge.

A *laboratory experiment* differs from a field experiment primarily in that its conduct affords the researcher greater control over the manipulation of the independent variable, measurement of the dependent variable, and the presence of nuisance variables. A simple laboratory experiment testing the effect of music on sexual urges might manipulate the independent variable by selecting two songs, one high in sexual content, the other low. These constitute the treatment conditions on the independent variable and subjects in the experiment would be randomly assigned to hear one song or the other. The songs could be played to individual teenagers to eliminate the nuisance variable of the listening partner. The researcher could measure physiological indications of arousal such as Galvanic Skin Response, or have each subject write an essay about what they planned to do that evening, to measure the dependent variable. Finally, the researcher would conduct the appropriate statistical test on the resulting data to compare the responses of the high and low sexual-content groups.

In a *field experiment*, the independent variable is frequently manipulated by the marketplace or social forces rather than the researcher. The researcher finds a way to measure the dependent variable, as well as find out what treatment condition the subject has been assigned to. A field approach to the "lyrics produce urges" question might involve subjects completing a questionnaire about their sexual activity and tastes in music, with the researcher once again performing an appropriate statistical test to determine the extent to which differences between groups were significant.

When cited during argumentation, scientific evidence may not seem that different from other types of evidence of fact or opinion. Because it employs statistical tests of significance, scientific evidence differs from other types of evidence of fact in that its statements of direct or indirect observation carry with them an estimate of the probability that the inferred cause-effect relationship could have been produced by chance or coincidence. Scientific evidence differs from evidence based on opinion in that its credibility derives from the rigor of its method of observation, rather than the prestige of the person drawing conclusions about those observations.

Evidence from Opinion

While factual evidence describes without judgment or evaluation, opinions are judgments and interpretations, someone else's perception of the facts. Anyone may render an opinion, but in argumentation evidence from opinion usually refers to the use of the opinions of experts in the field you are arguing. **Opinion evidence** consists of the interpretive and evaluative statements made by an expert in a given field in regard to factual material pertinent to that field.

The opinions of authorities in a field provide arguer and audience with access to their expertise. If we are discussing the economy, we might turn to nationally known and respected economists like Milton Friedman and Paul Samuelson for their opinions. Not all experts, however, are nationally recognized. To find an expert, we seek persons with credentials in the field we are discussing.

Because opinions perform the function of evaluating and interpreting factual information, they often appear to be claim statements. The only real difference between a claim you might make in constructing an argument and the opinion of an expert is that the expertise of the source of the opinion is a kind of proof in itself. The qualifications of the source give opinions their probative value. Representative Mineta quoted such an expert witness to support a claim that internment was motivated by racism and fear rather than military necessity.

> Gen. John L. DeWitt, head of the Western Defense Command and a key figure in the internment, actually managed, in speaking of the fact that no disloyal acts had been committed by Americans of Japanese ancestry, to say "The very fact that no sabotage has taken place to date is a disturbing and confirming indication that such action will be taken." (Japanese-American and Aleutian Wartime Relocation, 1984, p. 75)

To the extent that we are impressed by General DeWitt's historical role in the events under discussion, his statement supports Representative Mineta's claim of racism and fear without further verification.

When the qualifications of the source are omitted, the probative value of an opinion may rest solely on its isomorphism or agreement with what the listener or reader already believes.

> As Ellen Goodman stated in a recent column, rock ratings:
>
> The outrageous edge of rock and roll has shifted its focus from Elvis's pelvis to the saw protruding from Blackie Lawless's codpiece on a WASP album. Rock lyrics have turned from "I can't get no satisfaction" to "I am going to force you at gunpoint to eat me alive." (Record Labeling, 1985, p. 11)

In the absence of credentials, opinion is accepted as proof only by a listener or reader whose opinions are not contrary to it. In essence, the opinion of an uncredentialed source functions as proof only when it is viewed as a premise by the audience.

This raises an interesting problem. In magazines such as *Time* or national newspapers such as the *Washington Post*, in which Ms. Goldman's article appeared, the credentials of the author are not provided. In some instances, the author is not even identified. Can you use such material as if it were an expert's opinion? Yes. In this instance, nationally recognized news sources such as those mentioned are acknowledged as reputable sources of information. The publication's own reputation becomes the credentials backing the opinion. However, news sources are not infallible. It is usually wise to check the opinions they contain against those of acknowledged experts when you discover what you think might be worthwhile opinion evidence.

Often a news magazine or newspaper article with a named, or an unnamed, author will serve as a secondary source for the authoritative opinion of an expert as in the following example which deals neither with rock music nor internment:

> In *The Uses of Enchantment*, (Bruno) Bettelheim shows how irrelevant to the real needs of children the pro-social enterprise turns out to be. "Since the child at every moment of his life is exposed to the society in which he lives, he will certainly learn to cope with its conditions, provided his inner resources permit him to do so." In concentrating on mere outward behavior (cooperating, helping others), proponents of the pro-social neglect the child himself—the fearful, struggling child "with his immense anxieties about what will happen to him and his aspirations." The difficulties a child faces seem to him so great, his fears so immense, his sense of failure so complete, says Bettelheim, that without encouragement of the most powerful kind he is in constant danger of falling prey to despair, "of completely withdrawing into himself, away from the world." What children urgently need from children's stories are not lessons in cooperative living but the life-saving "assurance that one can succeed"—that monsters can be slain, injustice remedied, and all obstacles overcome on the hard road to adulthood. (Karp, 1984, p. 43)

In this instance, the credibility of the opinion derives as much, if not more, from the source Mr. Karp cited as it does from his own qualifications. While it would be best to read Bettelheim and quote him firsthand, the use of secondary-source material is acceptable.

In using opinion evidence as proof, remember that it does not provide facts but interprets or explains them. Expert or authoritative sources provide interpretations or judgments about facts and are always one step removed from the objects, statistics, and events that comprise their factual basis. Expert opinion is accepted by the listener or reader only when the expert is believed to be qualified to offer the interpretation or make the judgment, or when the expert states what the listener or reader already suspects or believes.

Summary of Types of Evidence

1. **Examples and illustrations** describe or report events, phenomena that exist; examples are brief statements, illustrations are more detailed accounts.

2. **Statistics** represent information about people, events, and phenomena numerically; they may be expressed in raw numbers or summarized in percentages or averages.
3. **Scientific evidence** reports the results of field and laboratory experiments on the effect of one variable on another.
4. **Artifacts** are actual exhibits of such things as objects, audiotapes and videotapes, photographs, and diagrams.
5. **Premises** are factual claims that exist as evidence on the basis of their being accepted as reflections of human belief or experience.
6. **Opinions** are interpretive and evaluative statements made by an expert in a field regarding factual information relevant to that field.

TESTS OF EVIDENCE

In addition to recognizing the types of evidence, you must be able to evaluate their reliability. There are specific tests that can be applied to each type of evidence and general tests of evidence with which the student of argumentation should be familiar. Tests of evidence give us the minimum requirements our proof must meet before it will be accepted as credible by our listeners and readers.

Tests of Facts

In testing evidence of fact, we are concerned with the accuracy and reliability of the observations being reported. In each category—example and illustration, statistics, and premises—certain tests can be performed to determine factual accuracy and reliability.

Tests of examples and illustrations concern the observations made. These tests ask questions about the accuracy and reliability of the report and the reporter.

Source Qualifications   Was the observer capable of making the observation in terms of the necessary physical and mental ability? A blind witness, for example, may have difficulty describing an automobile accident but may be able to describe minute variation in the sound of an automobile engine. Did the observer have the training and experience necessary to make the observation? Someone who has never driven, for instance, will have difficulty in describing the differences in handling between a front wheel drive and a rear wheel drive car.

Data Accuracy   Is the information reported in a straightforward manner or has it been manipulated to give it more or less importance? Prior to the 1988 campaign, for example, both print and electronic news media were accused of making more of George Bush's role in the Iran-Contra affair than was warranted by the facts, making it seem more serious than it actually was. Because information may be interpreted by the source reporting it, you must take care in checking the reliability of the interpretation.

Originality of Observation   Is the information obtained from first hand or second hand data collection? It is possible to make observations on the basis of someone else's data, but more reliable reports of fact are obtained from first hand observation. This does not mean you should never rely on secondary information; in some situations first hand reports are impossible to obtain.

Recency of Observation   In general, the more recent the information, the more reliable it will be. Some things remain relatively stable over time; however, many things do not. In using examples and illustrations taken from the reports of others, the recency with which the reporter made the observation can be very important. How easy is it for you to remember what happened last week or last month? The time that passes between an observation and when it is reported serves as an additional filter through which a reporter's account must pass. Arguments dealing with economic matters are a classic example of the need for up-to-date information. One need only examine the economic history of the United States over the past decade to appreciate how much inflation, unemployment, or the Dow-Jones average may vary in a short period of time.

Attitude of the Observer   Ideally, the best sources of factual reports should have a neutral attitude toward what they are observing. Since each person sees the world through unique perceptual filters, prejudice, emotion, and ambition may color the reporting of facts. Thus, a final test of examples and illustrations concerns the reporter's attitude toward what he is reporting. Try to find unbiased reports framed in relatively neutral language.

Tests of statistical evidence reflect our concern with verifying the reliability of our evidence. While statistics furnish us with an economical form of proof on a variety of subjects, they are more prone to distortion and misrepresentation than are other forms of proof. Statistical proof, you will recall, has a certain psychological appeal. The use of numbers seems somehow more credible, but you must take care that your statistics come from credible sources.

Source Reliability   The first test of statistics is to identify the source of the information. Certain agencies and institutions are in the business of gathering statistics. The United States Bureau of the Census, for example, may be regarded as a highly credible source ofdemographic information about the United States. The Bureau of Labor Statistics might be regarded as a worthy source regarding information on employment. By comparison, TV Guide is a less likely source of information on either population or employment, although it might be a source of information about America's television-viewing habits.

Statistical Accuracy   In addition to knowing who collected the information, we also want to know how it was collected. Statistical information is frequently collected by sampling techniques. Did the counting procedure fairly select a representative sample? If a statistic claims to sample the entire country representatively, it should draw information from each state or region. Along with the process of data collection, accuracy is also influenced by the length of time during which data were collected. Conditions change, and it would be a gross misrepresentation to claim that inflation went down, based on statistics for December that report a drop in inflation, if inflation increased during the months January through November.

Comparable Units Since statistics frequently inform through comparisons, it is important for the units being compared to be really comparable. Common sense tells us we cannot compare airplanes and microwave ovens because they don't have enough in common to render such a comparison meaningful. The same caution is necessary when dealing in statistical comparisons because statistics can appear to have been gathered on comparable entities. If you want to argue about technology in industrialized societies, for instance, before citing statistical information about the use of robotics in Canada, the United States, and Japan, be sure the term *robotics* has been defined in the same way by the agencies that compile each nation's statistics.

Data Significance Statistics are often expressed in terms of means, modes, medians, percentages, or standard deviations, and data may be created, concealed, or distorted by the method used to report them. Stating that the price of a loaf of bread increased from one dollar and fifty cents to three dollars in the last decade may not seem significant, but reporting a 200 percent increase in the cost of a loaf of bread in the last ten years does. Statistical measures can provide useful information, but those same data can yield different conclusions depending upon who interprets them.

Tests of Scientific Evidence are primarily concerned with the appropriateness of the methodology used in the experiment and possible effect of the laws of probability on its outcome. For that reason you should always understand the methodology of any scientific evidence you use, and be able to explain it to your listeners or readers. Three tests of scientific evidence should always be performed.

Generalizability of Setting and Subjects Laboratory experiments offer researchers greater control over the variables of interest than do field experiments. Some, however, question the generalizability of laboratory findings to real-world settings. If a subject behaves aggressively while alone in unfamiliar surroundings after exposure to sexually aggressive rock music, are we safe in inferring that same person would behave aggressively after hearing the same song at home, possibly in the company of parents, or more likely siblings, or peers? In addition some experiments are performed on nonhuman subjects such as mice or monkeys for ethical reasons. However, if a certain food additive produces disease in a laboratory animal, are we safe in inferring it will produce the same disease in humans? Applying these tests does not mean you should exclude all scientific evidence from laboratory studies or research using nonhuman subjects. Persons conducting such research often address these questions in describing their methodology and discussing the limitations of their study. Examine the arguments they present before dismissing their findings.

Variable Control and Manipulation   Whether in a laboratory or a field setting, a scientific researcher should take care to control as many as possible of the variables that could confound the results. If there is reason to believe that members of one sex may be naturally aggressive, or more easily influenced by rock music, the researcher should make sure that members of both sexes are assigned equally to each treatment condition of the independent variable. However, it is impossible to control all possible nuisance variables. Your own investigation of a topic will give you insight into whether the researcher attempted to control the important nuisance variables. In addition, you should look at the independent variable and the way it is manipulated. Is it capable of influencing the dependent variable, and is it manipulated in a meaningful way? Is hearing a song over the laboratory's intercom speakers likely to produce the same effect as listening to that same song on headphones at home? If a researcher manipulates the treatment groups in a way that takes this into account and a difference was found, does the researcher's methodology allow the determination of whether it was a consequence of lyrics, music, mode of listening, or the interaction of two or more of these variables? Fortunately, much scientific research is published in refereed journals in which the editorial board, composed of top professionals in that field, screens and rejects methodologically flawed submissions. Know your source's editorial policy, and apply some common sense.

Consistency With Other Findings   While external consistency is discussed under the general tests of evidence, it requires special attention in regard to scientific evidence. The conclusions of laboratory and field experiments rely on the application of statistical tests of significance to assess whether the independent variable may have had an impact on the dependent variable. When a researcher states that the effect of X on Y was significant at the 0.05 level, this means there are less than 5 chances in 100 that a phenomenon of the magnitude observed could have occurred by chance or coincidence. These findings would be considered tentative, and conditional on others repeating the experiment and getting similar results. The ability to replicate is at the heart of the scientific method, and the need to do so is the reason researchers publish their methodology along with their results. Even if the findings were true, probability theory suggests that if we replicated a study 100 times, randomly selecting a new set of subjects from the available population each time, our statistical test of the effect of X on Y might yield insignificant results on three or four occasions. If the conclusion of a piece of scientific evidence is inconsistent with other findings, you must be able to account for the difference. Was a different methodology used, or have relevant changes in the population from which samples were drawn taken place during the intervening time between the studies? If you are unable to find a reason for inconsistent findings, be extremely skeptical of them.

Tests of artifacts are usually performed by having the audience employ their own senses. There are only two tests of artifacts to consider.

Artifact Genuineness   In an age when the ability to edit audiotapes and videotapes has benefitted from astonishing technological advances, the authentication of artifacts used as evidence is a concern. Artifacts should be tested to determine their authenticity. Has a document or photograph been altered? The photographic and audiotape evidence supporting the claim that Elvis Presley is still alive offers a clear indication of the importance of document authentication.

Artifact Representativeness Artifacts are often used in value arguments concerning the worth of a product. Since it is usually impossible to examine all examples of a given item, a representative sample is used. When confronted by a large luscious hamburger in a television commercial, you probably ask yourself why it is not typical of the burgers you get at the local fast-food emporium. What you are applying is a test of the representativeness of the video-burger as an artifact.

Tests of premises are difficult because our belief in a premise is based on the notion that things will continue in the future as they have in the past. Since premises are valid because of the assumption that nothing will occur to invalidate them, you test premises by looking for indications that circumstances or our interpretation of them will not change. The decision to intern thousands of Americans of Japanese ancestry after the bombing of Pearl Harbor was based on the publicly stated premise that they represented a threat to the nation's security. The performance of Army units composed of the sons of these internees in the European Theater of World War II invalidated that premise. This example indicates the danger inherent in making policy on the basis of premises.

Summary of Tests of Factual Evidence

Examples and Illustrations
1. Was the report of fact made by a qualified source?
2. Was the information reported accurately?
3. Did the reporter make the original observation or is the report based on secondhand information?
4. Was the report based on a recent observation of phenomena?
5. Was the reporter relatively unbiased toward the material being reported?

Statistics
1. Were the statistics collected by a reliable source?
2. Were the statistics accurately collected from a sufficiently large sample over a sufficiently long period of time?
3. Are comparable units used in statistical comparisons?
4. Is the method of reporting the data an unbiased and fair account of what was measured?

Scientific Evidence
1. Are the results of the study generalizable beyond the setting in which the research was conducted and the subjects who were involved?
2. Are nuisance variables controlled and independent variables manipulated in a meaningful way?
3. Are the conclusions consistent with those of other studies conducted at roughly the same time using similar methodologies?

Artifacts
1. Is the artifact genuine or has it been altered in some way?
2. If the artifact is representative of a certain class of items, is it typical of that class of items?

Premises
1. Is there reason to believe that circumstances, or our understanding of them, has not changed in such a way as to invalidate the premise?

Tests of Opinion Evidence

Unlike facts, opinions are not directly verifiable. However, that does not mean we cannot test opinion evidence. Opinion evidence can seldom be judged true or false in the same sense as factual evidence. Since an opinion is someone's belief about facts, it is subject to contradiction by someone else's opinion of those facts. Keep in mind that some of the best minds of the sixteenth century believed lead could be turned into gold if only the right chemical formula could be discovered.

Source Expertise   In using opinion evidence, we are concerned with what the law refers to as the expert witness. While our opinions might all be of equal worth on some subjects, it is impossible for each of us to have the degree of experience necessary to make sound judgments about all the phenomena we encounter. If you want to know which automobile is most roadworthy, the opinion of a test driver for an independent consumer-testing agency might be more valuable than the opinion of your mother, who drives a twenty-year-old Ford. In testing the expertise of the source, we are concerned with the credentials that give this person the right to pass judgment. Investigate the training, background, and experience of the individual in her field of expertise. To the extent that your audience will accept those credentials, her opinion will have impact.

Source Bias   As a general rule, seek the most unbiased source of opinion evidence. Although it is virtually impossible for experts to remain totally unbiased about their fields, the more objectively the opinion is stated, the more credible it will be. In instances where bias cannot be avoided, it should be forthrightly acknowledged so the listener or reader is aware of it.

Factual Basis of the Opinion   As in the case of statistical information, the credibility of opinion evidence may be diminished if the opinion is based on secondhand information. Although many opinions on historical occurrences must, of necessity, be rendered long after the fact, the most credible judgments are those made by an expert observer on the scene at the time something is happening.

Summary of Tests of Opinion Evidence

1. Is the source a qualified expert in the field by training, background, or experience?

2. Is the source relatively unbiased?
3. Is there a reliable factual basis for the opinion?

General Tests of Evidence

The **reliability of evidence** as a source of support for your claims is your first general concern in selecting the evidence to include in an argument. The audience determines the reliability of evidence based on its accuracy and recency.

Accuracy In considering tests of factual information, we stressed that the accurate representation of that which was observed was a key factor in choosing evidence. In particular, reports of statistical information and observations of events should represent them as closely as possible. If evidence is to be considered reliable, it must be as credible as possible. Evidence of both fact and opinion must be tested for accuracy.

To assure accuracy in your use of evidence: (1) When quoting directly, do not take facts, statistics, or opinion statements out of context. Make sure you honestly portray what the source had to say. (2) When paraphrasing, make honest paraphrases. Sometimes, it is neither practical nor desirable to present a source's entire statement verbatim in your argument. When paraphrasing from books, speeches, or articles, do so honestly, in a manner which accurately reflects the author's intent or frame of reference. (3) When quoting or paraphrasing, accurately interpret your source; do not distort the information.

Recency Much real-world argumentation, and claim making of all kinds, is concerned with current events. Using recent sources of information adds potency to your arguments. This does not mean you should not research the history of your topic carefully. Knowing what has happened in the past helps us to hypothesize about the future. However, relying on out-of-date sources may cause you to miss recent developments.

The **quality of evidence** is also important. There is a temptation to confuse having a large quantity of evidence with having good evidence. Effective argumentation results more from having high-quality evidence than having great quantities of evidence. Quality results from choosing evidence that best helps the audience understand how you have arrived at the conclusions implied by your claim making. Quality evidence has the properties of being sufficient, representative, relevant, and clear.

Sufficiency Ideally, the best argumentation occurs when we know all of the facts and opinions of experts about our topic. Having all the evidence is seldom possible, particularly in our information-intensive society. Nevertheless, it is the arguer's responsibility to research the topic sufficiently and provide the support needed to make it possible for the audience to accept her claims.

Representativeness   Is the evidence you have selected to support your claims representative of all available evidence?   Just as we are concerned that statistical samples should accurately represent the populations from which they were drawn, the evidence of both the fact and opinion you choose to use should be representative of the available evidence on the subject.

Relevance   Is your evidence related to the claim it is supposed to support? In some cases, the relationship between grounds and claim in an argument is not always apparent. The reasoning process of the warrant, discussed in the next chapter, can help make it more apparent; however, the use of additional evidence in backing the warrant may be necessary. The important thing to remember is that evidence that seems to have little bearing on the claim will be of little use in supporting that claim.

Clarity   Will your evidence be readily understood by the audience?   The advice on the importance of defining terms in such a way that they render a subject more understandable to the audience also pertains to the selection of evidence. Facts and opinions that are too technical, or in some way beyond an audience's level of understanding, may be unsuitable for that audience. Vague or equivocal evidence will not contribute to the audience's understanding of the conclusions you are asking them to accept.

The **consistency of evidence** with itself, with other evidence on the same subject, or with human understanding contributes to grounding your claim making. Evidence that seems atypical, for whatever reason, is likely to cause the audience to disbelieve the claim it supports. Consistency is assessed on two levels.

Internal Consistency   Does your evidence contradict itself?   Evidence that comes from a single source should not state contradictory positions. Except in instances where a simple explanation can be provided, a piece of information that reports both an increase and a decrease, or a positive and a negative result, may pose serious problems for the arguer who attempts to use it.

External Consistency   Is your evidence consistent with other sources of information on the subject? Although new discoveries are being made constantly and two equally respected authorities in a field may interpret the same event very differently, we generally expect any piece of evidence to be consistent with others on the same subject. There is a natural tendency for a reader or listener to reject evidence that seems not to fit. A part of our need for external consistency is our expectation that the evidence used in argument will conform with what we already know in general. For example, because we expect the President of the United States to support American values and traditions, we might be skeptical when we hear the president quoted as condemning some intrinsic American value.

Audience acceptability is the last general test your evidence should meet. Will your listener or reader accept the evidence?   There is little utility in having the best evidence if the audience will not accept it. Evidence must be selected with the audience in mind. This does not mean you should be dishonest or distort evidence in such a way that the audience will be forced to agree. It does mean that audience values, predispositions, knowledge of the subject, and technical expertise must be taken into account as you select the evidence to use.

Arguers have the responsibility of addressing the rationality of their listeners or readers. If you fail to consider the requirements and tests of evidence, your ability to affect an audience instrumentally through the process of argumentation may be seriously impaired. Always consider the possible available types of evidence and their tests as you prepare to argue.

Summary of General Tests of Evidence

1. Is the evidence accurate in its report of fact or statement of opinion?
2. Is the evidence a recent report of fact or opinion?
3. Is the evidence presented sufficient in amount to support the claim effectively?
4. Is the evidence representative of the available evidence on the subject?
5. Is the evidence relevant to the claim being made?
6. Is the evidence clearly presented?
7. Is the evidence internally consistent?
8. Is the evidence consistent with other available evidence on the subject?
9. Is the evidence adapted to the requirements of the particular audience?

THE DISCOVERY OF EVIDENCE

Now that you know the kinds of evidence you can use in supporting a claim and how to determine the viability of evidence as a means of influencing belief or behavior, your next step is finding and recording evidence. Your college library will probably be your best available source for locating facts and opinions. Get to know its organizational system and make the acquaintance of the reference librarian. A working knowledge of how your library is organized and the assistance the reference staff can give you will save time and frustration in your search for proof.

Begin with a devout belief in the premise, "The probable truth of our question is out there to be found" (Ziegelmuller, Kay & Dause, 1990, p. 73). It is up to you to go out and find it. The sources of information described in this section are available in most college libraries. The resources of the reference section can be discovered through guides that provide bibliographies of reference materials. *American Reference Books Annual* has been published since 1970. It provides detailed explanations of such reference resources as dictionaries, general encyclopedias, specialty encyclopedias, foreign reference materials, selected government publications, abstracts, indexes, and some journals. It covers new editions of older references and annually describes references published in serial form. A second guide is *Introduction to Reference Work* by William A. Katz. It discusses the types of material common to the reference section of a library. If neither of these sources is available in your college library, consult the card catalog under the heading *reference bibliography*.

Books

Books—nonfiction unless you are arguing about literature— are a valuable source of evidence for argumentation. Your library's card catalog lists all books available in its collection. Card catalogs are usually arranged by title, author, and subject. Unless you are looking for the work of a specific author or you know the title of the book you wish to locate, begin with the subject index. Do not be discouraged if you find nothing listed under the subject you choose. Those responsible for creating the subject headings may not have given your subject the heading you are using. You need to be a sleuth. Think of a variation of, or synonyms for, your heading. If all else fails, ask the reference librarian for assistance.

Books are useful because they usually provide a more comprehensive treatment of a subject than a periodical or newspaper has space to provide. Books provide historical background on a topic, but they have certain limitations as sources of information. First, books have the disadvantage of quickly becoming outdated sources of fact and opinion. The process of researching, writing, revising, and publishing a single volume may span several years. In that time, the factual basis of the book may become dated, or superseded by new discoveries. Second, your library may have only a limited number of books on your topic, so you will be unable to find the quantity of information you had hoped for. You can overcome this problem by using the resources of other libraries through Interlibrary Loan, if your college library is part of such a system. Even if it is not, the books available will be good sources of information, but they have limitations. If you require an abundance of up-to-the-minute information, you must seek it from other sources.

Periodicals

Periodicals offer access to current fact and opinion and may offer it in quantity. Because they are so numerous and varied, it is impossible to generalize about which periodicals will be of most value to you in preparing to argue. Consulting one of several excellent reference guides to periodicals will help you find the ones most pertinent to your topic. A good place to begin is *The Reader's Guide to Periodical Literature,* which indexes what are commonly termed popular periodicals—*Time, Newsweek,* and *U.S. News and World Report,* for example. It indexes by subject heading, so the techniques you used in mastering the card catalog, if not the actual subject headings, can be applied to *The Reader's Guide.*

The Reader's Guide has one important limitation, however. It does not reference many scholarly journals or special-interest publications. If, for example, you are arguing about the unionization of public school teachers, finding out what is in *Newsweek* on this subject may be less valuable than finding out what is available in *The Journal of Collective Negotiation in the Public Sector.* Since the credibility of material from the latter is greater, you will need to examine specialty indexes. Most college libraries have the following indexes to scholarly or special-interest periodicals:

- *Agricultural Index*
- *Applied Science and Technology Index*
- *Business Periodical Index*
- *Education Index*
- *Human Resources Abstracts*
- *Index to Legal Periodicals*
- *International Index*
- *Psychological Abstracts*
- *Social Science Index*
- *Sociological Abstracts*

Once again, indexing is by subject. The difference between these indexes and *The Reader's Guide* is in what they do, not how they do it.

Newspapers

Not all college libraries offer current and back issues of a wide variety of newspapers, but your library will certainly have one or more major newspapers from your state and some national newspapers, such as *The New York Times*. The latter is an excellent source of material, not only because of its reputation but because it is indexed. This newspaper prints the text of major speeches, Supreme Court decisions, and documents such as the Pentagon papers. This is not to say there are not a number of other excellent newspapers, but they are not indexed.

In addition, a service known as *NewsBank* collects and reprints articles from fifty different papers. Although everything in a particular edition of a paper is not included, material on a given topic, the accident at the Soviet nuclear power plant at Chernobyl, for example, is available. *NewsBank* organizes by topic; so if your topic coincides with a *NewsBank* category, relatively recent information from a variety of papers across the country will be available to you.

A final note about newspapers in general and *NewsBank* in particular: Since most college libraries do not have unlimited space, newspapers are typically stored on microfilm or microfiche. Become familiar with the equipment for reading and photocopying film and fiche.

Government Documents

If you are interested in nutrition, how to prepare an income tax return, or treaty restrictions on foreign trade, the federal government has probably published one or more documents on the subject. Texts of the hearings of major and minor Congressional committees, information bulletins, treaties and agreements, all proceedings of legislative bodies, court decisions, and the like are contained between the covers of government documents, indexed in the *Monthly Catalog of United States Government*

Publications. This is not the only available index to these documents, or the easiest to use.

More and more indexes are being computerized, and many college libraries have not only computerized their card catalogs but also make various indexes available on CD-ROM. It will take a little time to learn, but the rewards are well worth the effort. We knew that hearings had been held on rock music in 1985. Searching the Government Printing Office (GPO) data base for "rock" turned up hundreds of documents that might have interested a geologist, "music" also gave us hundreds of possibilities. Asking for "lyrics" produced the following report (Figure 7.1).

This data base, like most others, allows the use of logical operators. AND, OR, and NOT, are logical operators. You can use them to combine and exclude terms from the search you request the computer to perform. Using AND tells the computer to report only on those documents in which the terms to both the left and right of the operator appear. For example, had we asked for "music" AND "lyrics" in the title of the document, we would have gotten the exact document we were looking for on the first try. A search using OR will report all documents in which either term appeared. Asking for "music" OR "rock" would have gotten us farther from, not closer to, the document we were looking for. A search using NOT will report all documents that contain the term to the left of the operator which do not contain the term to the right. Had we asked for "lyrics" NOT "music," we would have received a report that included the second document in Figure 7.1 but not the first. Our search would have missed the mark completely. Even with the false starts, our search took about as long as it has taken you to read about it.

Figure 7.1

SilverPlatter 1.6   GPO on SilverPlatter (7/76 - 12/89)

AN: 86013575
SU: Y 4.C 73/7:S.hrg.99-529
SU: Y4C737Shrg99529
CA: United States. Congress. Senate. Committee on Commerce, Science, and Transportation.
TI: Record labeling : hearing before the Committee on Commerce, Science, and Transportation, United States Senate, Ninety-ninth Congress, first session, on contents of music and the **lyrics** of records, September 19, 1985.
SO: Washington : U.S. G.P.O., 1985 (i.e. 1986).
SE: United States. Congress. Senate. S. hrg. ; 99-529.
IT: 1041-A, 1041-B (microfiche)

AN: 77016496
SU: LC 3.4/2:67/5
SU: LC 342675
CA: United States. Copyright Office.
TI: Poems and song **lyrics.**
SO: Washington : Library of Congress, Copyright Office, 1977.
SE: Circular ; 67.
IT: 802-A

Source: GPO on SilverPlatter (7/76 - 12/89). Newton Lower Falls, MA; SilverPlatter Information, Inc. 1990.

The *Congressional Record* is a government document that is a particularly good source for topics on public policy. It is issued daily while Congress is in session and provides complete transcripts of congressional debates and presidential messages. It also includes an appendix containing a variety of materials—newspaper articles, resolutions, excerpted speeches, and anything else that might pertain to business before Congress.

Almanacs, Fact Books, and Other Resources

A variety of sources that compile statistics and other factual information is available in the reference section of your college library. What distinguishes them is that they compile information in condensed form and are organized for quick access. *The Statistical Abstract of the United States,* and *The World Almanac* provide statistical information on such subjects as population, demographic characteristics and change, transportation, agriculture, trade, mining, national and international banking, energy use, and more. They are updated annually. *Facts on File* provides a weekly summary of news from major United States newspapers and magazines.

Your library probably contains several sources of biographical information that can be used to discover the credentials of authorities and experts. A particularly good source is *Current Biography Yearbook.* In its sixth decade of publication, it provides biographical articles about living leaders in all fields worldwide; it is updated yearly.

While the text of important speeches, court cases, or announcements by public officials can be found in a variety of sources, *Historical Documents of (Year)* collects and publishes these important United States documents annually. First published in 1972, it contains texts of public affairs documents, court decisions, government reports, special studies, speeches, and statements by public officials on domestic and foreign policy. If you wanted the text of the speech in which Reagan's "Star Wars" defense proposal was first presented, you could find it in *Historical Documents of 1983,* Ronald Reagan's March 23, 1983 televised address, "Defense in Space."

A resource that treats topics in much the same way as arguers do, developing pro and con positions on a topic, is the *Reference Shelf.* A yearly publication, each volume is devoted to a single topic on a subject of public interest. This source contains reprints of articles, excerpts from books, and opinions of experts. It suffers the same limitation of becoming dated as all other books, but it does provide a variety of sources of information. The series, which began in 1922, can be an excellent source of historical background information on how Americans have perceived many issues.

The foregoing is by no means a complete list of available reference sources, just some suggestions to get you started. To discover what else is available, browse through the reference section of your library, consult the librarian assigned to that section, or experiment with the various computerized services available in your library. As you become more experienced, you will find the process getting easier. We want to reemphasize that a good working knowledge of your library is the first step in the discovery of evidence.

RECORDING EVIDENCE

You should know how to record the material you research to render it most useful when the time comes to use it in constructing arguments. It is one thing to discover information in the library; it is quite another to organize it so that it will be readily accessible in the future. You may be a person who functions quite efficiently with a notebook full of bits of information or a file folder crammed full of photocopied pages. Most of us are not that efficient, however. What follows is a workable system of note taking based on the premise that an organized system of note taking will make you a better arguer. Failure to have a good system for recording and organizing material is one of the most common problems experienced by beginning and seasoned arguers alike.

The first step in efficient research is to have a clear idea of the evidence needed. Your analysis of the topic should help you get off on the right track. In the initial stages of working with a topic, attempt to discover what information is available by skimming summaries, prefaces, and opening paragraphs. Read for ideas as much as for examples, statistics, and opinion statements. Once you have surveyed the available information, look for specific things—a statistic grounding a relationship you want to claim, the opinion of an authority to back a warrant. Later you can become more concerned about the quality of the proof you are finding, but initially worry as much about quantity. The key concept to keep in mind is that you can only be efficient in looking for proof if you have a clear idea of the arguments you are trying to prove. Reading for ideas initially gives you a feeling for what can be proven with the resources available to you and keeps you from wasting time later looking for proof that may not exist.

Step two in the research process involves keeping an annotated bibliography and is performed in conjunction with step one. As you consider each source, record the title, author, publisher, date, and page numbers (where pertinent) on an index card; we recommend the four- by six-inch size. It is also a good idea to include the call numbers or reference numbers of all library materials so you can quickly find them again. In a few sentences, jot down the viewpoint of the author, a summary of what the source includes, and your personal evaluation of it. The purpose of this bibliography card is to give you a general idea of what a source contains. Make one card per source and have a system for keeping them in order, either alphabetically by author, chronologically, or conceptually by topic.

The third step in the research process involves excerpting specific facts and opinions in an organized system that will allow you to find what you need when you are ready to construct your arguments. The mechanics of the system need not be complex. Again, we recommend the use of index cards for recording each separate fact and opinion statement. Include the author, the author's qualifications, title, publication or publisher, date, and page number on the top of each card; then carefully record the fact or opinion. Accuracy is imperative. Omitting a word, punctuation mark, or phrase can seriously alter the meaning of the fact or opinion. Be especially careful in recording statistical information. In a moment of stress 3.6 million is less likely to be misread than 3,600,000. Also be sure the source stated million and not billion. It is easy to become confused when working with statistical information.

Once you have recorded information on a number of cards, you will have to arrange the cards in a fashion that will make it easy to find a particular piece of proof later on. If you require a particular opinion to back a warrant, you do not want to shuffle through sixty index cards to find it and then reshuffle through the same sixty cards to find the material to ground the next argument. An organizational system will help you avoid the paper chase. The fourth step in the research process involves developing a topical heading system to organize your index cards.

The system involves placing headings on each card that are brief, simple, and derived from the argument supported. The heading provides a two- or three-word summary of the information the card contains. Suppose you are arguing about drunk drivers. Some appropriate topical headings might be the following:

- State laws—California
- State laws—Nebraska
- Deaths per year
- Injuries per year
- Proposed solution—ignition interlock
- Proposed solution—random stop

These headings, commonly referred to as slugs, can help you organize large quantities of material into related categories and distinguish at a glance the cards pertaining to one category from all other cards. The important thing to remember about slugs is that they serve your purposes and should make sense to you. They reflect your impression of the contents of a particular card. Since you now have a lot of writing on a small card, confusion may be reduced somewhat if you record slugs in a different color of ink.

As a student of argumentation you may be required to both advocate and oppose the same proposition; therefore, you may end up with evidence on both sides of the proposition. Although most of our examples in this chapter were drawn from the examples of Value and Policy Advocacy in Action in Chapters 4 and 5, opponents use evidence to ground their claims and back their warrants as well. If you are not careful, it is possible that the evidence you find that is suitable to one side of the proposition will become mixed with evidence suitable to the other side. Using different colors of index cards for advocacy and opposition can avoid this situation. If you cannot find different colors, using cards of different sizes serves the same purpose. If your argumentation course involves working with more than one topic area, the color or size trick can be used to keep evidence for one proposition from getting mixed up with evidence for another.

Although this may seem needlessly complicated, we assure you it is important. Because evidence is vital in establishing claims, it is at the nexus of effective argumentation. The more systematic your approach to the discovery and recording of materials of fact and opinion, and the creation of a means to facilitate its retrieval, the better you will be in building arguments.

Knowing the types of evidence used in building arguments, the tests it must meet, and the means of finding and recording information enables you to begin preparing arguments. The next chapter discusses how to turn your ideas into arguments by considering the relationship of grounds, claim, and warrant in the reasoning process.

LEARNING ACTIVITIES

1. Find two samples of each of the following types of factual evidence: example, illustration, and statistic. Explain how each of your samples meets the tests for its type of factual evidence.
2. Choose a topic with which you are familiar. Find three sources that provide authoritative opinion evidence on this topic. Explain why each source is credible in terms of the tests of opinion evidence.
3. Find five examples of evidence based on premises. Consider each premise in terms of how it came to be held as true without needing further proof. Is there any reason to believe these premises might become invalid?
4. Review the definitions of fact and opinion in this chapter. Decide which of the following statements are facts and which are opinions.
   A. The Supreme Court has decided that legal counsel will be provided for those who cannot afford to pay for it.
   B. Humans are primates descended from earlier forms of primates.
   C. College tuition costs have stabilized.
   D. Germany and Japan will dominate world trade in the 1990s.
   E. Many professional educators believe that studying a foreign language will help students become more proficient in the structure and grammar of the English language.
   F. Railroads played an important part in the North's ability to win battles during the Civil War.
   G. Simply by visiting the Smithsonian, all may enjoy our nation's treasures.
   H. Natural-habitat zoos are more interesting than traditional caged-exhibit zoos.
5. Begin researching the topic area you have selected for future assignments concerning propositions of fact, value, and policy. Your evidence file should meet the following criteria:
   A. All sources of information should be identified on bibliography cards.
   B. Each item of evidence should be classified as to type.
   C. Each item of evidence should be evaluated as to credibility—meeting the tests of evidence.
   D. Each piece of evidence should be slugged according to the topic you have selected.

SUGGESTED SUPPLEMENTARY READINGS

Kimble, G. A. (1978). *How to Use (and Misuse) Statistics.* Englewood Cliffs, N.J.: Prentice Hall.
    Statistical and scientific evidence is used extensively in argumentation. This book provides useful insight into the scientific method and a thorough discussion of statistics, particularly the kinds used for significance testing in laboratory and field experiments. Its aim is the development of statistical literacy, rather than computational ability. We recommend it to students who foresee a specific need

to develop greater under standing of this form of analytical thinking, or who are particularly interested in the use of statistical and scientific evidence.

Windes, R. R., & Hastings, A. (1965). *Argumentation and Advocacy*. New York: Random House.
Although this is an older text, it is still useful for its discussion of the place of argumentation in society and its excellent examples of famous historical American controversies. Of greatest use, however, is its thorough discussion of the types of evidence: historical, legal, scientific, and journalistic. Even though the evidence samples are sometimes dated, these principles and the techniques for discovering evidence remain valid.

8

HOW DO I REASON WITH MY AUDIENCE?

Argumentation is a process of drawing inferences for instrumental purposes. As you discover information on a topic, you make guesses about how it fits together, and how it might support or fail to support your own ideas about the topic. You become concerned with creating viable arguments. What makes an argument viable? In part an argument is viable because the evidence used to ground the claim has been tested for validity, but there is more to the viability of an argument than the validity of the evidence that supports it. The relationship between evidence and the claim it supports is established through reasoning. When you study the reasoning process, you are concerned with the logic of the inference drawn when you ask your listeners or readers to agree that the evidence you provide warrants accepting your claim. In Chapter 3 we indicated that this inferential relationship is established by the warrant. A warrant can be tested for validity, and when it passes the test, we say the argument is viable.

The reasoning process is based on recognizing common patterns of experience. Consider a not uncommon experience of dormitory life: You encounter Dennis and Paul. Dennis has an empty bucket and Paul is dripping wet. What goes on in your mind? Since you were not on the scene to observe firsthand how Paul got wet, you probably inferred the cause of Paul's wetness. Experience suggests that the claim: "Dennis dumped a bucket of water on Paul" is viable. How reliably do the grounds, Paul's wetness and Dennis's empty bucket, support the claim? How probable is it that your claim describes what really happened? You do not know with any degree of certainty based on the grounds and claim alone, but a warrant increases your certainty of the relationship between grounds and claim. This chapter is about the reasoning process, the warrant step in the Toulmin model of argument.

In using the Toulmin model to study argumentation, it is important to remember that it is an idealized blueprint for creating and testing arguments. It graphically depicts the process of reasoning from evidence to a conclusion. The form an argument takes in the model may not represent the best way to articulate it in a speech or an essay. The actual wording of an argument for presentation depends on such factors as communicator style, audience needs, and how individual arguments combine to shape your speech or essay. As we guide you through understanding how the reasoning process works, we will state some examples in Toulmin model form, but we will provide other examples that show how arguments are typically authored. Chapter 10 addresses the question of how oral arguments are best presented more directly in its discussion of language, delivery, and brief writing.

While you are learning about argumentation, we strongly suggest that you employ all four elements—grounds, warrant, backing, and claim—in creating your arguments. As you develop skill in argumentation, you may find it unnecessary to articulate all of them all of the time and you will elect to use all of them only when your audience is likely to require them or want them supplied.

Reasoning is the inferential leap from grounds to claim made through the warrant in argumentation. In earlier chapters we noted that arguments may be developed in many different fields. Although the subjects about which inferences are drawn and the pattern of inference drawing that is favored may differ from field to field, the reasoning process does not change because it is based on patterns of common human experience. In this chapter we consider the forms of reasoning and the rules for testing the validity of warrants. In the chapter which follows, we will consider what happens when these forms and rules are not observed and fallacies in reasoning, appeal, and language use occur.

Six major forms of reasoning develop the relationship between data and claim: cause, sign, generalization, parallel case, analogy, and authority. In addition, two minor forms of reasoning are useful in certain circumstances: definition and dilemma. As you study these forms of reasoning, it is important to remember that reasoning—the warrant—is used to infer that *because these grounds exist, believing this claim to be true or probable is justified.*

ARGUMENT FROM CAUSE

Argument from cause is one of the most prevalent forms of reasoning in argumentation. When things are happening to us and around us, it is human nature to infer connections between them. *As a form of reasoning, argument from cause suggests a temporal connection between phenomena.* We claim that an event or condition of one kind is the cause of an event or condition of another. Consider these phenomena:

Phenomenon 1—A student does not read his assignments.
Phenomenon 2—The student receives an *F* on an exam.

It is useful to conceptualize events as existing on a time line (Ehninger, 1974). Phenomena along it may be connected, and it may be traveled in either direction. A present effect may be connected with a preceding cause; a presently existing cause may be identified to predict some future effect.

Argument from cause is based on the premise that things occur in an orderly fashion for some reason. Since neither the affairs of humanity nor nature are random, we assume we can rely on the premise, "Everything has a cause." In an argument from cause, the grounds, warrant, and backing must validate the claim on the basis of their temporal connection. If we are careful in researching phenomena, we can support claims that events or conditions of one kind are the cause of events or conditions of another.

As an illustration of how argument from cause works, let us consider some observable phenomena:

- American public schools are judged to provide an inadequate education.
- A shortage of math and science teachers exists.
- Teachers are poorly trained.
- At the secondary level, students are allowed to select courses from lists of electives rather than required to take a core of fundamental courses.

These phenomena may be organized into an argument from cause along the following lines:

GROUND 1   Teacher shortages exist in science and math.
GROUND 2   Teachers are poorly trained.
GROUND 3   In secondary schools, electives may be taken in place of fundamentals.
BACKING   The National Commission on Excellence in Education reported in May of 1983 that as a result of poorly trained teachers, failure to emphasize fundamentals, and the shortage of teachers in key areas such as math and science, a "tide of mediocrity" has lowered the standard of American public education.
WARRANT   Because inadequacy is caused by a mediocre system of public education.
CLAIM   Education provided by American public schools is inadequate.

In this example, the reasoning revolves around linking a series of existing causes with the effect specified by the claim. The time line examines what came first, three causes listed as grounds, in conjunction with their consequence, an inadequate school system. The warrant identifies what produced these observable effects, the mediocrity of the educational system. If you were to encounter this particular argument in a speech or an editorial, it would probably not be stated in this way. More likely, only the backing and claim would be presented as an argument from cause.

Consider the following example of an argument from cause taken from an article by Professor George Comstock on television's effects on children:

When science is asked a question difficult or impossible to address directly, its solution is to address lesser approximations that are within its means. . . . For example, we might design an experiment comparing the behavior of young people who have just witnessed a violent television or film portrayal with the behavior of those who have not. This has been done dozens of times, and the results have been consistent: those who saw the violent portrayal subsequently expressed a greater degree of punitiveness or aggressiveness against another person than those who did not. We might also design an experiment in which we observe whether children imitate the acts they have just seen on television or film. This too has been done dozens of times, and the results also have been consistent: those who saw an example of violent behavior behaved more frequently in a manner just like what they had seen than those who did not see the violent portrayal. . . . While these experiments have shown that violent portrayal can influence behavior within the context of an experiment, they have not told us much about everyday behavior. After all, an experiment is an artificial experience, abnormal in time frame and setting. In an experiment a person might display behavior that he or she would suppress in real life. . . . The next question, then, is whether aggressiveness and viewing of violent programming tend to go together in real life. Scientists would reply by collecting data on the television viewing habits of teenagers through self-report and data on their aggressive behavior from their peers. This has been done a number of times, and in a majority of the instances there has been a significant positive correlation between the two. Teenagers who viewed greater amounts of violent television programming were in fact more aggressive in everyday behavior than those who did not. (Comstock, 1982, pp. 187-88)

Dr. Comstock offers an argument about the cause-effect relationship between viewing violence on television and subsequently engaging in violent behavior. At the same time, he gives you an insight into how laboratory and field experiments examine cause-effect relationships. While he does not specifically state his warrant, it is implied to be: The scientific method can reliably identify cause-effect relationships. See if you can identify his grounds, backing, and claim.

In arguing causality, some precautions must be taken to ensure that our inferential leaps are justified. The most important question to ask is: Are the grounds sufficient to bring about or cause the conditions specified in the claim? Focusing on the grounds is an important first step in testing the strength of the argument from cause. Examine your arguments from cause using the following questions as guidelines:

1. Are other grounds likely to lead to the effect?
2. Is the asserted relationship between grounds and effect consistent, or are there instances in which this effect has not followed from these grounds?

When using causal reasoning, you are generalizing about the relationship between phenomena along the time line: In the presence of phenomenon A (cause), we can always find evidence of phenomenon B (effect); or if we can find evidence of phenomenon B (effect), it is likely to have been the consequence of phenomenon A (cause). The regularity with which this generalization has been true in the past warrants speculation about causes or effects that are undocumented or undocumentable. This is particularly useful when arguing about things that have not yet happened, as in the case of weighing the costs and benefits of some proposed course of action.

We take that course of action as a "cause" and speculate about the "effects," both good and bad, that it is likely to produce.

We also want to examine the generalizations produced by cause and effect reasoning to make sure they are really a cause and its effect, not simply two phenomena that happened to occur sequentially. Just because phenomenon A is followed by phenomenon B does not make A the cause of B. Many superstitions are based on this notion of false cause. A visit to Florida during the rainy season produced the following:

KARYN: (Raising umbrella in store) "I think I'll see if this works."
JANICE: "Putting up an umbrella indoors is bad luck."

Putting up an umbrella indoors only causes bad luck if you poke someone in the eye and that person sues you for all your worldly possessions.

Causality requires proof of more than chronological occurrence. When two things happen sequentially and you suspect a cause-effect relationship, consider whether the alleged cause is capable of producing the effect. Is the cause potentially strong enough to produce the effect? Two examples illustrate the danger of falling prey to believing false causes.

GROUNDS   In the 1968 presidential election, Karyn voted for Hubert Humphrey; in 1972, she voted for Eugene McCarthy; in 1976, she voted for Gerald Ford; in 1980, she voted for Jimmy Carter; in 1984, she voted for Walter Mondale; and in 1988, she voted for Michael Dukakis.
WARRANT   Because Karyn has never voted for the winner, the candidate she votes for will lose.
BACKING   In every presidential election in which she has voted, Karyn has always voted for the loser.
CLAIM   Karyn's vote for Michael Dukakis in 1988 cost him the presidential election.

That example may seem a bit foolish, so consider another from the 1980 presidential election.

GROUNDS   The hostages remained captive in Iran throughout the period of the 1980 campaign and election.
BACKING   Attempts to negotiate their release and the military rescue mission failed.
WARRANT   Because he was unable to bring the hostages home,
CLAIM   Jimmy Carter lost the election because of the hostage crisis.

Since the hostages were not released until Ronald Reagan had taken the oath of office, it is tempting to state that the hostage crisis alone cost Jimmy Carter the election.

Avoid being trapped by superficial connections between events by looking for alternative explanations of what happened. In both interpersonal and public relations, few things happen as the result of a single cause. The earlier argument on the inadequacy of the American public school system is a good example of the identification of multiple causalities. In the case of a presidential election, we can usually find several factors that contributed to one candidate triumphing over the other. For any given set of events, before placing too much faith in any single cause-effect relationship, look for possible alternative or multiple causes for the effect.

A cause may be discussed in terms of its being **necessary** and **sufficient**. A cause is said to be *necessary* if, without its presence, the effect will not occur. However, this cause may not be *sufficient* to bring about the effect all by itself. The difference between necessary and sufficient cause is illustrated by a traditional example, combustion (Ehninger, 1974). The presence of oxygen is a necessary cause of a fire's burning. If there is no oxygen, there is no fire. Oxygen alone, however, is not sufficient to produce a fire. You must raise the temperature of a material above its point of combustion in the presence of oxygen to produce a flame. A sufficient cause goes beyond that which is necessary to include all elements required to produce the effect. In the case of fire, fuel, oxygen, and a spark are all part of the sufficient cause.

Why is this distinction important? In determining whether a cause produced an effect, sufficient causes can always be counted on to produce predictable effects. Recall the education example. Is a shortage of math and science teachers a sufficient cause for poor-quality education in America's public schools? Do more deficiencies have to be discovered before a sufficient cause for poor quality can be found? The distinction between causes that are necessary and causes that are sufficient helps to emphasize the importance of always looking for alternative and multiple causes.

Summary of Argument from Cause

1. Argument from cause suggests a temporal connection between events in which one produces the other.
2. When we can document effects, we may reason as to their cause; when we can document cause, we may reason as to their effect.
3. A necessary cause is a factor that must be present to bring about an effect, but it will not in itself produce the effect.
4. A sufficient cause includes all factors needed to produce a particular effect.
5. Causality involves more than chronological order and may be tested by asking the following questions:
   A. Is the cause capable of producing the effect?
   B. Is the effect produced by the cause or does the effect occur coincidental to the cause?
   C. Are there other potential causes?
   D. Has this effect consistently followed from this cause?

ARGUMENT FROM SIGN

Unlike arguments from cause which link causes to their effects, *arguments from sign connect phenomena with conditions that merely exist.* **Signs** are indicators—observable symptoms, conditions, or marks—that tell us what is the case. Would-be naturalists often study the behaviors of animals and connect those behaviors to other events. Consider the following examples of sign reasoning in which the sign has no causal connection to the events they are used to predict:

- A robin is the first sign of spring.
- When the squirrels store extra nuts, it means we're in for a hard winter.
- If the groundhog sees its shadow on February 2, spring is only six weeks away.

What kinds of things serve as signs? Events are often observed to be signs of attitudes or activities. We observe that a certain product is selling well and take this as sign evidence of the product's quality or the effectiveness of its advertising. Statistics are often interpreted through sign reasoning. High employment and low inflation are said to be signs of a healthy economy. Public opinion polls signify attitudes about policies, activities, and persons. Let us turn to an example of sign argument:

GROUNDS   52 percent of American military leaders describe themselves as Republican, 43 percent as Independent, and only 4 percent as Democrats.
WARRANT   Describing one's party affiliation as Republican or Independent is a sign of politically conservative ideas.
BACKING   In the past, those who described themselves as Republican or Independent have tended to favor conservative policies; those who described themselves as Democrat tended to favor liberal policies.
CLAIM   American military leaders tend to hold conservative views.

The observable sign of political viewpoint used in this case is party affiliation: Republican, Democrat, or Independent.

Consider another example of this form of reasoning in an essay in which sex-role stereotyping in children's television is inferred on the basis of certain observable signs:

> Children's TV tends to reinforce traditional sex-role behaviors and personality traits extant in society. Thus, females are portrayed as being more passive in behavior and paying more attention to social relationships. They rate lower in aggression, and in self-concept and achievement-related behaviors—i.e., they seem less confident. They also display the virtues of unselfishness, kindness, and warmth, while being weaker, more peaceful, more dependent and more passive than males. These conclusions hold true for most females. The exceptions are female heroes . . . however, both female heroes and villains were rarely found. Out of 471 major dramatic characters, there were only 13 female heroes and six female villains. (Barcus, 1983, p. 61)

Mr. Barcus lists several behavioral characteristics of female characters on television to ground the claim expressed in the first sentence. The warrant is implied rather than stated: The portrayal of passive behaviors and the small percentages of female heroes and villains are signs that television programs for children reinforce traditional sex-role stereotypes.

There are some cautions to observe in arguing on the basis of signs. The most important is to be sure the sign you are using is reliable. We have longed for spring months after the groundhog's first appearance. The problem with finding a reliable sign is that signs are only circumstantial evidence in many instances. We can never be absolutely sure that party affiliations are related to conservative or liberal attitudes. Both the Democratic and Republican parties have conservative and liberal elements. Things we observe to be signs may not really warrant any claim unless backing for the warrant can be found.

A second caution regarding sign reasoning is that signs should not be confused with causes. A good rule to follow in distinguishing sign from cause is this: *A sign tells what is the case, while a cause explains why it is the case.* Arguments from cause attempt to analyze events in terms of antecedents and their consequences. Arguments from sign concern themselves with what the sign will signify. They tell us what we can expect to observe as a result of having first observed the sign.

A final caution about sign reasoning is that we must be concerned with the strength of the sign. Sign arguments draw conclusions about what was, is, or will be. Sign reasoning is presented as a factual claim about the sign and what it signifies. It must be tested the way we test any factual claim, by examining its grounds. We want to know if the grounds, the sign, always or usually validate the prediction of that which it signifies, the conclusion drawn in the claim. Examination of the grounds might include asking if sufficient signs are present. After all, one robin does not constitute spring, but a flock of robins and other species, buds on trees, and the absence of snow may reliably lead us to conclude that spring is at hand.

Summary of Argument from Sign

1. Signs are observable symptoms, conditions, or marks used to prove that a certain state of affairs exists.
2. Signs should be reliable so that the grounds point to the conclusion drawn, not to some alternative conclusion.
3. Sign reasoning must not be confused with causal reasoning. Signs describe the situation; causes analyze the situation.
4. Sign reasoning is assessed on the basis of there being a sufficient number of signs or the certainty of an individual sign's strength.

ARGUMENT FROM GENERALIZATION

Generalizations, based on sampling populations to draw conclusions about wholes, are very common. Much social science research studies a small sample of people or events and generalizes about the group they represent. A generalization states that what is true in some instances is true in all or most instances. *Generalizations are a form of inductive reasoning in which one looks at the details of examples, specific cases, situations, and occurrences and draws inferences about the entire class they represent.*

Generalizing may be the form of reasoning you have experienced most frequently in forming your attitudes, values, and beliefs. If you have had a negative experience with a course in Department X, you may reason that all courses offered by Department X aren't worth taking. Prejudices against people and nations are often formed on the basis of generalizations. This does not mean, however, that generalization is not an effective and efficient form of reasoning.

What we see on commercial television is determined on the basis of reasoning from generalization. The Nielsen ratings of the popularity of various television shows are based on sampling viewing habits in a few American homes and generalizing that what is true of the viewing habits of the sample is true of the viewing habits of all Americans. Consider another example of generalization regarding the effect of Music Television (MTV) on young children:

> Much of what they see is sexist, violent, or some mix of both. Educators and others worry about the effects such images have on impressionable young minds. . . . Action for Children's Television, a Boston-based watchdog group, has logged calls from pediatricians and child psychologists who report kids unable to sleep after viewing Michael Jackson's horrific "Thriller" video. (Barol, Bailey, & Zabarsky, 1984, p. 48)

Generalizations may be restricted in nature, arguing from some to more, as in the example given. Notice the qualifier "much" in the opening statement. The arguer does not assert that all rock videos are sexist or violent; it is left to the reader to determine whether all young minds are impressionable and therefore subject to harm, itself an argument from cause. The use of qualifiers in claim statements facilitates generalization when the behavior of an entire population, or the qualities of an entire class of objects, cannot be validly predicted. You may have owned three cars made by The Motor Car Company, experiencing great dissatisfaction with each, but would it be warranted for you to generalize that "The Motor Car Company produces lemons"?

Generalizations may also be universal, arguing that what is true of some members of a group will be true of all members of that group. In making a universal generalization the arguer needs to be careful that the sample on which the generalization is based is adequate to warrant the conclusion. Much of what was said in Chapter 7 about the verification of factual and statistical evidence applies to generalizations. There are four generic tests to apply to arguments from generalization. Applying them helps determine whether a generalization should be universal or restricted.

First, sufficient cases or instances should be cited as grounds to assure a reliable generalization. It would be unreasonable to argue on the basis of what happens in one state that enforcement of laws to reduce drunk driving is inadequate nationwide. A sample composed of states from each region might be needed to show a national trend. How large must the sample be? Large enough that the addition of more instances does not change the conclusion. Ultimately, the audience is the final arbiter of how many cases are needed to support the claim. The more familiar your audience is with the topic, the fewer instances you will need to cite.

The second test of generalizations is sample representativeness. Do the individuals or items cited in the grounds fairly represent the group or class about which the generalization is made? Items or individuals must be typical of a class if they are to represent it. One of the recurring criticisms of Nielsen ratings is that they are not representative. In addition to being representative of items in a class, all items must actually come from the same class, and it makes a difference how you define the class. For example, generalizing about a class of objects called sports cars may be problematic if your definition allows the inclusion of cars capable of carrying more than two passengers or cars with automatic transmissions.

The third test of generalizations is that instances must be taken from random samples of populations. If in attempting to generalize about laws to control drunk driving you include only those states in one region of the country, distortion may occur. The region you have selected may have laws that are more or less stringent than those in other regions, and thus they will not accurately represent the national trend in laws relating to driving while intoxicated.

The final test of generalizations asks if negative instances have been accounted for or explained. A generalization will not hold up if too many instances exist that contradict it. Including a rebuttal statement to modify such a claim is absolutely necessary. If in preparing an argument on drunk driving laws you discover that one region has particularly stringent laws while the rest of the nation does not, you would use a rebuttal to account for the existence of stringent laws in a few states and their absence everywhere else.

Summary of Argument from Generalization

1. Generalizations argue that what is true of some members of a group will be true of more or all members of the same group.
2. Generalizations should be based on a sufficiently large sample of cases if a conclusion about an entire group is being drawn.
3. Instances cited in making the generalization should be representative of all members of the group.
4. Instances should be randomly selected to avoid distortion.
5. Negative instances should be explained or accounted for.

ARGUMENT FROM PARALLEL CASE

Argument from parallel case is used when we have all the particulars about a given case and we reason from it, comparing the known case to a similar unknown case. *Arguments using parallel case involve reasoning on the basis of two or more similar events or cases.* Government policy makers and organizations such as universities often use argument from parallel case to frame their thinking. Those who set academic policies and regulations governing graduation requirements may study what is happening at other similar schools, reasoning that what is appropriate at college 1, college 2, and college 3 should be appropriate at our college.

In arguments based on parallel case, grounds involve the case, or cases, that are in some critical way similar to the case about which the claim is made. The warrant, backed by additional evidence when necessary, explains how the case described in the grounds and the case identified in the claim are truly parallel cases. An example of an argument reasoning from a parallel case is found in this discussion of the Olympic Games, which makes a historical comparison:

> Politics and professionalism may well destroy the modern Olympic movement, but the greater danger we must overcome is our willingness to delude ourselves. In our despair over the modern Games, we are holding history hostage; we like to think that once, long ago, the Olympics were somehow unspoiled and innocent.
>
> In fact, the Games of the Greeks were just as flawed as our own. It was the Greek tyrant Pheidon of Argos who seized Olympia in the seventh century B.C. and presided over the games for the glorification of his strong-arm regime. Two neighboring city-states, Elis and Pisa, fought for generations over the right to control the Games and to collect their revenues. Sometimes such conflicts ended in an "An-Olympiad" or non-Olympics: the Games did not always go on.
>
> Indeed, the ancient Greeks would be baffled by our belief in a bygone age of athletic innocence. Then, more so than now, winning was everything. If there were no shoe contracts or cereal endorsements, there were also no second- or third-place awards. The winner took all and it generally amounted to quite a fortune in victory benefits. Hundreds of inscriptions survive which were set up in honor of athletes, and from these we learn of free lunches for life and of professional "circuits" for runners and wrestlers. (Holt, 1984, p. 16)

The argument that historian Frank L. Holt developed about the Olympics is based on examining the parallel cases of ancient and modern Olympiads. To the extent that his readers perceived fundamental similarities between them, the argument demonstrates his point.

There are two tests to apply to arguments from parallel case, and both involve scrutinizing the similarities between the cases cited. First, ask yourself, "How similar are the cases cited?" If we claim we can better understand the modern Olympic Games by comparing them to those of ancient Greece, we must be able to find enough similarities between them to make the comparison hold up to the audience's scrutiny. The second test to apply to arguments from parallel case is to ask, "Are the similarities cited key factors?" In general, the more critical the factors common to both cases, the more force the argument will have. In particular, the similarities cited must have relevance to the claim being made in the argument. Holt claimed that the Olympic ideal of ancient Greece should not serve as a standard for modern Olympics because the ancient games were no less political than the modern ones. Notice the similarities he identified.

Summary of Argument from Parallel Case

1. Argument from parallel case reasons on the basis of two or more similar events or cases; because case A is known to be similar to case B in certain ways, we can appropriately draw inferences about the ways in which their similarities are unknown.
2. For the argument from parallel case to be valid, the cases must not only be similar but their similarities must pertain to important rather than trivial factors.

ARGUMENT FROM ANALOGY

Analogies represent a special form of comparison in which the cases compared do not have a sufficient degree of similarity to warrant argument from parallel case. *Arguments from analogy assume some fundamental sameness exists between the characteristics of dissimilar cases.* The argument proceeds much as it would if it were an argument from parallel case. A claim that is true of case 1 should be expected to be true of case 2 because both share a sufficient number of relevant characteristics. The essential difference between an analogy and an argument from parallel case is found in their forms of comparison. Analogies are figurative, often used as rhetorical devices to add style to an argument, while arguments from parallel case are literal.

Consider the following example derived from Douglas Ehninger's (1974) discussion of analogy:

GROUNDS   As everyone knows, the free and unimpaired circulation of the blood is essential to the health of the body.

WARRANT   Information is the life blood of society,

BACKING   Just as blood carries important "nourishment" to various parts of the body and assists in the elimination of impurities that would eventually poison it, information "nourishes" society and assists it in dealing with problems that would eventually poison it.

CLAIM   Therefore, the free flow of information is essential to the well-being of society.

If you were using this analogy in a speech or an essay, you would be more likely to phrase it more eloquently: "Just as the free and unimpaired circulation of the blood is essential to the health of the body, so is the free and unimpaired flow of information essential to the well-being of society," (Ehninger, 1974, p. 69)

Comparisons in analogies are based on the function of a thing. Blood and information have little in common. In the example, the strength of the argument rests upon how similar their functions can be made to appear. The use of analogies can help listeners and readers better understand how something functions.

> No sane parent would present a child with a fire engine, snatch it away in 30 seconds, replace it with a set of blocks, snatch that away 30 seconds later, replace the blocks with clay, and then replace the clay with a toy car. Yet, in effect, a young child receives that kind of experience when he or she watches American television. (Singer & Singer, 1979, p. 56.)

Because of its figurative nature, analogy has been classified as the weakest form of argument (Eisenberg & Ilardo, 1980; Toulmin et al., 1984; Ziegelmuller, Kay & Dause, 1990). It is said that the comparison of dissimilar cases is a rhetorical device and cannot actually warrant a claim. The analogy's usefulness is primarily confined to illustrating, clarifying, or making an argument more memorable or striking.

As Ehninger (1974) suggests, the position you ultimately adopt on the use of analogy will be determined by how you define argument and by the degree of probability you expect an asserted relationship to possess before you are willing to regard it as proven. If your definition of argument is restricted to instances where the relationship between grounds and claim produce conclusions that have a high probability of being true, you will probably not be satisfied with arguments from analogy.

Argument from analogy can be useful in instrumental communication. Since rendering the form of an argument understandable to the audience is a requirement for effective communication, there will be times when an analogy is the most appropriate argumentative choice. Analogy fulfills several critical functions in argumentation (Wilcox 1973). It helps organize and clarify thought by relating terms. It enables us to learn new information and adds style to our reasoning.

Should you choose to argue from analogy, there are two tests to apply to determine the viability of your analogy. First, the cases alleged to be similar must be sufficiently similar in function in all important ways. An analogy will not hold up if the functions compared are so dissimilar that the analogy is incomprehensible to the audience. Second, the dissimilarities between the cases compared must not be so great as to influence perception of the implied similarities adversely. Since analogies compare things that are essentially dissimilar, those dissimilarities must not overshadow their similarities.

If you decide to use this form of argument, search for analogies that will add force to your argument. While there is probably a point of diminishing returns in the use of analogy, it is possible to use more than one analogy to help your audience make connections between the available evidence and the claims you wish to advance.

Summary of Argument from Analogy

1. An analogy is a comparison of fundamentally dissimilar cases that draws attention to the common function they perform.
2. Analogies are commonly used as rhetorical devices, providing figurative rather than literal comparisons.
3. The dissimilarities between the cases should not be so great as to nullify the validity of the comparison being made.

ARGUMENT FROM AUTHORITY

In Chapter 7 we said arguers often use the opinions and research of experts as evidence. Society has become so complex that we are no longer confident of our own expertise on many subjects, so we rely on the knowledge of authorities. Textbooks, including this one, are examples of the reliance on authority to shape inferences about the nature of things. Watch the news on television, read an article in a magazine, or listen to the opinions of friends; it will not take long to discover how reliant you are on authorities.

Who are these people we turn to for opinions and interpretations of fact? We label as an authority a person or group determined to possess expertise in a given field. Their expertise may come from education or experience, from having published in their field, or from being a well-known professional—a scientist, physician, jurist, artist, or the like. In addition leaders, public figures, government officials, and spokespersons for well-known institutions, groups, and organizations are acknowledged as authorities.

In an argument from authority, the inference is that the claim is justified because it is consistent with the opinion, interpretation of fact, or research findings of an authority. *As a form of reasoning, argument from authority relies on the credibility and expertise of the source to warrant acceptance of a claim.* Since authorities use the same patterns of reasoning as the rest of us, an argument from authority may appear to be an argument from cause, sign, generalization, parallel case, analogy, definition or dilemma. What distinguishes argument from authority is that the warrant identifies why the audience should regard the authority as credible rather than drawing some other inference linking grounds and claim.

Arguments from authority can be structured in one of two ways. In the first form, the arguer states his or her own opinion as the claim and reasons that accepting the claim is justified because an authority provides the grounds for it. In a sense, this is the form nearly all arguments in academic argumentation take. Through research, you discover as much as you can about a topic, and determine the opinions you hold on it and how those opinions will be formed into claim statements. Then you find the appropriate evidence from credible sources to ground these claims. In the second form of argument from authority, the arguer takes an authority's view, restates its main point as the claim, and uses evidence taken from the authority's view as grounds for the claim. The warrant in either form of argument from authority is a statement that the authority should be considered credible, and backing applies one of more of the tests of argument from authority to establish that credibility.

Before turning to the tests used to establish the validity of an argument from authority, let us examine an example of this type of reasoning.

CLAIM   Membership in labor unions will continue to decline.

GROUND   Professor Greensmith states: My examination of the decline in union membership reveals that labor organizations have experienced an average decrease of 1.73 percent every year since 1974. Barring some revolutionary change in worker attitudes, there is no indication that this pattern will reverse itself.

WARRANT   We should accept Professor Greensmith's projection based on her expertise in the field of labor research.

BACKING   Professor Greensmith is an Associate Professor of Labor Relations in the Department of Management and Organization al Behavior at Northern State University and a consultant to the United States Bureau of Labor Statistics. Her findings are consistent with the membership declines reported by the American Federation of Labor-Congress of Industrial Organizations.

What makes our fictitious professor's opinion reliable is your willingness to accept her experience as a teacher and a consultant as establishing her expertise. The backing statement also indicates that her views are consistent with information from other sources. As you read the tests of argument from authority, notice how the backing statement met these tests.

Because argument from authority involves evidence that expresses an opinion, interprets fact, or reports research findings, many of the tests of evidence discussed in

Chapter 7 may be appropriate. The specific tests of argument from authority seek answers to the question: Can the authority be regarded as credible?

The first test of argument from authority is to determine whether the source is a qualified expert in the field by reason of training, experience, or background. The academic degrees a person holds, the length of their experience, and the nature of their background are all ways of verifying that an alleged authority is indeed an expert. To be recognized as an authority, some demonstration of expertise must be made.

The second test of argument from authority examines the context in which the source offered an opinion or presented information. Is the statement made within the context of the alleged authority's area of expertise? Public figures express a variety of opinions that may not necessarily be within their field of expertise. For example, prominent members of the entertainment industry have expressed opinions about the environment, but are ecology and industrial policy within the context of their field of expertise?

The third test of argument from authority examines the source's degree of involvement. Is the alleged authority relatively unbiased? The office or position a person holds may induce bias in a certain direction, and a person who is trying to protect tenure in an office or position will reflect such biases. We would expect the president of the American Medical Association to reflect some bias in expressing an opinion about government regulation of physicians' fees or the cost of malpractice insurance. While all authorities have a vested interest in their field, the important thing to look for in examining their biases are obvious conflicts of interest or self-serving statements.

The fourth test of argument from authority examines the source's statement in relation to those of acknowledged experts in the field. Does the alleged authority reflect a majority or minority view? In legal argument, each side may have its own expert witnesses, amply qualified, who express diametrically opposite views. Experts often disagree with each other on subjects inside and outside their field of expertise. Just because a view is different, it is not automatically invalid. However, an alleged authority may also express a totally isolated point of view. While many accepted principles were once minority opinions, if you cite an authority whose view does not reflect majority opinion, be prepared to establish the credibility of that view by providing the backing for the warrant in your argument.

The fifth and final test of argument from authority examines the factual basis on which the source's statement rests. Is there a reliable factual basis for the alleged authority's opinion? Remember, it is not the image or stature of the alleged authority that grounds the claim, but the factual basis on which opinions are offered. When someone with prestige, office, or an academic reputation offers an opinion, we assume there is some basis for it. This may not be the case. They may be bluffing, expressing a point of view which is contradicted by the evidence, or speaking outside his field of expertise, relying on reputation alone to support his view (Wilson, 1980).

Because of the special nature of this pattern of reasoning, a final caution about argument from authority is offered. Arguments from authority can be used to circumvent the reasoning process when authority is cited to prevent further consideration of a matter. In Chapter 9 this error in reasoning is discussed in more detail.

Someone is properly regarded as an expert because they possess special knowledge, not because they are famous. The warrant in an argument from authority should reassure the listener or reader that the person cited is an expert because of special knowledge, not because of his status as a public figure. Backing is used to verify the basis of the alleged authority's expertise. It is important to include both steps in creating arguments from authority.

Summary of Argument from Authority

1. Argument from authority relies on the credibility of the source of information to warrant acceptance of the claim it grounds.
2. The source should be a qualified expert in the field by reason of training, experience, or background.
3. The statements of authorities are only credible within the context of their field of expertise.
4. The authority should not be unduly biased.
5. If the authority expresses an opinion at odds with those of the majority of experts in the field, the arguer should establish the credibility of that view.
6. The authority's opinion should have a basis in fact.

ARGUMENT FROM DEFINITION

A definition of terms is frequently offered within an oral or written argument, and the arguer must justify it. *An argument from definition specifies how something shall be defined or classified.* How something should be defined or classified may become a source of controversy. Dictionaries can be useful sources of definitions, however, in arguing the basis of a definition, how a term is used within an "entire communication environment" may be more satisfactory (Toulmin et al., 1984). Consider the following explanation of how the term *children's programming* should be understood.

> WATCH (Washington Association for Television and Children) defines children's programing as including (1) those programs expressly designed for a child audience (the definition adopted by the FCC), (2) those programs watched by a large number of children, (3) those programs which have been made into cartoons such as *Mork and Mindy* and *Gilligan's Island*, and (4) those programs which generate lines of toys for marketing to children such as the *Dukes of Hazard*. WATCH also believes it is appropriate to define children as a wider group than the two- to eleven-year-old market. We would include adolescents in the wider group due to the fact their needs only partially overlap with those of an adult audience. WATCH sees childhood as a developmental continuum and we stress that arbitrary divisions into preschool, school age, and adolescent are convenient groupings rather than actual categories. (Children and Television, 1983, p. 199)

The important test of arguments from definition is that they must provide a clear explanation of the contested term and draw upon a common source of knowledge within the audience. In the sample definition, examples the listener or reader is likely to be familiar with were used to add precision to the definition.

ARGUMENT FROM DILEMMA

This final type of reasoning deals with choice making. *An argument from dilemma forces a choice between two unacceptable alternatives.* Economic policies are common sources of arguments from dilemma. Consider the international financier's dilemma: Which alternative causes the least amount of harm, renegotiating lower interest rates on loans to third-world countries on the verge default or allowing them to default on billions of dollars in loans? During the Vietnam War, critics of the Johnson administration argued that the nation could not have both guns (the war) and butter (social welfare programs) without serious harm to the economy.

Regardless of the number of alternatives suggested in the argument, the validity of a dilemma depends upon its identification of a true either-or situation. The grounds presented must identify the options available; and these alternatives must indeed be different, mutually exclusive choices. The goal of argument from dilemma is to point toward the one suitable or least objectionable choice, or to place the opposing arguer in the position of having to decide which of two equally objectionable choices he is willing to accept.

> The First Amendment of the U. S. Constitution guarantees freedom of speech and of the press. This freedom has never been absolute, however. It is unlawful to speak or write so as to incite others to illegal acts, and communities may censor communications that are obscene or profane by their own standards. Those concerned about the effects of television on children have often threatened to use legal means (such as withholding a TV license renewal) to censor what they consider to be unacceptable content. Boycotting of advertisers, which has also been suggested at one time or another, may also be considered a form of censorship. Others, however, have expressed grave concern about placing *any* censoring function in the hands of a government agency or ideological group. These individuals say that the idea of generating lists of "approved" television programming for children frightens them more than anything they have seen so far on entertainment television. (Liebert, Sprafkin, & Davidson, 1982, p. 12)

In this example, the dilemma takes the form of a forced choice between freedom and control. The reasoning pattern that indicates this represents a true either-or situation is implied rather than stated. The reader is expected to recognize that a dilemma exists, that choosing to maximize one value minimizes the other.

Reasoning makes the connection between claims and the evidence used to ground them. Although in actual argument the warrant and its backing are seldom stated, it is only through the presentation of the warrant that the arguer's reasoning is explicitly stated to her reader or listener. In your early attempts to frame arguments from dilemma, we suggest you include at least four elements of the Toulmin model— grounds, warrant, backing, and claim—as a means of developing facility with this technique of reasoning.

When you reason, you make an inference that establishes relationships between observed or known facts and the probable truth or validity of a claim. The purpose of reasoning is to assist in determining that probability. In the process, warrants are offered in the form of argument from cause, sign, generalization, parallel case, analogy, authority, definition, or dilemma. Each form has some specific tests associated with it that help determine the validity of the reasoning process. However, these tests do not identify all the potential errors in reasoning that can occur in argumentation. In the next chapter, these errors are discussed as we consider some of the common fallacies that can impair the quality of your arguments.

LEARNING ACTIVITIES

1. Conduct a discussion of argument from cause on one or more controversial topics such as gun control, abortion, euthanasia, or a campus controversy. What necessary and sufficient conditions establish cause in each case? Are these instances in which multiple causality may apply? What would be necessary to prove cause in each case?

2. Find examples of public opinion polls on an issue such as gun control, pollution, or presidential popularity. Construct an argument from sign based on the statistical information. Explain the strengths and weaknesses of this sign in establishing the probable truth of your claim.

3. Conduct a discussion on the inferential leaps made in going from grounds to claim in the examples of Value and Policy Advocacy and Opposition in Chapter 4 and 5. Why must this inferential leap be made? What inferences were drawn in each, what type of reasoning (cause, sign, generalization, parallel case, analogy, authority, definition, and dilemma) were used? Applying the tests of reasoning, how reasonable were the various inferential leaps that listeners were asked to make?

4. Examine the text of several speeches from a recent issue of *Vital Speeches*, or other similar sources, for examples of the use of analogies. Share your examples in class. Which analogies succeed in creating comparisons that make the unknown more easily understood? Which seem to fail, and why do they fail? On the basis of this experience, are analogies a useful reasoning technique?

5. For each of the following (a) identify the kind of reasoning used and (b) apply the appropriate tests of reasoning.
   A. In a sense we have come to our nation's capital to cash a check. When the architects of our republic wrote the magnificent words of the Constitution and the Declaration of Independence, they were signing a promissory note to which every American was to fall heir. This note was a promise that all men, yes black men as well as white men, would be granted the unalienable rights of life, liberty, and the pursuit of happiness. It is obvious today that America has defaulted on this promissory note insofar as her citizens of color are concerned. Instead of honoring this sacred obligation, America has given the Negro people a bad check; which has come back marked "insufficient funds." But we refuse to believe that the bank of justice is bankrupt. We refuse to believe that there are insufficient funds in the great vaults of opportunity in this nation. So we have come to cash this check—a check that will give us upon demand the riches of freedom and the security of justice. (Martin Luther King, Jr., "I Have A Dream," 1963)
   B. We watched the U.S. falsification of body counts, in fact the glorification of body counts. We listened while month after month we were told the back of the enemy

was about to break. We fought using weapons against " oriental human beings," with quotation marks around that. We fought using weapons against those people which I do not believe this country would dream of using were we fighting in the European theater or let us say a nonthird-world people theater, and so we watched while men charged up hills because a general said that hill has to be taken, and after losing one platoon or two platoons they marched away to leave that high (ground) for the reoccupation by the North Vietnamese because we watched pride allow the most unimportant of battles to be blown into extravaganzas, because we couldn't lose and we couldn't retreat, and because it didn't matter how many American bodies were lost to prove that point. And so there were Hamburger Hills and Khe Sanhs and Hill 881s and Fire Base 6s and so many others. Now we are told that the men who fought there must watch quietly while American lives are lost so that we can exercise the incredible arrogance of Vietnamizing the Vietnamese. Each day—each day to facilitate the process by which the United States washes her hands of Vietnam someone has to give up his life so that the United States doesn't have to admit something that the entire world already knows, so that we can't say that we have made a mistake. Someone has to die so that President Nixon won't be, and these are his words, "the first President to lose a war." (John F. Kerry, "Vietnam Veterans Against the War," April 22, 1971)

C. But when Miltiades stood on the Plain of Marathon, he and his Athenian spearmen defended Greek civilization against barbarian invaders. As the Polish cavalry centuries later fell back before the German panzer divisions, they fought to defend their land from the Nazi aggressor. And in most wars throughout history—for all their immorality and tragedy— their waste and cost and stupidity—there has been the essential distinction between the Athenians and the Persians—the Poles and the Nazis—the defender and the aggressor—the protector and the destroyer of international order. And to ignore that distinction is to deny the existence of a fundamental and moral choice—the distinction between the peaceful pedestrian and the thug who assaults him in the city street—between the thief and the sleeping householder. (Adlai E. Stevenson, "Foreign Policy: The Shades of Gray," June 1, 1965)

D. It should not be difficult for you here in Europe to appreciate this. Your continent passed through a longer series of revolutionary upheavals, in which your age of feudal backwardness gave way to the new age of industrialization, true nationhood, democracy and rising living standards—the golden age for which men have striven for generations. Your age of revolution, stretching across all the years from the Eighteenth Century to our own, encompassed some of the bloodiest civil wars in all history. By comparison, the African revolution has swept across three quarters of the continent in less than a decade; its final completion is within sight of our generation. Again, by comparison with Europe, our African revolution—to our credit, is proving to be orderly, quick and comparatively bloodless. (Albert J. Luthuli, "Africa and Freedom," 1961)

E. It is harder and harder to live the good life in American cities today. The catalog of ills is long. There is the decay of the centers and the despoiling of the suburbs. There is not enough housing for our people or transportation for our traffic. Open land is vanishing and old landmarks are violated. Worst of all, expansion is eroding the precious and time honored values of community with neighbors and communion with nature. The loss of these values breeds loneliness and boredom and indifference. Our society will never be great until our cities are great. Today the frontier of imagination and innovation is inside those cities and not beyond their borders. New experiments are already going on. It will be the task of your generation to make the

American city a place where future generations will come, not only to live, but to live the good life. (Lyndon B. Johnson, "The Great Society," 1964)

F. No government or social system is so evil that its people must be considered as lacking in virtue. As Americans, we find Communism profoundly repugnant as a negation of personal freedom and dignity. But we can still hail the Russian people for their many achievements—in science and space, in economic and industrial growth, in culture, in acts of courage. Among the many traits the people of our two countries have in common, none is stronger than our mutual abhorrence of war. Almost unique among the major world powers, we have never been at war with each other. And no nation in the history of battle ever suffered more than the Soviet Union in the second world war. At least 20,000,000 lost their lives. Countless millions of homes and families were burned or sacked. A third of the nation's territory, including two-thirds of its industrial base, was turned into a wasteland—a loss equivalent to the destruction of this country east of Chicago. (John F. Kennedy, "The Strategy of Peace," June 10, 1963)

G. But when television is bad, nothing is worse. I invite you to sit down in front of your television set when your station goes on the air and stay there without a book, magazine, profit-and-loss sheet or rating book to distract you—and keep your eyes glued to that set until the station signs off. I can assure you that you will observe a vast wasteland. You will see a procession of game shows, violence, audience participation shows, formula comedies about totally unbelievable families, blood and thunder, mayhem, violence, sadism, murder, Western badmen, Western good men, private eyes, gangsters, more violence and cartoons. And, endlessly commercials— many screaming, cajoling and offending. And most of all, boredom. True, you will see a few things you will enjoy. But they will be very, very few. And if you think I exaggerate, try it. (Newton N. Minnow, "Television: The Vast Wasteland," 1961)

H. Great leaders are almost always great simplifiers, who cut through argument, debate, and doubt to offer a solution everybody can understand and remember. Churchill warned the British to expect "blood, toil, tears and sweat"; FDR told Americans that "the only thing we have to fear is fear itself"; Lenin promised the war-weary Russians peace, land, and bread. Straightforward but potent messages. (Korda, 1981, p. 7)

I. The economy we inherited after almost five decades of Communist rule is in need of thorough overhaul. This will require patience and great sacrifice. This will require time and means. The present condition of the Polish economy is not due to chance, and is not a specifically Polish predicament. All the countries of the Eastern bloc are bankrupt. The Communist economy has failed in every part of the world. One result of this is the exodus of the citizens of those countries, by land and by sea, by boat and by plane, swimming and walking across borders. This is a mass-scale phenomenon, well known in Europe, Asia, and Central America. (Lech Walesa, "Poland: Solidarity and Freedom," November 15, 1989)

J. My friends, eight years ago this economy was flat on its back—intensive care. We came in and gave it emergency treatment—got the temperature down by lowering regulation, got the blood pressure down when we lowered taxes. Pretty soon the patient was up, back on his feet and stronger than ever. And now who do we hear knocking on the door but the doctors who made him sick. And they're telling us to put them in charge of the case again. My friends, they're lucky we don't hit them with a malpractice suit! (George Bush, "Acceptance Speech," August 18, 1988)

K. Most of the time, when you hear the phrase, "sex education," you think of class time devoted to human reproductive biology, including carefully phrased explanations about the use and abuse of the male and female genitalia. I'm told that young people call these classes "organ recitals"..."sex education" means more to me than just an "organ recital." "Sex education" ought to deal with relationships betwen men and women that are loving, caring, respectful, and tolerant. Such relationships include some fulfilling sexual activity, but they are not defined only by that activity. (C. Everett Koop, "Educating Our Children about AIDS," January 23, 1987)

L. We (the United States and the Soviet Union) share cultural ties: poetry and music, basketball and hockey, and most of all a love for literature, from Chekhov to Bellow. Back in 1966, as a student traveler, I can remember leaving the Soviet Union by car into Hungary and being detained four hours until the Soviet border guard had his fill of perusing my copy of Steinbeck's *Of Mice and Men.* (Bill Bradley, "Soviet-American Relations: A Congressional View," August 27, 1987)

M. Would it not stabilize this hemisphere as a whole if the five Central American states had a long period of domestic tranquillity and freedom from outside interference or subversion? Could that come about if a James Madison of Costa Rica, an Alexander Hamilton of Honduras, joined in calling for a meeting like our Annapolis Convention in 1786, followed by a call for a meeting like ours here in Philadelphia, to "form a more perfect union"? (Warren E. Berger, "Keeping Faith with the Vision of the Founders," September 18, 1987)

N. Six years ago I was here to ask the Congress to join me in America's new beginning. Well, the results are something of which we can all be proud. Our inflation rate is now the lowest in a quarter of a century. The prime interest rate has fallen from the twenty-one and a half percent the month before we took office to seven and a half percent today, and those rates have triggered the most housing starts in eight years. The unemployment rate, still too high, is the lowest in nearly seven years and our people have created nearly thirteen million new jobs. Over sixty-one percent of everyone over the age of sixteen, male and female, is employed—the highest percentage on record. (Ronald Reagan, "State of the Union (1987)," January 27, 1987)

O. When I addressed the Congress on the twenty-sixth of February last, I thought that it would suffice to assert our neutral rights with arms, our right to use the seas against unlawful interference, our right to keep our people safe against unlawful violence. But armed neutrality, it now appears, is impossible. Because submarines are in effect, outlaws when used as the German submarines have been used against merchant shipping, it is impossible to defend ships against their attacks as the law of nations has assumed that merchantmen would defend themselves against privateers or cruisers, visible craft giving chase on the open sea. (Woodrow Wilson, "War Message," April 2, 1917)

SUGGESTED SUPPLEMENTARY READINGS

Bettinghaus, E. P.   *The Nature of Proof.* Indianapolis: Bobbs-Merrill.
The focus of this book is making the message believable for the audience. It considers the use of evidence and reasoning and discusses the Toulmin model as a means of structuring thought. This is a useful book for examining the relationship between audiences and the arguments aimed at them.

Kahane, H. (1984) *Logic and Contemporary Rhetoric* (4th Ed.). Belmont, CA: Wadsworth.
This book examines inductive and deductive reasoning and discusses how news media, advertising, and textbooks create distorted world views. It has three chapters on fallacies that offer extensive discussion and excellent examples of reasoning errors. The chapter on language fallacies is especially interesting in its treatment of the problem of "double speak."

McDonald, D. (1983) *The Language of Argument* (4th Ed.). New York: Harper & Row.
Although intended for composition courses, McDonald's discussion of reasoning techniques, which focuses on induction, deduction, and fallacies, can be adapted to speaking as well. He provides a

good discussion of the uses and abuses of statistics. The bulk of the text is composed of examples that could serve as useful discussion material.

Walter, O.M., & Scott, R.L. (1984) *Thinking and Speaking* (5th Ed.). New York: Macmillan.

This is a popular public-speaking text that focuses on persuasive theories used in creating and delivering speeches. Chapter 7, "Thinking and Speaking About Causes," provides extensive discussion of reasoning from cause. The historical basis for causal analysis, numerous examples of how cause-effect reasoning has been used and misused, and a thorough discussion of conditions influencing cause are highlights of this chapter.

9

WHAT SHOULD I AVOID?

The strength of your arguments is determined by the use of reliable evidence, sound reasoning, and adaptation to the audience. In the process of argumentation, it is sometimes possible to make a mistake. At this point, it is important to distinguish between things done deliberately to distort or deceive and things done in error. The message appears the same, whether the mistake is the product of intentional deception or the honest error of an arguer who has failed to examine his or her own arguments critically. These mistakes are generically termed **fallacies**.

For some (Crable, 1976; Sproule, 1980), fallacy is a litmus test for distinguishing a misrepresentation of the truth from a piece of sound reasoning. Ethical problems occur when argument is used to distort and deceive by falsifying, fabricating, or twisting the meaning of evidence, deliberately using specious meaning, or deceptively hiding your intent as a communicator (Minnick, 1968).

Rather than identifying all possible ways in which deliberate distortion and deception can occur, focusing on some of the most common errors to avoid will better serve your development as an arguer. Through the theme "What should I avoid?" this chapter suggests how you can not only improve your skills as an advocate or an opponent of change, but also hone your critical thinking skills to become a more discerning consumer of argument by becoming aware of common fallacies in reasoning.

Since most errors in logic result from faulty reasoning or problems in language choice, we want to emphasize the need to pay careful attention to the structure of arguments, the nature of the appeals they make, and the language used to phrase them. Consider these problems from the perspective that:

> The study of fallacies can be thought of as a kind of sensitivity-training in reasoning. It should attune the student to the omnipresent dangers to which we are exposed as a consequence of imprecise expressions—vague, ambiguous, or misdefined terms—students should also be alert to unarticulated assumptions and presumptions. (Toulmin et al., 1984, p. 132

FALLACIES IN REASONING

Hasty Generalization

When you make a hasty generalization, you have committed the error of jumping to conclusions. You will recall that in describing argument from generalization, two tests were that the generalization must be made on the basis of a sufficient number of cases and that the cases comprise a representative sample of all cases. The fallacy of hasty generalization occurs when the claim is not warranted, either because insufficient cases were used or because they constitute a nonrepresentative sample.

If you are arguing the claim "Dioxin contamination is a national problem" grounded on instances of dioxin being found in Michigan and Missouri, you have fallaciously based the claim on insufficient instances. The argument is salvageable, provided a warrant indicating that problems in Michigan and Missouri constitute "a national problem" can be backed. If backing cannot be found, or does not exist, the claim may be made, but it must be qualified to reflect its limitations better. Since Michigan and Missouri are both midwestern states, you could claim "Dioxin contamination is a problem in the Midwest."

Sometimes the generalization cannot be qualified. When you come across an atypical example and attempt to reason based on it alone, the generalization will be fallacious. Consider the following generalization:

GROUNDS   The Big Burger has "secret sauce."
WARRANT   Since it is typical of fast food,
CLAIM   All fast food has "secret sauce."

In part, this example is fallacious because the warrant has no backing. It underscores the importance of our earlier suggestions that arguers include all elements of the primary triad in the Toulmin model of argument and that they back their warrants. "If we are forced to spell out the warrants on which our arguments rely and the backing on which those warrants depend, it will usually become clear at once when our grounds are based on too small a sample of cases or on examples that are quite *untypical*" (Toulmin et al., 1984, p. 154).

Many fallacious generalizations occur when arguers become victims of the temptation to try to squeeze more from a generalization than is actually warranted. This is similar to the problem of relying on insufficient cases in that the arguer makes an unqualified claim when only a qualified one is warranted. Consider the following example of overgeneralization:

GROUNDS   There are an estimated 350 synthetic organic chemicals in the nation's drinking water.

WARRANT   Because these chemicals can lead to an increase in the incidence of cancer,

BACKING   Dioxin, a synthetic chemical, was found leaking out of a dump at Niagara's Love Canal. Since then, the residents of the area have had a high percentage of birth defects, miscarriages, liver disorders, and various types of cancer.

CLAIM   There are a significant number of synthetic chemicals in our water that can cause cancer.

Because the claim is unqualified as to cause, we are asked to believe all 350 chemicals are capable of "causing" cancer. The warrant and its backing does not justify this conclusion. Recall the discussion of necessary and sufficient causes in the previous chapter. Before the medical community attributes cause, it conducts what are called epidemiological studies over a period of years using a large number of subjects. At best, the backing for this warrant justifies the use of *may* instead of *can* in the claim, and even that could possibly be an overgeneralization. Since generalization is one of the most frequently used forms of reasoning, you are well advised to examine the generalizations you make and hear very carefully.

Transfer

Transfers extend reasoning beyond what is logically possible. There are three common types of transfer: *fallacy of composition*, *fallacy of division*, and *fallacy of refutation*.

Fallacies of composition occur when a claim asserts that what is true of a part is true of the whole. In the dioxin example, the degree of certainty we place in the causal connection between dioxin and cancer is unrelated to the degree of certainty we can place in that same relationship for the other 349 synthetic substances mentioned as grounds. When claims assert that what is true of a part is true of the whole, the warrant and its backing must be carefully examined, since they are what justifies the inferential leap from part to whole.

Fallacies of division are the opposite of fallacies of composition. The error arises from arguing that what is true of the whole will be true of its parts. When you break a whole into its parts and attempt to make claims about them, you may create an unwarranted transfer from the whole to its parts. "Speech courses are fun, and argumentation is a speech course; therefore, argumentation is fun." This may be true, or it may be false, but the transfer from whole to part is not sufficiently warranted in this example. Consider a common example of this type of fallacy: "The Motor Car Company makes expensive cars. The windshield wiper blade is one part of those cars. Therefore, the windshield wiper blade on The Motor Car Company products is expensive." As with avoiding committing fallacies of composition, arguing that what is true of the whole will be true of its parts must be carefully warranted and that warrant backed.

The fallacy of refutation is the final transfer fallacy, also known as the *straw-man argument*. It occurs when an arguer attempts to direct attention to the successful refutation of an argument that was never raised or to restate a strong argument in a way that makes it appear weaker. It is called a straw-man argument because it focuses on an issue that is easy to overturn. It is a form of deception since it introduces a bogus claim, one that was not part of the argument, or misrepresents the original claim. Notice the creation of a straw man in the following:

LISA: Our high schools are graduating a bunch of functional illiterates and mathematical incompetents. Why achievement by seventeen-year-olds is down by over 4 percent in mathematics from what it was just five years ago; and besides, what you need to know to be competent today is a lot more extensive than what you needed then, and a lot less than you'll need to know five years from now.

ANDREA: Wait a minute! Did those seventeen-year-olds graduate from high school? Maybe they dropped out. Aren't you assuming they didn't learn anything in their senior year? You can't say that the high schools are pumping out students who are incompetent unless you look at how they score when they graduate!

Fallacies of this sort are relatively easy to commit, even when you are not attempting to distort and deceive. Like Andrea, we often raise a series of questions, thinking they are sufficient responses to the arguments of another. When we are uninformed or ill prepared, we unintentionally create straw man arguments because of our ignorance. If we do not carefully examine the degree of similarity or the number of cases used when we create comparisons, generalizations, and analogies, it is easy to shift the focus of argumentation accidentally in an inappropriate direction. However, responding to an argument perceived to be weak with a strong argument of our own does not mean we are necessarily creating a straw man, since the quality of proof can vary from claim to claim, depending on both the competence of the arguers and the availability of evidence.

Irrelevant Arguments

An irrelevant argument is one that does not seem pertinent in terms of the claim it advances, or on the basis of the proof it offers. Such fallacies are also known as *non sequiturs*, Latin for "It does not necessarily follow." The critic of defense spending who argues that we should stop spending money on "Star Wars technology" since millions of Americans do not have adequate food and shelter may be making an unwarranted assumption about how federal monies are allocated, that funds that would have been spent on programs for the needy are being diverted to develop high-technology weapons. Unless proof is offered that such diversion actually takes place, the basic assumption of the argument is fallacious.

Circular Reasoning

Also known as begging the question, arguments that are circular support claims with reasons identical to the claims themselves.

CLAIM   Guns don't kill, people do.
WARRANT   Since a person must pull the trigger,
GROUNDS   A gun is an inanimate mechanical object, it can't shoot by itself.

In this example, the meaning of grounds and warrant are equivalent to the meaning of the claim itself. Strictly speaking, this is a nonargument, since it makes no inference from grounds through warrant to claim. It is an example of a fallacious attempt to support a claim by simply repeating the essential aspects of the claim using different words.

Avoiding the Issue

Any attempt to shift attention away from the issue at hand is an error because it denies the integrity of the reasoning process to ignore an issue rather than discuss it. While we suspect that some avoidance behaviors are intentional, it is more likely that arguers pay insufficient attention to the task at hand. Monitor your own behavior and that of others for these common errors.

Simple evasion is the first type of avoidance. Changing the subject for no apparent reason, or bypassing a critical issue, diverts attention from the issues central to the argument. This error is most likely to occur when insufficient time has been spent analyzing the topic to determine which issues are inherent to the proposition.

Attacking the person not the argument is the second avoidance behavior. Known as an *ad hominem argument*, it shifts attention to the personality or appearance of the arguer, her ability to reason, the color of her skin, or the values she holds, all of which tell us nothing about the validity of her arguments. "She goes away to college for one semester, and now she's an expert on everything" is a parental response which ends some family discussions over Christmas break. While we may never become more than children in our parents' eyes in the familial context, it is essential that the worth of ideas behind claims be given primary consideration in the argumentative context.

Shifting ground is a third fallacy of avoidance. Shifts of ground occur when an arguer abandons his original position on a particular argument and adopts a new one. It is probably one of the easiest errors in reasoning to commit. In everyday social communication, most of us do not decide what we plan to say in advance. There is a tendency to adapt, to modify our thoughts and the manner of their expression to those around us. This becomes a real problem when we are involved in argumentation, because shifting ground gives the impression of evasiveness. We need to be careful to stick to our claims. This does not mean you can never change your mind or admit an error in argumentation. However, if you find it necessary to move away from your original claims, take special care to explain what has caused you to shift ground.

Seizing on a trivial point is the final error of avoidance. When you locate another's weak or indefensible argument and magnify it out of all proportion to discredit her entire position on the proposition, you have committed the fallacy of seizing on a trivial point. For example, she quotes an article from *Time*, September 31, 1989. You note that September has only thirty days. She argues that unemployment is running at about 8 percent. You concentrate your attack on the fact that unemployment is presently 7.92 percent. The accuracy of factual information is of great importance, but focusing all your attention on minor inaccuracies and trivial points is an unsound argumentative technique.

Forcing a Dichotomy

A forced dichotomy is one in which listeners or readers are presented with an oversimplified either-or choice, phrased in such a way that it forces them to favor the arguer's preference between the options. The fallaciousness of the forced dichotomy rests on its failure to consider alternative choices fully. A popular bumper sticker of recent vintage provides an example of this error in reasoning: "America, love it or leave it." The only alternatives presented are unquestioning acceptance or absolute rejection.

The forced dichotomy is also known as the false dilemma. You may recall that in discussing dilemmas as a form of reasoning, we said that the either-or situation they create may force choosing the better of two options. The false dilemma, or forced dichotomy, is a fallacy in reasoning because the choice making that it forces is too simplistic. The argument "Either we unilaterally freeze the development and production of nuclear weapons or face a nuclear holocaust" appears to preclude other alternatives: multilateral treaty negotiations, or claims that development and production of more nuclear weapons may reduce the probability of their use. The either-or rhetoric of a forced dichotomy in this instance forestalls consideration of too many potential issues. In human affairs, it is seldom the case that choice amounts to selecting between two alternatives. Examine your own reasoning and that of others to avoid being trapped into arguing or accepting forced dichotomies.

Summary of Fallacies in Reasoning

1. *Hasty generalizations* offer conclusions based on insufficient information, basing reasoning on too few instances, atypical examples, or overstatements that claim more than is warranted.
2. *Transfer fallacies of composition* result from the unwarranted assumption that what is true of the part is true of the whole.
3. *Transfer fallacies of division* result from the unwarranted assumption that what is true of the whole is true of its parts.
4. *Irrelevant arguments*, *non sequiturs*, make assumptions which do not follow from the information provided.
5. *Circular reasoning* offers as warrants and grounds statements equivalent in meaning to the claims they are supposed to support.

6. *Avoiding the issue* is an error in reasoning that shifts attention from the issue under consideration. It commonly takes the form of a simple evasion of the issue, an attack on the arguer rather than the argument, a shift of ground, or seizing on a trivial point rather than the central issue.

7. *Forcing a dichotomy* puts the listener or reader in the position of having to choose between oversimplified either-or options.

FALLACIES OF APPEAL

When you construct an argument, you do not do so in a vacuum. You have an audience in mind and develop your arguments accordingly. This can lead to your committing a series of fallacies based on the appeals you decide to make. In particular we must be careful when appealing to emotion, rather than the ability to reason. There is nothing intrinsically wrong with emotional appeals, but problems can arise when you use these appeals to avoid arguing the issues at hand. Appeals that bypass reason are usually based on the feelings, prejudices, or desires of the audience. The fallacies of appeal we shall discuss are some of the more commonly occurring lapses that arguers experience which reduce the rationality of their arguments. Again, we emphasize that emotional appeals are an important part of the process of persuasion, and we caution that in argumentation emotion should not supplant reason.

Appeal to Ignorance

Appeals to ignorance, known by the Latin term *ad ignoratium*, ask the audience to accept the truth of a claim because no proof to the contrary exists. Something is true simply because it cannot be proven false. "Evidence does not exist to prove teenagers are harmed by rock music" does not demonstrate that rock music does not harm them, only that evidence of harm cannot be found. Even more troublesome is the technique of claiming because we cannot prove something has not happened or does not exist it therefore must have happened or must exist. "The inability to disprove the existence of flying saucers and extraterrestrial visitation to earth confirms the existence of the former, and the occurrence of the latter."

Can you make nonfallacious claims about what the absence of proof may mean? Yes, to a certain extent. An absence of evidence suggests the possibility of a claim's validity. For example, drugs are tested for side effects and are presumed safe when none occur. The problem with using this type of reasoning is that backing for the warrant becomes the assertion that the lack of evidence is, in itself, evidence. This tends to trivialize the meaning of evidence as a concept (Toulmin et al., 1984).

There is one important exception: Artificial presumption may be assigned in such a way that failure to prove something leads to the conclusion that its logical opposite is true. When the prosecution fails to present a prima facie case against the accused, we conclude he must be innocent. In other cases, the absence of contrary evidence may strengthen a claim, but it in no way proves it. The absence of evidence may simply mean that research regarding the phenomenon has not been very thorough.

Appeal to the People

Also known as the bandwagon appeal, or an *ad populum argument*, appeals to the people address the audience's prejudices and feelings rather than the issues. When a claim is justified on the basis of its alleged popularity—we should do or believe something because the majority of people do or believe it—an appeal to the people is being made. For example, an advocate might argue for a change in laws governing the ownership of handguns because a majority of Americans are of the opinion that private ownership of handguns should be outlawed. In cases like this, the line between sound and unsound argument is blurred.

On the one hand, common sense suggests that when matters concerning "the people" are discussed, their will should be taken into account. In the case of a future law, this allows us to forecast whether it would likely be obeyed or violated. On the other hand, to make popular opinion the sole criterion of a claim's worth, and to appeal to this opinion in order to discourage consideration of pertinent facts, will inevitably result in less informed and less thoughtful decisions. In recent years, for example, voters in some states passed a series of tax reforms reflecting the popular belief that taxes were too high. After a few years of lower taxes, citizens in these same states are experiencing anguish over the loss of revenues for education. Critical consideration of the issues should take precedence over popular opinion.

Appeals to Emotions

As we suggested, the use of emotional appeals is not necessarily bad, nor is it possible to be entirely rational. Nevertheless, strong appeals to emotion are no substitute for careful reasoning. Any emotion may be a source of appeal. Here we will concentrate on the two used most frequently in poor argumentation: appeals to pity and fear.

Traditionally, the use of the appeal to pity was taught as a means of creating audience sympathy for an individual or group. Such appeals are common on topics that address the suffering of those unable to overcome misfortune without the aid of others. No fallacy is committed when such appeals are used in conjunction with sound reasoning. However, when pity is the only basis on which an alteration of belief or behavior is justified, argumentation has been abandoned in favor of persuasion. Consider the effect the following argument might have if it were not placed in the context of other issues:

GROUNDS Amerasian children fathered by American servicemen, besides being social outcasts in Asian countries, have a high incidence of tuberculosis, malaria, and even a few cases of leprosy.

WARRANT Because it would be cruel and heartless to turn our backs on children who should rightfully be American citizens when their condition is so desperate,

CLAIM We must accept all Asian children seeking refuge in this country who can prove American parentage.

The action ultimately taken, based solely on this criteria, might lack those qualities of administrative and economic feasibility that an effective remedy must possess. In a situation where an opponent was present to confront this advocate, some of these problems would certainly be addressed. However, in a situation in which a respondent for the other side of the question is not present, the arguer must place any appeals to pity in a context of sound proof and reasoning.

The appeal to fear is another form of emotion seeking, arousing concern over potential consequences. The opponent of our hypothetical advocate of the rights of Amerasian children would generate more heat than light if he succumbed to the temptation to counter the appeal to pity with the following appeal to fear.

GROUNDS   It is openly admitted that these people have dangerous, contagious diseases like tuberculosis, malaria, leprosy, and who knows what else.

WARRANT   Because we can't bring them into this country without bringing their afflictions right along with them,

CLAIM   Letting these children into this country will threaten the health and safety of your children.

As with appeals to pity, the use of an appeal to fear is a matter of appropriateness and balance. There are occasions when a little fear is needed to move people to action, but to appeal to fear alone may produce disastrous consequences. When fear dictates behavior, rash decisions may result, such as the blacklisting that destroyed careers during the McCarthy era or granting powers that deprived citizens of Japanese ancestry of their civil liberties.

Appeal to Authority

An argument from authority that utilizes the opinions and testimony of experts is a legitimate form of reasoning. However, care must be exercised to ensure that the argument from authority does not become a fallacious appeal to authority. An appeal to authority is fallacious when a seemingly authoritative source of opinion either lacks real expertise or prevents a fair hearing of the other side of the issue. Instead of being used to ground a claim or back a warrant, the authority is characterized as infallible and is used to shut off further discussion of the issues. Abuses of authority commonly involve the Bible, the Constitution, revered persons, or testimonials by celebrities. We have become accustomed to this last form of appeal to authority. Football star Joe Montana promotes soft drinks, basketball player Ervin "Magic" Johnson tells us where to bank, and former quarterback Roger Staubach once endorsed antacid tablets.

Are all testimonials fallacious? Not necessarily. The validity of the warrant in testimonials depends on the backing that establishes the authority's credentials. Consider the following:

GROUNDS   Life insurance is available from Veterans Life to any individual who is a U.S. military veteran.

WARRANT   Because Roger Staubach knows the needs of veterans,

BACKING   He graduated from Annapolis and served in the United States Navy before playing
    professional football.
CLAIM   They should buy this insurance which he endorses.

The audience is asked to accept the claim "You should buy this insurance" based on
the testimony of someone who is a veteran first and a retired quarterback, who is
therefore recognizable, second.

Be prepared to defend your choice of experts. Unknowingly, your choice may
represent a fallacious use of authority if you cite someone outside their acknowledged
field of expertise. While we might take Joe Montana's advice on football, is he likely
to be an expert on soft drinks? Making this distinction is sometimes difficult because
an individual may be an expert in more than one field. At one time, comedian Bill
Cosby appeared in a series of computer commercials. We might acknowledge his
expertise on issues of comedy or acting, but what about education, the major claim
advanced in these commercials? In fact, Bill Cosby has advanced degrees in psychology and education, has produced several educational films, and has also lectured on
race relations in education and student motivation. This illustrates why it is always
important to provide information documenting the qualifications of those you cite.

Appeal to Tradition

We normally have strong ties to tradition, and learning the historical background of a topic is a good way to prepare to argue it. However, asking an audience
to accept something because it is customary, rather than because of the issues
justifying it, commits the fallacy of appeal to tradition. Before the issue was put to
rest with the nomination of Geraldine Ferraro, it was typical to hear appeals to tradition
that simultaneously begged the question, "A woman should not be on the ticket,
because in the over-200-year history of American politics, no woman has had
sufficient experience or national exposure to be the presidential or vice-presidential
nominee of a major party."

Comparisons, which reference tradition, are not necessarily inappropriate.
Value claims often involve matters of taste derived from tradition. A thorough
analysis of the reasons behind a tradition provides a valid basis on which to argue its
future violation or veneration. However, it is important to realize that arguing on
behalf of a belief or behavior solely on the basis of tradition gives the audience
insufficient understanding of the issues that justify opposing a proposed change in that
belief or behavior.

Recalling our discussion of presumption, you may think something is amiss.
Doesn't presumption favor *tradition*, that which is already in existence? Yes, and
opponents in argumentation find themselves arguing on behalf of the benefits of
continuing to believe or behave as we have in the past. However, when the opponent
uses such argument, it must provide good and sufficient reasons to justify maintaining
that tradition and not merely appeal to tradition alone.

Appeal to Humor

Appeals based on humor can be problematical for several reasons. The arguer who resorts to a series of jokes about women drivers to refute criticism of auto safety standards uses humor to entertain rather than enlighten. When humor is used to such an extent that it becomes the focal point of the discussion, the point of argumentation is lost. A series of commercials for a low-calorie beer features celebrities and retired sports figures. These commercials are so humorous that many viewers are unable to name the product being promoted but can recount the antics of the people promoting it.

Humor is also misused when it takes a claim to its most extreme and therefore absurd meaning. This is known as *reductio ad absurdum*. Reducing a claim to absurdity is a particularly troublesome kind of fallacy because it sometimes occurs in an effort to employ style but results mainly in decreasing the discussion's rationality. One of the premises of the National Rifle Association is frequently seen on bumper stickers: "I support the right to bear arms." This claim is reduced to the absurd by another bumper sticker: "I support the right to arm bears!" While such a turn of phrase may be witty, it has the effect of trivializing a serious issue.

This is not to say that humor cannot be an effective device. Humor can have a positive effect, creating good will or lessening tensions in a heated situation. During the summer of 1930, President Carter had the unpleasant task of informing farmers in the southwest that the economic aid they desired would not be forthcoming. Just before his helicopter landed in the drought-stricken Dallas-Fort Worth area, there was a sudden rainfall. President Carter began an address to a group of farmers saying, "Well, you asked for either money or rain. I couldn't get the money so I brought the rain" (Boller, 1981, p. 346).

Summary of Fallacies of Appeal

1. *Appeals to ignorance* ask the audience to accept a claim solely because no proof exists to deny its validity.
2. *Appeals to the people* ask an audience to accept a claim because it is supported by majority opinion.
3. *Appeals to pity* arouse sympathy for individuals or groups to encourage the redress of some wrong or misfortune they have suffered.
4. *Appeals to fear* attempt to gain the audience's acceptance of a claim by arousing concern over the consequence it alleges.
5. *Appeals to authority* encourage reliance on some ultimate source of knowledge in place of reasoning as the basis of a claim.
6. *Appeals to tradition* ask an audience to accept a claim because it represents a customary belief or course of action.
7. *Appeals to humor* either fail to make a serious point or reduce another's claim to its most absurd level.

FALLACIES IN LANGUAGE

Since language is the vehicle of your argument's meaning, you must be concerned about how you use it in constructing arguments. We have already indicated some concerns about the way in which claims are phrased and we stressed the importance of defining terms. We now discuss the care that must be exercised in choosing language appropriate to all aspects of argumentation. In any use of language, but especially in using it to alter belief or behavior, it is important to remember that meanings are in people, not in words. The meaning we attach to the words of others is a consequence of their passing through our own perceptual filters. Become aware of your own language habits and biases to avoid falling victim to the fallacies of language described here.

Ambiguity and Equivocation

The ambiguity of language interferes with effective argumentation when a term is used differently by both parties to the dispute. This "meanings are in people" problem may occur unintentionally, with both arguers operating on the basis of legitimate, but entirely different, meanings for a term. Consider the plight of the musician, the dentist, the billiards player, and the engineer engaged in an argument concerning the best way to use a *bridge*. This example may seem frivolous, but consider a real-world example. If you have ever handed a paper in late and the professor, emulating Benjamin Disraeli, has told you, "I shall lose no time in reading this," you have experienced the uncertainty that ambiguity engenders.

Like the errors resulting from the ambiguity of language, errors of equivocation occur because words have multiple legitimate meanings. An error of equivocation occurs when a term appears to have two or more meanings within the arguments of one person. When you shift the meaning of a term in an argument, you are equivocating. The statements of candidates for public office frequently contain equivocations which are used intentionally to avoid offending part of the electorate. One candidate declares, "I stand for revenue sharing or an equalization of the tax burden," leaving uncertain whether the phrase following "or" restates the phrase preceding it or names an acceptable alternative. Another announces, "I favor appropriations adequate to ensure our national defense, which will not place an undue burden on the taxpayers of this nation."

Since the audience is a part of the process of argumentation, it will be impossible for you to avoid all instances of ambiguity. However, by exercising care in phrasing arguments and defining key terms, you can avoid many errors of equivocation. You should be cognizant of language in the arguments you construct and scrutinize the language used in the evidence these arguments contain, especially when it is opinion evidence.

Emotionally Loaded Language

The arguments of everyday life are frequently condensed to what fits on a picket sign carried at a march or rally, a bumper sticker, or a T-shirt. "War is unhealthy for children and other living things." "Abortion is killing." "A boy of quality is not threatened by a girl of equality." In addition to serving as a vehicle for the denotation of ideas, language is a powerful instrument for the expression of attitudes and feelings. Your choice of language can reveal your attitude toward a topic. One of our favorite illustrations of the connotative property of language is the following list of questions "for sexists only":

Why are forceful males referred to as charismatic while females are domineering?

When speaking about people who are talkative, why are men called articulate and women gabby?

Why are men who are forgetful called absentminded, when forgetful women are called scatterbrained?

Why are men who are interested in everything referred to as curious, but women of the same type are called nosy?

Why are angry men called outraged, while angry women are called hysterical?

Why are women who are ironic called bitter, while ironic men are called humorous?

Why are lighthearted men called easygoing, but the same type of women are called frivolous?

Why are devious men considered shrewd, when devious women are scheming?

Why are men who are thoughtful called considerate, while thoughtful women are called oversensitive?

Why are women who are dauntless considered brazen, when dauntless men are considered fearless?

Why is it that men of ordinary appearance are called pleasant looking, when ordinary women are called homely?

(Communication Research Associates, 1983, p. 107)

In various forms of imaginative or creative speaking and writing, language that fully expresses feeling or attitude is highly prized. Indeed, if language did not possess the power to express and elicit feelings, most of the world's great literature would not exist. In arguments, however, emotionally loaded language, which exceeds the natural warmth that marks a sincerely expressed belief and earnestness of purpose, becomes an impediment to rational decision making and represents a poor choice.

Technical Jargon

The use of the technical terminology of a field becomes a problem when it so confuses listeners they lose sight of the issues or when it is used in place of reasoning on the issues. Beginning arguers frequently become so involved in the topic being argued they forget that not everyone is as conversant with its jargon as they are. Technical terminology may be important to understanding the issues involved, but it is possible to send an audience into semantic shock if you ask them to deal with too many new terms at once.

When jargon replaces the real issues as the focus of the argument, an error has been committed. We would expect people arguing about education to be sufficiently informed to be able to discuss the advantages and disadvantages of *mainstreaming*. But if the argument centered on a disagreement over what should properly be included on a list of the different kinds of mainstreaming or the medical technicalities of the handicaps of those to be mainstreamed, we may, as an audience, lose sight of the real issues.

Summary of Fallacies of Language

1. *Ambiguity* occurs when a term is used in legitimate but different senses by two or more persons involved in argumentation.
2. *Equivocation* occurs when an individual uses a term in different ways in the context of the same argument.
3. *Emotionally loaded language* is a problem when we use terms that show more about our feelings on the issues than about the rational basis from which those feelings derive or when we use emotion as the sole means to alter the belief or behavior of others.
4. *Technical jargon* becomes a problem when the audience is overwhelmed with too many new terms or when jargon is used to impress the audience or replace sound reasoning.

The foregoing is a set of guidelines for the sorts of errors in reasoning, appeal, and use of language that you should avoid in constructing your own arguments and it is a yardstick you should use in evaluating the arguments of others. You should now be able to construct valid arguments, patterns of proof and reasoning that are sufficient to support claims. You are ready to begin putting it all together. In the final chapter, we will look at how advocates and opponents of change can most effectively present their ideas before an audience.

LEARNING ACTIVITIES

1. Return to the examples of Value and Policy Advocacy and Opposition in Chapters 4 and 5 and identify the fallacies of reasoning and appeal in these arguments. Discuss what causes each instance of fallacious reasoning or appeal.

2. Discuss current examples of advertising in the mass media. Which seem to have fallacies? What kinds of fallacies are they? Which examples of advertising, if any, employ sound reasoning according to the tests in Chapter 8?

3. Each of the following statements represents a fallacy of the types discussed in this chapter. Identify the type of fallacy in each statement and explain why the reasoning, appeal, or use of language is in error. Some statements contain more than one error, so be sure to identify all fallacies.

   A. In reference to high levels of defense and social spending, the government should have learned from the Vietnam experience that you can't have guns and butter at the same time.

   B. By definition, since a housewife is someone who doesn't work, it follows that all housewives are unemployed.

   C. When you've seen one zoo, you've seen them all.

   D. The Democratic party has always been the party of the working man and woman. It makes no sense for the AFL- CIO to endorse a Republican candidate.

   E. Obviously, the authors of this book want to make us schizophrenic. They want us to learn how to both advocate and oppose a proposition on the same topic.

   F. Your argument that drunk driving causes death and injury is very interesting, but what about all the people who weren't wearing their seatbelts at the time of the accident? Aren't you assuming that every person involved in an automobile accident has been drinking? You can't really make that claim until you look at some of the other information.

   G. We outlawed prayer in schools and look what happened! Within ten years of that sacrilegious court's decision, the divorce rate is approaching 50 percent, students are becoming functionally illiterate, drug abuse abounds in our schools, and juvenile crime is increasing.

   H. Cheating on exams must surely be acceptable. After all, most college students cheat on an exam at least once.

   I. The advocate has obviously misanalyzed the situation. The Supreme Court ruled in favor of freedom of choice in the matter of abortions in 1973, not 1972.

   J. The Motor Car Company's new Q-Body designs have had serious problems with their brake systems. I'd be suspicious of all their products.

   K. Rolling Valley Vineyards must produce good wines. Their commercials state that they are the only American winery that doesn't use pesticides to control insect damages to the crop. We should all be concerned about pesticides in what we eat and drink.

   L. The chairman of the rules committee says that our bylaws have been incorrectly developed. He ought to know. After all, he's the chairman of the rules committee.

   M. We shouldn't be surprised that Northern State University's basketball team was cited for recruiting violations. Recruiting players has always been a matter of which college could offer a prospect the best deal.

   N. Professional athletics is a hotbed of drug abuse. Why just last week, three more football players were arrested for using cocaine.

4. Read the essay "A Mole Among the Gerbils?" in *Newsweek*, March 11, 1985, pp. 14-15, and list the various fallacies it contains. You should be able to find more than just the one obvious fallacy. Comment on how effective it is as a piece of argumentation, remembering the intended audience. Is this the most effective way to get the message across to this particular group?

5. In the essay "Reflections on a Hockey Helmet" in *Newsweek*, March 12, 1984, p. 13, the fallacies in reasoning, appeal, and use of language are less obvious. Read it and identify

the fallacies it contains. To what type of audience do you believe this argument was addressed?

SUGGESTED SUPPLEMENTARY READINGS

Fearnside, W. W., & Holther, W. B. (1959). *Fallacy: The Counterfeit of Argument.* Englewood Cliffs, N.J.: Prentice Hall.
This is one of the most comprehensive sources on the nature of fallacies. The authors provide an excellent classification system to cover fallacies of logic, emotional appeal, and language use. Despite its age, this book remains usable since most of the examples are taken from well-known historical sources or common communication situations.

Toulmin, S., Rieke, R., & Janik, A. (1984) *An Introduction to Reasoning* (2nd Ed.). New York: Macmillan.
Part IV, Chapters 14 through 20, examines what causes fallacies in reasoning in detail. It provides an excellent analysis of the warrant and how to avoid common reasoning errors in using it. The examples are varied, and the Toulmin model, of course, is used in many instances to show how reasoning has broken down.

10

HOW DO I PRESENT MY ARGUMENTS TO AN AUDIENCE?

Up to this point, we have been primarily concerned with preparing the ideas which communicate your views to an audience, constructing rational units of thought. Presenting your arguments and having them accepted by an audience depends not only on the quality of your reasoning but the clarity and expressiveness of your technique as a communicator as well. In Chapter 1 we told you that argumentation is part of persuasion. In addition to argumentation, the logical subset of persuasion, there are two other subsets: ethos and pathos. Today, we refer to these as the communicator's credibility and the communicator's ability to create a particular psychological climate in the minds of audience members.

Logical arguments, the arguer's credibility, and the creation of a favorable mind set combine to make up the persuasive presentations of advocates and opponents of change. In this concluding chapter, we will make some suggestions about the persuasive presentation of arguments which derive from skills of audience analysis, style and language use, brief writing, delivery technique, and credibility building.

Argumentation is audience-centered communication. To be of any use, to have any impact, your preparation and presentation of arguments must center on the receiver. Without considering who your audience is, argumentation becomes nothing more than an exercise in your ability to construct units of argument. Successful argumentation involves much more, adapting those units of arguments into a message that is both appropriate and compelling to your receivers.

Adapting arguments to an audience in public communication is generally known as using *rhetorical strategies*. A rhetorical strategy is a choice you believe will increase the probability that an audience will see your message as both appropriate and compelling. Your choice of a rhetorical strategy begins with the units of argument you construct—the claims you make, the evidence you use, the reasoning process that allows you to ask the audience to accept these claims based on the evidence you provide. Rhetorical strategies also include the choices you make in framing individual units of argument through style and language choices, organizing your arguments into a complete message, selecting appropriate delivery techniques, and building your credibility. The first step in choosing the most effective rhetorical strategies is analyzing your audience.

AUDIENCE ANALYSIS

Perfecting your technique in presenting arguments begins with a consideration of your audience. We can consider the audience on two levels: The general audience suggested by the field in which argumentation takes place and the specific individuals who make up the audience you address your message to.

The General Audience

As we have indicated throughout this textbook, a field of argument is the context in which argumentation takes place, such as medicine, law, film, or politics. The field of argument sets up expectations about how arguments will be presented. The field also determines the *rules of engagement* under which arguments are created and presentations are made (Toulmin 1958 and Toulmin et al., 1984). Some fields, such as law, have very rigid rules of engagement. In legal argumentation, if the rules are not closely followed, a jury's decision may be overturned "on a technicality." The rules of engagement for academic debate, which specify what advocates and opponents must do to "win" the debate, are presented in the appendix which follows this chapter.

The rules of engagement for a particular field also specify the *degree of precision* the general audience will demand in the arguments they hear and read. Audiences have predispositions, based on their knowledge of the field, about how much accuracy in the use of evidence and reasoning they expect from arguers. In scientific fields, standards of accuracy may be rigidly predetermined; in artistic fields, accuracy may be more open to interpretation by the arguers (Toulmin et al., 1984).

The way in which argumentation is concluded, its *mode of resolution*, is also a part of the rules of engagement. People argue to achieve specific outcomes—to determine a winner, to reach consensus, or to justify or clarify a position they have taken. The rules of engagement in a field specify the kind of outcome arguers seek. In intercollegiate debate, the losing side does not concede the accuracy or justness of the winner's case, even though the debate judge names a winner and a loser. In other fields, such as the deliberations of legislative groups, the goal of argumentation is usually to reach a consensus that produces a majority coalition voting for or against a piece of proposed legislation. A third goal, justifying or clarifying a position, is represented in the argumentation a corporation might use in stating its case for a change in the laws concerning environmental protection.

To be a successful arguer, you must understand the unique demands of the field in which you argue. How much formality is expected? What demands for accuracy in the use of evidence and reasoning exist? What goal or outcome does an arguer in this field pursue? Your ability to meet the expectations of the field is an important factor in how successful you will be in presenting arguments in that field.

The Specific Individuals in Your Audience

In discussing the concept of presumption, we said that it has important implications for audience analysis. By virtue of being associated with a field of argument, you can make some guesses about who makes up your audience and what they will expect of you. Within a field, however, there can be a lot of variety among the individuals who make up the audience that actually hears your message. The rhetorical strategies you should choose in adapting your message to these receivers can be discovered by asking certain questions about them:

- What does the audience think is important?
- What issues concern them?
- What kinds of things does the audience value?
- How knowledgeable are they on this topic?
- Do they share my views?
- What opposing views might they hold?
- What sources of evidence are they likely to respect?
- What reasons are they likely to find most persuasive?

Sometimes you will have the opportunity to answer these questions specifically by surveying members of the audience, asking them these questions before preparing your argumentative message. Lawyers prepare for trials by surveying sample jurors, selected at random from jury lists, just as real jurors will be drawn. They ask questions about prejudices, understanding of evidence, or beliefs about issues to determine how the real jurors are likely to respond to a line of argument. Political candidates survey voters to determine their understanding of issues, what they strongly believe, and what qualities they think a candidate must have to obtain their votes. In your classroom exercises in argumentation, you can find the answers to many of your questions about your classmates as an audience by asking directly or by listening to what they have to say in class discussions.

When a survey or direct questioning is not feasible, it is still possible to learn much about those who will make up your audience by turning to other sources. The same sleuthing techniques used to discover evidence to present to an audience can be used to discover information about the audience itself. Professional polling and survey research are constantly being done and reported by the mass media. If you want to know what audiences composed of individuals from the business field value and perceive to be important, you might find information from the Bureau of Labor Statistics, the Commerce Department, the Federal Trade Commission, the President's Council of Economic Advisers, the *Wall Street Journal, Business Week*, or Cable News Network's financial programming useful.

Finding out as much as you can about an audience's expectations and the extent of their knowledge is a key factor in making a successful presentation before them. In addition to knowing the rules of engagement under which you must argue and the demands of the field of argument for precision in creating your arguments, audience analysis will also help you discover what style and language use will be most acceptable to your audience, which delivery techniques are likely to be preferred, and what you must do to be perceived as a credible arguer.

LANGUAGE CHOICE AND STYLE

Language and style are the vehicle for communicating your ideas to the audience. Both language and style choices influence the ability of the audience to understand your arguments as you wish them to be understood. You maximize your chances for being understood by paying attention to your use of language.

Words as Symbols

The smallest unit of language is the word. In communication we typically refer to words as *symbols*, because a word only represents something else. The symbol is not the thing it represents, but is used to represent someone's direct experience with people, places, objects, and concepts. This makes choosing words a tricky business, since the meaning you assign to a symbol is not necessarily the same meaning your audience will assign.

You can improve your chances of having an audience correctly assign meaning by considering your symbol choices in terms of what you know about your audience. Choose the most concrete term. For example, when arguing about something "the government" (a more abstract term) does, refer to the specific government office or agency such as "the Federal Trade Commission" (a more concrete term). In adapting your language to your audience, choose the symbols your audience is most likely to assign meaning to in the same way that you do. Define key terms, particularly if they may be unfamiliar to your audience. When you are uncertain about what meaning they will assign a term, provide the appropriate interpretation for them.

There is another aspect of language that is important to consider to make sure your choice of word-symbols does not impair an audience's ability to understand your arguments properly. The language you choose reveals your attitudes, prejudices, and values. Language choices act as a filter for a person's view of the world. In communication, language is said to act as a *terministic screen*, that choice of a particular term sets limits, directs attention in a certain way, or creates a certain feeling, based on the symbol chosen.

Being insensitive to how you choose your language can lead to problems in how your audience perceives your arguments. For example, if every reference to people in general used the terms "mankind," "men," "he," or "manpower," these choices all function as a male terministic screen. Your audience may perceive that you view the world as male-dominated and feel that only men are important. You would be guilty, at a minimum, of using sexist language.

Terministic screens are a product of the connotative and evaluative dimensions of language. Your own terministic screens are not necessarily bad, but you should become aware of them and how your use of language works to convey meaning. Defining terms creates the specific terministic screen through which you want your audience to interpret meaning. Devoting equal care to choosing the language in the remainder of your message prevents your audience from becoming caught up in the screen your choice of language dictates. Be sensitive to connotative meanings and the evaluative properties a word might have for an audience. Avoid language that conveys sexism, racism, or other types of discrimination. Of equal importance, be conscious of the language choices you make in terms of how your audience assigns meaning to those terms. Understanding the fallacies of language use, discussed in Chapter 9, can help you avoid some of these problems.

The Elements of Style

The arrangement of words into complete thoughts and of those thoughts into units of argument reflects style in argumentation. Style includes the rules of correct English usage, the necessity to be clear, and the quality in using language termed *eloquence*. Style in communicating arguments is the element that makes them interesting to the audience. While good style will not compensate for poorly reasoned arguments, good reasoning alone does not guarantee your audience will be receptive to your message. Audiences expect good argumentation to possess eloquence as well as substance.

The first characteristic of effective style in argumentation is that the arguer must follow the rules of English usage. This means using grammar, spelling, and punctuation correctly in written argument and using correct grammar and pronunciation in oral argument. The sentence is the basic unit of thought in English and constructing sentences to provide variety and interest improves style. Sentence structure can be varied by using clauses, compound sentences, repetition of phrases, and using active rather than passive verbs. Knowing the rules of English usage and following them in creating arguments will improve your credibility, since we tend to estimate the intelligence and competence of someone based on how closely he or she follows the rules of grammar, spelling, punctuation, and pronunciation.

The second characteristic of effective style in argumentation is that the arguer must strive for clarity. You can improve your ability to be clear by paying attention to language choice and how you organize both individual units of argument and the several units of argument that comprise your case. Clarity is a product of the economical use of language. Do not use more words than you need to express an idea and use repetition only when it helps your audience follow your main lines of argument or ideas. Specifically choose language that quantifies, names, or describes things in concrete terms. Always choose the simplest term, avoiding insofar as possible jargon, or ambiguous or vague terms. Just remember, there are differences in how you achieve clarity in oral and written style.

The principal difference between oral and written style is that written style tends to be more formal and more closely observes the rules of English usage. Oral style uses less formal modes of expression that are not appropriate for formal written style, including colloquialisms, contractions, interjections, and sentence fragments. Oral arguments need to be expressed with a more restricted vocabulary than written ones. Personal pronouns and rhetorical questions are more frequently used in oral style. Oral argument tends to use more direct quotations of evidence, connotative words, elaborate figures of speech, and restatement of key ideas. Oral style must be punctuated nonverbally by the speaker's use of pauses, gesture, facial expression, voice, or movement.

The final characteristic of effective style in argumentation is the eloquent expression of ideas. Eloquence refers to the beauty of using language. While you want to exercise care in making language choices, avoiding choices that interfere with your audience's assigning the meaning you intended, you do not want them to become bored and tune out your message. If you are advocating a proposal to solve the problem of homelessness in America, you should present clear statistical evidence and reason that these statistics point to a need for your proposal. However, that argument may not be very compelling because it does not capture the interest of your audience. To be persuasive, you must do more. Make the audience visualize what it is like to be a part of those statistics. You want the audience to sense the experience of homelessness so they will support your proposal.

The hallmark of an eloquent style is that it uses imagery and creates interest for the listener or reader. To create imagery in arguments, use descriptive language that calls up a sensory experience in the receiver's mind. An illustration or example vividly describing what it is like to live on the street will shape that sensory image. Combined with your reasoning and use of a statistic enumerating the extent of homelessness, the illustration or example will make your argument much more persuasive.

Although oral style typically uses more figures of speech than written style, both depend upon these devices of style to create imagery and stimulate interest. The following list represents figures of speech commonly used in speaking and writing (Rybacki & Rybacki, 1991).

- *Alliteration* is the repetition of opening sounds of two or more words in sequence: The slippery slope of symbol selection. A related figure of speech, *assonance* is the repetition of vowel sounds: Take now our counsel.
- *Allusion* refers to shared cultural heritage, usually referencing a legend or myth: We are like Johnny Appleseed, planting the seeds of a federal deficit from which future generations will harvest bitter fruit.

- *Antithesis* contrasts two opposing ideas: From our darkest hour can come our finest moment. When the contrast is stated in inverted parallel phrases, it is called a *chiasmus*: Let us never negotiate out of fear, but let us never fear to negotiate.
- *Climax* builds to a high point: At the local level the homeless are a nuisance; at the state level, a budget item; but at the national level, they are a reflection of our inhumanity.
- *Hyperbole* uses great exaggeration: Listening to this argument is about as compelling as watching paint dry.
- *Metaphor* compares things that are different: The drug problem is a cancer, eating away at our society. *Analogies* are more fully developed metaphors. Metaphors and analogies are the most commonly used devices of style in argumentation.
- *Metonymy* substitutes a given name or title for something the name or title is associated with: The White House held a press conference today. *Synecdoche* substitutes the whole for a part or a part for the whole, but does not necessarily use a formal name or title: Science does not recognize the efficacy of homeopathic medicines (using the whole "science" for the part "physicians").
- *Oxymorons* are seeming contradictions in language use which may or may not represent actual contradictions: The silence following the advocate's speech was deafening.
- *Personification* gives human characteristics to nonhuman things: The defense budget is fat with waste. Congress needs to put it on a diet.
- *Repetition* repeats words or phrases: We shall arrest them where they live; we shall arrest them where they work; and we shall arrest them where they play.
- *Rhetorical questions* do not ask the audience for an overt response, but instead asks them to focus their thoughts in a particular direction: We must ask, are we really our neighbor's keeper?

These devices of style help create the psychological climate within which you want the audience to interpret your arguments. Figures of speech help provide the terministic screen through which you want the audience to view the world. One of the most important functions of devices of style is that they help the audience remember what you had to say, making your words more memorable. We may no longer recall all of Abraham Lincoln's analysis of how to establish peace between halves of a warring nation, but we remember the psychological climate he created in the conclusion of his second inaugural address of 1865.

> With malice toward none, with charity for all, with firmness in the right as God gives us to see the right [repetition and assonance], let us strive to bind up the nation's wounds [personification], to care for him who shall have borne the battle and for his widow and his orphan [synecdoche], to do all which may achieve and cherish a just and lasting peace among ourselves with all nations. (Andrews & Zarefsky, 1989, p. 296)

Achieving eloquence in argument is a matter of choosing figures of speech wisely to create imagery and add interest. A cautionary note on style: It can be a stimulating mental exercise to see how many figures of speech you can include in an argument, but be careful not to overdo eloquence. A speech or essay that uses too many figures of speech may be perceived as empty eloquence rather than substantive argumentation. You do not want to become so caught up in creating images that you lose sight of what you were trying to achieve through reasoning.

BRIEF WRITING

The actual oral or written presentation of an argument should be preceded by the preparation of an argumentative brief. *The brief outlines the essential elements of the advocate's or opponent's development of arguments on the proposition.* At a minimum, the advocate's brief contains the following elements:

1. A full statement of the proposition.
2. A definition of key terms.
3. An interpretation of the proposition of fact, value, or policy that establishes how the advocate will argue the proposition.
4. The development of each stock issue through units of argument which include the claims and evidence that make up the body of the case. Warrants and their backing should be included only as necessary.

The minimum requirements for the opponent's brief include the following:

1. A full statement of the proposition from the opponent's perspective.
2. Any counter arguments on the definition of key terms. Note: Since the opponent is free to accept the advocate's definition of terms, this step may be omitted.
3. A statement of philosophy that forecasts the opponent's choice of strategies to be used in responding to the advocate's case.
4. The claims and evidence that make up the opponent's arguments, warrants and backing included when necessary.

The idea of using a brief in developing an advocate's or an opponent's arguments into final message form is adapted from the field of law and legal brief writing. In preparing for trial, or in appealing a decision to a higher court, a lawyer develops a written brief that includes all of the arguments and evidence. The brief provides a system for organizing the lawyer's arguments into a whole that will make sense to the intended audience. Like a lawyer's legal brief, an argumentative brief is an outline of claims to be made and the evidence to be used in advancing them.

Argumentative briefs are organized as an outline. "An outline is a visual representation of the relationships among ideas" (Campbell, 1982, p. 222). Earlier, in discussing how propositions of fact, value, and policy are argued, we provided suggestions for patterns of organization that are appropriate to each. All of these patterns can be described as *logical structure*, because each arranges units of argument in a logical relationship. As an advocate, you would obviously arrange your units of argument in terms of the case structure your approach to the proposition will take— interpreting fact; applying value criteria to a value object; comparing two value systems; describing a problem and its solution; a goal and the proposed policy that better meets it; or the consequences of two policies, one existing and the other proposed. As an opponent, your brief would contain what you intend your response to be if an advocate argues a particular claim, and your actual presentation would include that response only if the advocate's presentation warranted it.

Organizing your arguments in a logical outline increases your ability to present your reasons for or against change clearly. The key to organizing logically starts with the proposition and the issues you discovered while analyzing it. Each issue is a main point on the outline. In argumentation, a main point is called a *contention*. Under each contention, you will arrange the individual units of argument that develop that contention. The claim statements from these units of argument form the outline's substructure. A third level of substructure under the claim statements would be individual pieces of evidence, warrants, and backing supporting your claims. While you do not always need to supply the warrants and backing, when you prepare your first argumentative brief it is a good idea to include all of the third level of subpoints in your outline. Writing out the warrant is a good way to test the soundness of your reasoning; and providing the backing ensures that you have it in case audience analysis suggests you need to back a particular warrant.

Since the purpose of the brief is to promote clarity, paying attention to the rules of outlining is important. In talking about claims, we emphasized the importance of phrasing a claim as a complete, declarative statement. If you have followed that advice, you already have the basis for a logical outline. As you construct your outline, follow these rules of effective outlining:

1. State each contention as a complete, declarative sentence.
2. Each contention is a main point and must have appropriate subpoints. A claim must be subordinate to the contention it develops, and stated as a complete declarative sentence.
3. At the third level of subordination, the evidence that grounds a claim must be stated. Warrants and backing may also be included.
4. Use a consistent set of alpha-numeric symbols to show subordination. Contentions are typically given Roman numerals, with capital letters used for claim statements under each contention, and Arabic numbers used for evidence, warrant, and backing under claim statements.

The logical outline lays out the essential elements of your case in brief form. A brief, however, is not the final form your presentation will take, it just provides the essentials of case content. The conventions of effective speaking and writing also mandate that arguers have introductions, make transitional statements between main ideas, and offer conclusions. The differences between oral and written style further influence the final form your message will take. However, whether you are speaking or writing, there are some basic principles of introductions, transitions, and conclusions that will help you make your presentation a polished whole.

In argumentation, an effective introduction accomplishes four things. First, it gains the audience's attention. Second, it states the proposition from your perspective on the controversy. Third, it gives the audience a reason to listen or read further, establishing what they stand to gain from accepting your point of view on the dispute. Fourth, the introduction should connect you personally to the dispute. This last step helps to establish your credibility by revealing your motives for engaging in argumentation.

There are several rhetorical strategies that help create an effective introduction. In oral argument it is sometimes customary to greet the audience and acknowledge the occasion for your speaking to them. You may want to begin with an appropriate quotation from a respected authority who sees the issues as you do or who expresses a perspective that supports your development of the proposition. Alternative beginnings include using statistics that show significance, rhetorical questions to focus the audience's attention, or a statement of the values you will be supporting through your arguments. A reference to the field of argument and the place of your arguments in that field can also be effective. As part of your introduction, you may also provide a presummary to overview the main points you will develop. In complex situations, where it is necessary to develop several contentions, a presummary is a useful strategy.

Transitions are used to move from one contention to the next and to link units of argument to the contentions they support. Transitions can enumerate the point or subpoint you are arguing, restate claims, or forecast the subpoints you are about to argue. In speaking and writing, transitions tell the audience that one unit of argument is finished and another is about to begin. Oral style tends to make greater use of transitions that summarize, because they help the audience retain what has been said.

Since the conclusion is the last thing the audience hears or reads, it is particularly important to have a memorable conclusion. The passage from Lincoln's second inaugural used to illustrate the use of figures of speech contains one of Lincoln's most often quoted thoughts: "with malice toward none, with charity for all." The conclusion is your final opportunity to create credibility for yourself as an arguer.

An effective conclusion must accomplish three things. First, it must underview or summarize the main ideas in your message. Second, it must reference the role of the audience in the process of argumentation, acknowledging their part in the rules of engagement as decision makers, judges, or those asked to concur with one side or the other in a controversy. Third, the conclusion must provide closure for your advocacy or opposition by telling the audience what you want them to do on the basis of having heard your arguments.

A final summary of main ideas, a synopsis of one or two key pieces of evidence or reasoning, or a restatement of your strongest argument are effective techniques for concluding. Your final words might be an appeal for the audience to respond favorably to your stand on the proposition, or you might choose an appropriate quotation or a reference to the field of argument that has given you the opportunity to present your message to the specific audience.

The number of contentions you advance and the number of claims used as subpoints under each contention will be determined by your analysis of the issues and research on the proposition. A brief will contain the elements illustrated in the example which follows, part of an argumentative brief prepared as part of a classroom exercise in policy advocacy. It contains multiple pieces of evidence for some claims to show proper outlining technique when multiple grounds or the backing for warrants are included.

Proposition:

The federal government should alter the availability of performance-enhancing drugs to athletes.

Definition of key terms:

1. federal government—The Food and Drug Administration
2. performance enhancing drugs—anabolic steroids
3. athletes—amateur athletes, including all secondary school, college, and U.S. Olympic athletes

Introduction:

1. Attention step:
   Jack E. Swagerty, Assistant Chief Postal Inspector, testified before Congress that "according to a recent study by the American Medical Association as many as 500,000 high school students may be taking steroids." (Anabolic Steroid Restriction Act, 1989, p. 32)
   According to Representative William J. Hughes of New Jersey, "estimates indicate that there are over one million users of anabolic steroids in the country today, with adolescents accounting for one-quarter to one-half of the users." (Anabolic Steroid Restriction Act, 1989, p. 5)
2. Proposition statement:
   (Deferred for use as the transition statement into the body of the speech.)
3. Reason to listen:
   This indiscriminate use of steroids can affect you, members of your family, your neighbors, or even the person sitting next to you in this class.
4. Motivation for speaking:
   As a student at this university, I am concerned about the manner in which some of my friends and classmates who are student athletes are tempted to use anabolic steroids to improve their performance on the field at the cost of their future well-being.

Transition to body of the speech:

Because steroid use is widespread, I believe the Food and Drug Administration should alter the availability of performance-enhancing steroids to amateur athletes.

I. Current steroid use is medically unsupervised.

    A. Athletes obtain steroids without the help of a doctor.

        1. Ethical physicians will not provide such drugs for the purpose of enhancing performance, but the amateur athlete who wants to use them need not find an unscrupulous doctor in order to obtain them.

        2. According to Mr. Swagerty, "steroids may be obtained with relative ease. Under the laws of many countries steroids may lawfully be purchased and then may be unlawfully imported into the United States, sometimes in highly concentrated solutions which can be diluted under far less than clinically acceptable conditions into individual doses. Within the United States it appears that the mails and common carriers are the primary media for distribution." (Anabolic Steroid Restriction Act, 1989, p. 32)

    B. Athletes administer steroids without the help of a doctor.

        1. Athletes at all levels can be disciplined if they are discovered to be using steroids. The NCAA will suspend an athlete for as much as a full season for violating its ban on steroids, and Ben Johnson was stripped of a gold medal at the 1988 Olympics.

        2. The fear of detection does not prevent steroid use, but it does drive it further underground and away from medical supervision.

        3. Dr. Charles E. Yesalis III, Professor of Health and Human Development at the Pennsylvania State University testified that "the study we did at Penn State last year showed 6.6 percent of male high school seniors use the drug. Forty percent of those people were hardcore users already. By their senior year in high school these males had used five cycles. A cycle is an episode of use of 6 to 12 weeks or more...Thirty eight percent of the kids were injecting these drugs. Forty four percent were using more than one steroid at a time." (Anabolic Steroid Restriction Act, 1989, p. 46)

Transition:

What are the consequences of this clandestine, medically unsupervised use of black market steroids?

II. Current steroid use is potentially lethal.

    A. Steroid users obtain drugs of questionable purity by themselves and administer them to themselves, oblivious to the warnings.

        1. According to Representative Hughes, "in too many instances these young people and athletes are unconvinced or ignorant of the deleterious effects of these drugs." (Anabolic Steroid Restriction Act, 1989, p. 5)

        2. This may represent a previously unreported side effect of steroids, or more likely indicates the feeling of invulnerability that so many young people have.

    B. The dangers of steroid use are numerous.

        1. Mr. Swagerty noted "there are many published reports indicating the use of steroids can be very harmful. These reports indicate adverse medical consequences such as heart attacks, strokes, cancer, liver disease, sterility, elevated cholesterol levels, and stunted growth in adolescents." (Anabolic Steroid Restriction Act, 1989, p. 36)

        2. One study of male and female power lifters who used steroids concluded that "the demonstration of these atherogenic markers (high serum total cholesterol, low HDL2-C, low HDL-C to total cholesterol ratio and low apoA-I levels) in our subjects supports the belief that male and female athletes who ingest anabolic steroids may be exposing themselves to a significant risk of premature coronary artery disease." (Cohen, Faber, SpinnlerBenade, & Noakes, 1986, p. 136)

Transition:

Will current drug-testing policies and programs deter steroid use by detecting users and punishing them? No!

III. Current steroid use goes undetected for all intents and purposes.
   A. The message of Ben Johnson's getting caught was that it was a fluke.
      1. According to Olympic gold medalist Carl Lewis, "even though Ben Johnson was caught, how many kids came out of that race realizing, well, he finally got caught? Or they may read in the paper 2 months later he beat the test 19 times. So he was caught 1 out of 20 times in testing procedures throughout his career." (Anabolic Steroid Restriction Act, 1989, p. 17)
      2. With odds like those and the potential rewards of an athletic career in the balance, the temptation to use steroids is great.
      3. According to Dr. Yesalis, "one of my colleagues recently completed a study in which four subjects received anabolic steroids...up to 300 milligrams a week of testosterone esters for 6 weeks. That 300 milligram dose exceeds the dosage used by many strength athletes in the 1960s and early 1970s and exceeds what is used by most track athletes today. They had six injections. At the end of 6 weeks he obtained urine samples, submitted the samples to a laboratory, and they all passed their test. They submitted the backup samples. They all passed their test." (Anabolic Steroid Restriction Act, 1989, p. 45-46)

Transition:

The reasons that Ben Johnson's case is considered a fluke is that the athletes are always one jump ahead of any testing program.

   B. Athletes know how to beat the testing system.
      1. Carl Lewis: "They have found masking agents to mask the actual drug use in their system. So they are able to use more and use them closer to performance time. They have diuretics that can flush it out of your system. They have been able to integrate B12 and different vitamins with the steroid use to help everything work better." (Anabolic Steroid Restriction Act, 1989, pp. 22-23)
      2. If you know how to beat any system, whether it's the radar police use to catch speeders or the testing procedures used to catch athletes on drugs, that system won't do much to deter behavior.
      3. Dr. Yesalis: "Some athletes have had themselves tested by laboratories in order to titrate the doses of particular AS (anabolic-androgenic steroids) to their own biochemistry; thus they know when to stop use prior to official testing during competition." (Anabolic Steroid Restriction Act, 1989, p. 49)

Transition:

Even if the present system of drug testing were effective, it can't keep up with new developments in the pharmacopeia of sports.

C. Medical science keeps producing new enhancers that are undetectable to the existing technology.

    1. "Dr. William Taylor, a U.S. Olympic Committee adviser on drugs, says that if it (human growth hormone) were administered to a child in combination with anabolic steroids it could produce a 'lean 7-foot 6-inch, 350 pound athlete.' Its use would be difficult to detect." (Axthelm, 1988, p. 62)

    2. New enhancers cause present standards of drug testing to be ineffective.

    3. Our athletic director acknowledges that the tests administered to our athletes probably don't catch some of the new drug combinations.

Of course, the advocate's brief went on to propose a policy to resolve the inherent harms caused by attempts to control steroid use, and an appropriate conclusion. The proposal lifted the ban and mandated medical supervision. In preparing a brief, remember that it is not the finished product in argumentation. The finished product is a speech or essay. The brief initially provides a logical framework that organizes your arguments. It is refined for oral or written presentation. For oral argument, you can usually think of the brief at this stage of development as a speaking outline. For written argument, it would serve as a very rough first draft that you would revise, rewrite, and polish into a completed essay.

Practitioners of argumentation in the real world use similar briefing techniques to those we recommend for exercises in academic argumentation. The following is an excerpt from the written statement which supplemented testimony by Dr. Joe Stuessy during the hearings from which our examples of Value Advocacy and Opposition in Action in Chapter 4 were drawn. Notice the briefing structure that we, as students and practitioners of argumentation, would label Dr. Stuessy's third contention.

IV Is There, Then, Reason to Think That Heavy Metal Can Affect Human Behavior? (Or, "So what!")

    A. Most of the successful heavy metal music projects one or more of the following basic themes:

        1. extreme rebellion

        2. extreme violence

        3. substance abuse

        4. sexual promiscuity/perversion (including homosexuality, bisexuality, sado-masochism, necrophelia, etc.)

        5. Satanism

Testimony by Mr. Jeff Ling will provide more than ample evidence of heavy metal's projection of these themes.

    B. These five basic themes are projected by overt messages. Let us now see how the music works to affect behavior, as based upon the principles discussed in Section II above.

        1. Remember that music reinforces verbal retention. The messages of commercial advertisers are more easily retained in our memory because they are set into a musical context. If you can still recall "See the USA in your Chevrolet," (assuming you are old enough to remember it from 30 years ago!), we can conclude that the message was firmly stored in your subconscious for later

retrieval. Similarly, heavy metal lyrics, especially "hook lines" like "We're not gonna take it anymore," or "Lick it up," or "Eat me alive" are going to be stored in the current teenager's subconscious. The teen may or may not <u>act</u> upon this information, but we can be relatively certain that the mind has stored it away for future reference.

2. We said that repetition reinforces the message. With heavy metal,there are two kinds of repetition. I refer to them as primary and secondary repetition. Primary repetition is integral to a given song <u>per se</u>. Catchy hook lines are repeated over and over within a song. For example, in "Lick It Up" by KISS, the hook line (the title) is repeated thirty times in this four-minute piece. That's an average of one time every eight seconds. If I were to repeat a short message to you thirty times in the next four miutes, I'll bet you would remeber it for quite a while! And remember that as an additional retention aid, the hook line is set to music. The hook line (and title) "Eat Me Alive" by Judas Priest is repeated eighteen times in 3 1/2 minutes. Twisted Sister's line "We're Not Gonna Take It" is repeated 24 times in three minutes and forty seconds. Let's face it: You never heard "See the USA in your Chevrolet" that often, yet your subconscious can still retrieve it.

Secondary repetition is more elusive. Adults often have difficulty understanding the words to heavy metal rock songs. And guess what! So do kids. But they are determined to grasp every profound nugget of wisdom their heavy metal mentors spew forth! So they put on headphones and play the songs over and over, for hours if necessary, in order to decipher the words. Often they write them down in notebooks. In the process, more repetitive listening reinforces the message even further.

3. Recall that coordinated multi-sensory input also reinforces messages. The message of heavy metal music bombards our senses from every direction. The album covers display Satanic symbols, portrayals of violence, open and free sex, and angry defiance. The names of the groups, the song titles, the names of the performers (e.g., Blackie Lawless), the words of the songs, and the liner notes reinforce one of more of the basic themes. The facial expressions, the hair, the clothes all contribute to the same messages. The videos and the histrionic antics of the live stage performance add a strong visual impact. The light shows, the smoke devices, and the sheer volume add impact. One can literally <u>feel</u> the music at a live concert, as the rib cage vibrates with every beat. Heavy metal is a media expert's dream-come-true. If the youngsters at the live concert happen to be smoking marijuana (as a great many do), please add the sense of smell and taste. That about rounds out all five senses: You hear it, you see it, you feel it, you taste it, and you smell it.

4. As mentioned earlier, "exclusionary" input enhances the impact of a message. The phenomenon usually results from the parents' yelling for the teenager to "turn it down," or "turn it off," or "go to your room to listen to that stuff!" Often, they do just that. They go to their rooms, and put on the headphones (volume up, of course). When that happens, exclusionary input takes over. Now all distracting or competing input is blocked out. The heavy metal becomes the sole point of concentration. Now the teenager's mind need not be distracted by dishes rattling in the kitchen, little brother watching sitcoms in the next room, the dog barking, or even the telephone ringing (now <u>that's</u> a problem!). Literally, they can't hear it thunder! But heavy metal now has a direct, unfettered freeway straight into the mind.

5. Finally, we suspect that stimulative music (heavy metal surely qualifies) may stimulate certain bodily functions while actually sedating others (much like alcohol). The simplicity, the repetitive beat, and the uniformity of timbre and dynamics may contribute to a lowered level of consciousness. This may be why parents report that when their youngsters sit in apparent headphoned reverence while listening to music, they seem almost trancelike. If this is true (and we must admit that this phenomenon has yet to be scientifically substantiated to my knowledge), it would imply that while in such a state, the listener has a greater susceptibility to suggestion. When our conscious mind "dozes off," our subconscious is left with its guard down and rather indiscriminately accepts all input. Further study of this possible phenomenon is needed. (Record Labeling, 1985, pp. 123-125)

Many of the traditions of argumentation in our society have emerged from oral debate and discussion. In certain fields such as law, oral argument seems to dominate, although written argumentation is important. In the classroom, even when written assignments are used, it is common practice to present them orally as well. To assist you in the practice of oral argument, the next section of this chapter covers specific delivery techniques that can be strategically employed in turning your brief into a speech.

DELIVERY TECHNIQUES

Delivery refers to presenting arguments before an audience physically. Delivery includes appropriate use of your voice and body to communicate, and the effective use of visual aids in communicating ideas.

Use of Voice

The properties of voice include articulation and pronunciation, pitch, volume, rate, and the use of pauses. By knowing what each appropriately involves, you can improve your oral presentation of arguments.

Articulation is the formation of intelligible sounds by human vocal mechanisms. The tongue, teeth, lips, hard and soft palate, and the vocal chords all work together to produce sounds by manipulating the air you exhale. The intelligible production of various vowel and consonant sounds of English is articulation. Good articulation neither adds anything to nor omits anything from each sound. While some people have articulation problems caused by a physical impairment in the vocal mechanism, most speakers can clearly articulate the sounds of the English language. The most common problems in articulation are caused by laziness, not paying attention to how sounds are made, and haste, trying to say too much too rapidly.

Pronunciation is often confused with articulation. While both are a matter of agreement, articulation represents only the sounds of English, while pronunciation concerns agreement on the sounds and the order in which they must be articulated in uttering a particular word. Agreement on pronunciation is not as universal as agreement on articulation. The correct pronunciation of a word may vary from region to region. In some parts of the nation "apricot" is pronounced with the long "a" sound, in other parts it is pronounced with the short "a."

Standards of correct English pronunciation were first codified in the eighteenth century and reflected the pronunciation of the British upper class. The first American standards of pronunciation were the work of language scholars. In today's dictionaries the first pronunciation given is usually the preferred one, with regional alternatives listed second. One factor influencing American standards of pronunciation is the mass media. Radio and television have promoted a standard of American speech that is primarily middle-western. The regional accents of the upper east coast, New York and New Jersey, the deep south, and the southwest are obliterated. Aside from the potential for confusion, the biggest problem with mispronouncing words, or failing to follow standards in pronunciation, is that it can undermine an arguer's credibility.

Pitch is the tonal range, the highness or lowness of the voice produced by the vibration of the vocal folds. Women's voices are generally higher pitched and men's voices are generally lower. Whether you are female or male, you can still vary your pitch by practicing. One of the uses of a pitch change is to punctuate thoughts, slightly raising pitch toward the end of a sentence asking a question, slightly lowering it when making a statement. A problem occurs when the same pattern of raising and lowering pitch is used habitually, producing a sing-song vocal pattern.

Volume is the loudness or intensity of the voice. Speaking too softly can cause your audience to tune you out because they must work too much to hear, let alone understand you. Good speakers vary their volume as a way of focusing audience attention on a key idea or word. Increasing volume can also be used to drown out extraneous noise, to compensate for speaking in a large room with poor acoustics, or to overcome a normally soft speaking voice. However, speaking too loudly can cause your audience to perceive you as harsh and strident.

Rate of speaking is the speed with which words are uttered. Audience-preferred rates of speaking range from 160 to about 200 words a minute. Anything less gives an audience too much time to drift away mentally. Anything over 200 words a minute is a rate of speaking that is too taxing for all but the most skilled or practiced audience members to listen to. Like volume, the rate of speaking can be varied to keep the audience's attention focused on what you are saying, slowing down to emphasize key words and ideas for example.

Pauses punctuate speaking and also give the speaker time to draw a breath. A pause of a few seconds draws the audience's attention back, if for no other reason than to see if the speaker has finished. Pauses are used most effectively to signal the end of a complete thought or point, to allow the audience time to reflect on a rhetorical question, or to emphasize a key point. Vocalizing the pause, "uh," "um," "er," "OK," or "you know," is a distraction rather than an effective delivery technique. It is probably impossible to rid your speaking of vocalized pauses completely. Discover which vocalized pauses you are most prone to use and work to eliminate as many as possible from your speaking.

Taken together, these characteristics add up to *voice quality*. Whether a voice is described as rich, smooth, polished, and pleasing or harsh, nasal, scratchy, and irritating depends upon how the speaker manages use of voice. It is important to learn your own voice quality. Working with an audio or video tape will allow you to determine the characteristics of your speaking voice. If you discover you have a serious problem with some aspect of using your voice, it may be worthwhile to take a course in voice and diction, work with a therapist, or get advice from a speech coach. Most problems, however, are minor and can be effectively managed by carefully listening to yourself, determining your vocal strengths and weaknesses, and practicing to eliminate weaknesses while maintaining strengths.

A final consideration of voice quality concerns the attitude your voice communicates. Pitch, volume, rate, and pauses all send a nonverbal message to your listeners about your attitude. How you feel about the arguments you are advancing will come across in your voice. If you do not sound enthusiastic, like you believe in your message, the audience may not accept you as competent, sincere, or credible. You should try to project a sense of belief in and commitment to your arguments through your voice.

Use of Body

The properties of your body that communicate include eye contact, facial expression, gesture, posture, and movement. The verbal elements of your arguments can be undermined if conflicting messages are sent nonverbally. Just as an unenthusiastic voice that is hard to hear can influence how an audience interprets your message; casual, sloppy, informal, or random body communication can also undermine your arguments.

Eye contact is the person-to-person impression of communication you create by looking directly at the people in your audience. Eye contact is one of the most important aspects of effective delivery. In our culture, failure to make eye contact may be associated with a lack of honesty or self-confidence on the part of the speaker. Your eye contact with an audience should be frequent and take in the whole audience. With very large groups, this can be difficult, but can be managed by consciously looking at people in all areas of the room. Be sure you do not favor one side of the room over the other and that you actually look out at the people to whom you are speaking, rather than gazing over their heads.

Facial expression communicates feelings. The human face is very expressive in showing anger, fear, concern, joy, sadness, and the whole range of human emotions. In addition to your voice, your facial expression also indicates your belief in what you have to say. Speakers who believe what they say tend to have animated faces.

Gesture refers to the movement of hands and arms. Probably the most common gesture in oral argument occurs when speakers enumerate points on their fingers. Gestures also reach out to the audience, pointing or extending the arm and hand. For this to be effective, gestures have to be natural. The two greatest weaknesses of inexperienced speakers are that their gestures are either wooden and unnatural or so numerous that the speaker's hands and arms seem to be constantly in motion, like the wings of a bird ready for flight. To observe gesture as a natural communication device, watch people in conversation. Almost no one talks as though they were sitting on their hands. Instead, the arms are raised, moving in circles or from side to side, and the hands are in motion. Take these basic techniques, enlarge the movement to compensate for the increased distances imposed by the speaker-audience setting, and beware of overusing a gesture to the extent that it loses its potential to communicate.

Posture is how a speaker stands before the audience. Ideally, posture should communicate the sense that the speaker is in control of the situation, and has confidence in what is being said. A speaker should stand up straight, avoiding leaning on the podium or slouching, both feet flat on the floor. Good posture conveys a sense of formality that tells the audience the speaker is a competent person who can be trusted.

Movement is the speaker's use of space. How you occupy and use space are a means of establishing control over the speaking situation and projecting confidence in yourself and your arguments. You want to avoid standing rigidly in one place, as though you had been planted on that spot. Coming out from behind the podium, taking a step forward, or moving to one side can be used to signal a transition between points or to emphasize a point. The most important caution to keep in mind, to ensure that your use of movement is effective, is that movement should occur for a reason. Avoid wandering around or setting a pattern of pacing back and forth.

Use of Visual Aids

In discussing kinds of evidence, we talked about the use of artifacts—objects, photographs, audio and video tapes, and diagrams. Using these artifacts in an oral presentation involves the use of visual aids. *A visual aid offers a visible demonstration or representation of information in an oral presentation.* Because so much evidence, particularly statistics, can bewilder or bore an audience, visual aids are fairly common in speaking. Charts, tables, graphs, and diagrams can be used to present statistical information visually, making it easier to understand. Visual aids can be used effectively to show changes, compare data, point out significance, or establish trends. It is also possible to use a flip chart with a brief list of key ideas to help the audience keep key points in mind and follow the progression of arguments.

In choosing visual aids, there are two principles to keep in mind. First, a visual aid must be visually pleasing in its presentation of information. If the audience cannot see it, if it is messy, or if it crowds too much information into too little space, as frequently occurs when a speaker uses a single visual aid when several would be more appropriate, the visual aid is useless. Using the graphic capabilities of a computer to generate charts, graphs, and the like, and using the printed output to produce transparencies are good ways to create visual aids. You can also create visual aids without a computer if you remember to keep your lines straight, your lettering neat, and the contrast between foreground and background high.

The second principle to keep in mind when you plan on using visual aids is that you must practice with them before actually giving your speech. Practice ensures your visual aid will fit more smoothly into your presentation and you will feel comfortable using it. Observing the following requirements in your practice sessions will help you effectively incorporate visual support for arguments into your delivery:

1. Use the visual aid as a form of support for your argument; explain the visual aid as you are using it.
2. Talk about the visual aid while you are using it; do not assume that the audience will figure out what it is supposed to mean.
3. Remove the visual aid from sight after you are finished with it.

Visuals aids are much like figures of speech in terms of their ability to enhance recall, add interest, and focus an audience's attention. Like figures of speech, overusing visual aids can be a hindrance rather than a help. Use visual aids sparingly and make sure you relate them to the unit of argument they support. If you are using electronic equipment, it is extremely important to practice using it. Few things will undermine your credibility as a speaker more than spending several minutes fumbling with an overhead or slide projector, searching a videotape to find the right spot, or discovering that your electronic equipment has malfunctioned.

The effectiveness of your delivery can make or break your credibility with the audience. While your analysis of the audience, choice of language and use of style, and the organization of your case are all important factors to your being perceived as a competent, credible advocate or opponent of change, poor delivery of an oral presentation will surely diminish your effectiveness.

BUILDING CREDIBILITY WITH AN AUDIENCE

Credibility refers to an audience's perception of a speaker's reliability. It is not something you automatically have, although what you do in preparing and presenting your arguments has a strong impact on whether your audience will perceive you as credible. There are two kinds of credibility: external credibility, which is the product of your prior reputation, and internal credibility, which is the product of an audience's direct experience with you and your arguments.

External Credibility

Initially, external credibility is a more important factor in determining how an audience perceives an arguer. A person's prior reputation determines the degree to which an audience is willing to trust his words and consider his arguments credible. External credibility is a product of what the audience already knows about the arguer's socio-economic status, profession, education, race, sex, and established position on the issues or the proposition being argued.

The field of argument is important in assessing prior reputation. Someone who is either respected or notorious in a particular field has an established prior reputation with potential audiences. For locally or nationally known individuals, mass media coverage may have helped establish their prior reputation. The field of politics and candidacy for public office provides one of the best demonstrations of the effect of prior reputation. Long before elections are held, in some cases before campaigning has gone on very long, voters are made aware of the most intimate details of the candidates' lives along with their stands on issues. In other fields, external credibility occurs in the same way. For example, Oliver Stone's success as a maker of award-winning films gives him external credibility that a less successful filmmaker might not have, something which he himself has acknowledged, giving him the ability to get skeptical studios to listen to his proposals for projects they would not otherwise consider. The more information about an arguer that an audience has prior to experiencing his arguments directly, the more likely they are to have formed strong opinions about the arguer's credibility.

Internal Credibility

A speaker may not have the kind of public reputation that produces strong positive or negative feelings in an audience prior to their direct experience with his or her ideas. Internal credibility, that which is assigned by the audience as a result of their direct experience is ultimately more important in determining whether the audience perceives an arguer as credible. While you cannot always manage your prior reputation with an audience, you can manage the part of your credibility that is a product of your audience's exposure to your message.

In Chapter 1, we said that in argumentation, you have ethical responsibilities to research the proposition thoroughly, to promote the common good of society, to use good reasoning, and to observe the rules of free speech in our society. Managing your internal credibility with an audience is a matter of demonstrating how effectively you have met these responsibilities. Internal credibility is also influenced by your skill in organizing your case, being clear and specific in your use of language, and how effectively you perform as a public speaker while presenting your case.

Managing Your Credibility

First, arguers with high credibility are perceived to be competent and trustworthy. You want to be perceived as an expert, thoroughly prepared to argue your side of the proposition. If you follow the rules for selecting and using evidence presented in Chapter 7, you will build your credibility as an arguer. This means using qualified sources of evidence which will be recognized by your audience as authoritative, accurate sources of information. Acknowledging and explaining any biases or inconsistencies in your evidence will further enhance your credibility. Competence and trustworthiness are also demonstrated by using sound reasoning and avoiding fallacies of reasoning and inappropriate language use.

Second, arguers with high credibility are well organized. It is not enough simply to create sound units of argument. You must organize them in a way that makes sense to your audience. Following the recommendations for brief writing in developing messages on propositions of fact, value, or policy will help you present arguments that are clear and easy to follow and understand. Being organized in presenting arguments will increase the probability that your audience will perceive you as competent. Moreover, you will be free of any suspicion of attempting to conceal things from them by clouding the issues with disorganization, thus increasing your trustworthiness.

Third, arguers with high credibility demonstrate that they are fair and have their audience's best interests in mind. Managing your image as fair and concerned for the common good of your audience is a matter of associating your arguments, or your perspective on the proposition, with that which your audience values. Analysis of your audience should take into account what they might value. In business, an audience may value success, progress, scientific research, or beating the competition. Relating your position to something your audience values and explaining how your position reflects their own interests in terms of achieving or maintaining that which they value will build your credibility in their minds.

Fourth, arguers with high credibility are sincere. This final element in managing internal credibility combines elements of language use, style, and delivery. Sincere arguers project social responsibility by avoiding prejudicial uses of language and examples. Sincere arguers avoid ambiguity by being clear and direct in expressing both their intentions for arguing and their arguments. Sincerity is also a product of delivery techniques that cause a speaker to be labeled a vital, interesting person, whose message is worth the audience's attention. This means projecting confidence in speaking, while avoiding apologetic phrases or nonverbal mannerisms that contradict this air of confidence.

Ultimately, your audience decides whether you are credible. Deciding which rhetorical strategies will help you manage your credibility begins with your audience analysis. Knowing what expectations they have, what sources of information and reasoning techniques they find credible, what language and delivery techniques they find appealing, and what they believe to be in their own best interests can be used to choose rhetorical strategies which enhance your credibility.

Remember, if the field of argument has rules of engagement stating a winner and loser must be determined, losing does not necessarily mean you had no credibility with your audience. Whatever credibility you built in the course of presenting arguments becomes part of your reputation with the audience and may influence them to give credence to your arguments in the future.

Presenting your arguments to an audience involves more than constructing sound arguments through effective issue analysis, and the use of evidence and reasoning. Your arguments and the manner of their presentation must be adapted to your listeners or readers. This means taking an audience-centered perspective on argumentation. You must consider the field in which you are arguing and the audience expectations it creates. You must also consider who will make up your actual audience and the role they play as decision makers or participants hearing or reading your message. Adapting your arguments into an effective message involves making appropriate language choices, using appropriate techniques of style and organization, and, in oral argument, practicing appropriate delivery skills. Together with the content of the arguments in your message, these presentational aspects of oral argument will influence your credibility and the probability that your audience will perceive you to be a competent, trustworthy advocate or opponent of change.

LEARNING ACTIVITIES

1. Analyze the "Statement of Dr. Joe Stussey" from a field perspective. What is the field in which his argumentation takes place? What rules of engagement and what mode of resolution exist in this field? How much precision and accuracy in the use of evidence and reasoning techniques does the field expect of him?

2. Analyze the people in your class as an audience for your argumentative messages. What do members of the class think is important about the subject you are going to argue? Which issues might concern them most? What values do they hold in regard to this subject? Are they likely to share your views or oppose them? How knowledgeable are they on this subject? What sources of evidence are they most likely to find compelling? What reasons will they find most persuasive?

3. Find an essay or opinion piece in *Time* or *Newsweek* and a speech from *Vital Speeches* on the same subject. Discuss the differences between oral and written style demonstrated by the two examples.

4. In each of the following speech excerpts, identify the style device the speaker used.
   A. He was the original interior decorator of this economic house of ill repute. Now that the sirens are sounding and the bust is due, he has his story ready. He was only the piano player in the parlor, He never knew what was going on upstairs. (Lane Kirkland, "Solidarity, Indispensable Key to the Future," November 16, 1981)
   B. It is indeed an Alice-in-Wonderland world when one arm of government is constantly pushing for greater use of pesticides at the same time another agency is restricting their use; or when one branch of the federal bureaucracy is demanding weight-adding safety features for automobiles even as another agency is promoting lighter-weight cars to reduce gasoline consumption. (William S. Anderson, "Meeting the Japanese Economic Challenge," September 25, 1980)
   C. It [not teaching values] is the greater crisis in American education, for the "rising tide of mediocrity" is in morality and manners far more than in mathematics and manufacturing. (Jeffrey R. Holland, "A 'Notion' at Risk: The Greater Crisis in American Education," March 22, 1984)
   D. Religious values cannot be excluded from every public issue—but not every public issue involves religious values. (Edward M. Kennedy, "Tolerance and Truth in America," October 3, 1983)
   E. [W]e [the U.S.] have tried to help friendly governments defend against aggression, subversion, and terror. We have noted with great interest similar expressions of peaceful intent by leaders of the Soviet Union. I am not here to challenge the good faith of what they say. But isn't it important for us to weigh the record as well?
   —In Afghanistan, there are 118,000 Soviet troops prosecuting war against the Afghan people.
   —In Cambodia, 140,000 Soviet-backed Vietnamese soldiers wage a war of occupation.
   —In Ethiopia, 1,700 Soviet advisers are involved in military planning and support operations along with 2,500 Cuban combat troops.
   —In Nicaragua, some 8,000 Soviet bloc and Cuban personnel, including about 3,500 military and secret police personnel. (Ronald Reagan, "Speech on the 40th Anniversary of the United Nations," October 24, 1985)
   F. If our young ladies do not use a wide variety of cosmetics and hair lotions and body perfumes they are excoriated by their peers and relegated to a life of barren spinsterhood. (David Manning White, "Mass Culture: Can America Really Afford It?" September 24, 1982)

    G. America's cities are the windows through which the world looks at American society. (Henry G. Cisneros, "A Survival Strategy for America's Cities," February 26, 1982)

    H. Our ultimate strength is an eternal idea, not a gun. The constant lamentations from Washington that Russia has more weapons, that we must arm and arm and arm to protect ourselves from annihilation or subjugation, fails to ask the ultimate question, Arm for what purpose? (Terry Sanford, "Is America a Leader?" May 16, 1983)

    I. Never in that time has the State of Black America been more vulnerable. Never in that time have black people so strongly felt themselves under siege. Never in that time have black economic and civil rights gains been under such powerful attack. Never in that time have so many black people been so alienated from their government. (John E. Jacob, "The State of Black America," January 18, 1982)

    J. How can I, a mother of small children?

    How can I, who live in a remote area or small town?

    How can I, who don't want to run for office?

    How can I make a real difference in the public policy of my town, my city, state, or nation?

    Let me suggest a way—and it's one I have learned the hard way—it is one that worked for me. Most of us are anxious to participate, and we spread ourselves too thin. We join too many organizations, go to too many meetings, feel frustrated and ineffectual. The key I suggest to you, is not to do that. Instead, select an area—one area—of your interest and concern. (Diane Feinstein, "Women in Politics: Time for a Change," September 28, 1983)

    K. Ask any of these black leaders if my office isn't always open to representatives of the black community. We may not agree on how to resolve these issues and problems, but the dialogue goes on. Progress can and in fact is being made, and the charge that this administration has written off the black segment of American society is dead wrong. The door to the Reagan White House is open to leaders of the black community. It's been open and will always remain open. (George H. W. Bush, "A Wall of Misunderstanding," July 5, 1983)

  5. Make an audio tape of yourself delivering an oral argument. Analyze your voice in terms of your articulation, pronunciation, pitch, volume, rate, and use of pauses. How would you characterize your voice quality? What aspects of your voice do you think need improvement? How can you make these improvements?

  6. Conduct a discussion of the external credibility of members of your class. After you have determined how each class member's external credibility has been established, analyze ways of managing internal credibility with the class audience.

SUGGESTED SUPPLEMENTARY READINGS

Campbell, K.K. (1982). *The Rhetorical Act.* Belmont, CA: Wadsworth.

    This is an advanced public speaking text that provides information on all aspects of speech construction and public speaking technique. We recommend Chapter 11, "The Resources of Language," for a complete discussion of language use as a rhetorical strategy, using figures of speech, and the concept of what constitutes oral style.

DeVito, J.A. (1990). *The Elements of Public Speaking* (4th ed.). New York: Harper & Row.

    This is a more basic public speaking text that also provides information on all aspects of speaking. We recommend Part Six, "Delivery and the Public Speech," for its very thorough discussion of technique. The author offers several useful drills and suggestions for improving delivery skills.

Hanna, M.S. & Gibson, J.W. (1989). *Public Speaking for Personal Success* (2nd ed.). Dubuque, IA: Wm. C. Bown.

This basic public speaking text has the best chapter on the use of visual aids of any text. We recommend Chapter 10, "Supporting Ideas Visually," for its extensive consideration of various kinds of visual aids and its guide to choosing and using audio-visual media. What makes this chapter especially useful for students of argumentation is its discussion of how to show problems, solutions, and their advantages visually.

Warnick, B. & Inch, E.S. (1989). *Critical Thinking and Communication: The Use of Reason in Argument.* New York: Macmillian.

Chapter 10, "Language and Argument," provides a good discussion on the nature of language, the problems of abstraction, and how to overcome them. The authors also discuss the six functions language performs in communication—emotive, phatic, cognitive, rhetorical, metalingual, and poetic—and explain how each function can be present in argumentation.

APPENDIX

One specialized format for argumentation is competitive debate. The setting in which argumentation takes place is formalized, and specific time limits and responsibilities are imposed on those who participate. Debates may take place in argumentation classes as a learning experience, or you may find yourself involved in debate in an intercollegiate contest between teams representing different schools. There are even national debate championship tournaments.

Since the orientation of this book has precluded a focus on the specialized form that is competitive debate, this appendix provides an introduction to debate. Entire books are devoted to the tactics and strategies of competitive debate, as well as numerous articles in the *Journal of the American Forensic Association*. Once you have learned the basic skills of arguing, you may choose to delve further into debate technique. This appendix will assist you in recognizing debate formats and introduce you to debate technique. Winning debates is a matter of your skill and preparation. Had we cast this appendix in the interrogative paradigm of our chapter titles, we would have called it *What Are the Rules of the Game?*

DEBATE FORMATS

While there are many different debate formats, and there are different kinds of propositions argued, academic debate in general has the following characteristics:

1. Teams of debaters, usually two to a side, will be prepared to argue both sides of a proposition. In debate parlance, they are called affirmative and negative rather than advocate and opponent.
2. All teams will argue the same proposition, often a policy proposition, for the entire year, although value topics that change at midyear are used by the Cross Examination Debate Association (CEDA). Propositions address broad issues of national concern.
3. The debate is judged by a single individual or a panel of three, five, or seven individuals who determine the "winner" of the debate based on which team demonstrated the greater skill or had the better arguments.

Like all communication, debate is rule-governed behavior. One set of rules pertains to the order in which members of both teams make their presentations and the length of time they have for each presentation. This is commonly referred to as the **format** for the debate. While slight variations may be found, most debates use one of two formats. The first is called the **traditional format,** in which each team member presents a constructive and a rebuttal speech. While the time limits for the speeches may vary, the format looks like this:

Traditional Format

First Affirmative Constructive Speech	10 minutes
First Negative Constructive Speech	10 minutes
Second Affirmative Constructive Speech	10 minutes
Second Negative Constructive Speech	10 minutes
First Negative Rebuttal Speech	5 minutes
First Affirmative Rebuttal Speech	5 minutes
Second Negative Rebuttal Speech	5 minutes
Second Affirmative Rebuttal Speech	5 minutes

Notice that the affirmative team has the first and last speeches, and that the negative team has two speeches in a row. (We will have more to say about this when we discuss the responsibilities of the speakers.) We should also point out that the debate may take longer than an hour to complete, since it has become customary to allow both teams a total of five or ten minutes preparation time during the course of the debate. This is time that may be used as the team members see fit.

The second commonly used format is the **cross-examination format.** The order and length of constructive and rebuttal speeches stays roughly the same, but both teams are given the opportunity to interrogate each other. The format looks like this:

Cross-Examination Format

First Affirmative Constructive Speech	10 minutes
Cross-Examination of the First Affirmative Speaker	3 minutes
First Negative Constructive Speech	10 minutes
Cross-Examination of the First Negative Speaker	3 minutes

Second Affirmative Constructive Speech	10 minutes
Cross-Examination of the Second Affirmative Speaker	3 minutes
Second Negative Constructive Speech	10 minutes
Cross-Examination of the Second Negative Speaker	3 minutes
First Negative Rebuttal Speech	5 minutes
First Affirmative Rebuttal Speech	5 minutes
Second Negative Rebuttal Speech	5 minutes
Second Affirmative Rebuttal Speech	5 minutes

The length of constructive and rebuttal speeches is some times shortened to eight and four minutes respectively to reduce the time it takes to complete the debate, since preparation time is generally provided. The Cross-Examination Debate Association does this in its debates on value propositions. Regardless of the subtle variations, debate formats establish fixed amounts of speaking and preparation time and give equal time to both parties to the dispute.

Less common than either of these formats for debates between teams of individuals is the **Lincoln-Douglas Format,** named after the historical one-on-one debates between these two candidates for the Senate. This format is often favored for in-class debating. The variations in this format are numerous. The basic rules for Lincoln-Douglas debating are that "Each speaker presents a constructive position, questions the opponent, replies to questions, refutes the opponent's position, and defends his or her own position" (Patterson & Zarefsky, 1983, p. 13).

SPEAKER RESPONSIBILITIES

In both the traditional and cross-examination styles of debating, each speaker has certain duties he or she must perform. The order of presentation, with affirmative speakers beginning and ending the debate, is based on presumption, which lies with the negative, and the requirements of the burden of proof, which fall on the affirmative. The debate begins with the **first affirmative constructive speech.** This presentation establishes the basis of the affirmative case and normally includes all the claims, evidence, and reasoning that would, if unanswered, allow the judge to vote in favor of adopting the proposition.

In value debate, this would involve presenting a case as discussed in Chapter 4. Identifying the value object, establishing the criteria by which it is to be evaluated, and providing arguments supporting the appropriateness of judging the value object in this manner. In policy debate, the first affirmative speaker might only discuss the first stock issue, reason for change, if the affirmative is employing the traditional need-plan pattern of organization. However, if one of the other patterns of organization is used, the first affirmative is responsible for presenting both a proposal and a reason for change. Regardless of whether the proposition is one of value or policy, and irrespective of the pattern of organization followed, the first affirmative speaker establishes her team's interpretation of the proposition. The second affirmative may add new arguments that further develop, or in the case of the traditional organization pattern complete, that interpretation; but if the first affirmative speech fails to establish a prima facie position, the affirmative has lost before the debate has even begun.

Assuming a prima facie case has been presented, what are the duties of the **first negative constructive speech**? The first negative speaker establishes the philosophy of the negative team—its stand on the proposition. If the negative team plans to question the definitions of key terms offered by the affirmative, those questions are raised in this speech and alternative definitions are offered. If the affirmative definitions are so outrageous that their case appears to be nontopical, the first negative speaker normally argues this as well. If the negative team intends to defend the present system of values or policies, the first negative presents these arguments. This speech responds directly to the first affirmative presentation and establishes the points of clash between the two teams. In policy debating, this speech usually focuses on the first stock issue, leaving the second and third stock issues to the second negative speaker. This is called *division of labor*, and you will see the wisdom of it when we discuss the rebuttal speeches.

The **second affirmative constructive speech** attempts to repair the damage done to the affirmative case by the first negative speaker. Since the initial points of clash between the two teams were defined by the first negative, the second affirmative must respond point by point—for three reasons. First, if there are arguments relating to definitions or topicality, the affirmative will be unable to carry argumentation forward successfully unless an attempt is made to resolve these disputes in the affirmative's favor. Second, the negative team is about to get two turns at bat, back-to-back. If the second affirmative does not respond to the first negative arguments, the first affirmative rebuttalist will be swamped. Third, it is a rule in debate that *while new evidence may be introduced in rebuttal speeches, new arguments may not be.* The constructive speeches are the appropriate place for presenting original arguments.

In addition to repairing any damage, the second affirmative should point out arguments that still stand, arguments with which the first negative chose not to clash. This is best accomplished if the second affirmative responds to the negative arguments in terms of the basic case structure used in the first affirmative constructive speech. Finally, in policy debating, the second affirmative must present the proposal for change if it was not included in the first affirmative's speech. In general, the second affirmative has the responsibility of rebuilding and extending the affirmative case.

The **second negative constructive speech** is the final speech in the constructive phase of the debate. The second negative generally deals with the stock issues his partner left unargued. In value debate this frequently takes the form of examining society's willingness to accept the new value hierarchy proposed by the affirmative. In policy debate this means examining the affirmative proposal in terms of solvency, circumvention, workability, and disadvantages.

The second negative speaker must be careful to listen to his partner so that their arguments are not contradictory. The easiest way for the affirmative team to get off the hook on a disadvantage or solvency argument is to point out that one of the first negative's inherency or minor repair arguments reduces the disadvantage's impact or eliminates the solvency problem. Affirmative speakers have to listen to each other as well, but they usually do not have as much of a problem with contradictions since they know where they want to go, and don't want to go with their case. They have argued it many times before. The negative may be hearing it for the first time, grasping for anything to defeat it.

The **first negative rebuttal speech** begins the final phase of the debate. These back-to-back speeches are sometimes called the negative block. If the negative speakers do not maintain a clear division of labor, the first negative will waste time repeating what the second negative has just said; thus, any advantage that might have been gained from consecutive speeches will have been squandered. The first negative rebuttalist's responsibilities are similar to the second affirmative constructive speaker's—rebuild and extend on the points of clash established in the constructive speeches. It is important for the first negative rebuttalist to respond to the second affirmative's arguments, not merely repeat his own. This rebuttal should identify arguments the negative has "won" outright because they were not contested by the second affirmative. It should crystallize the important arguments to which the affirmative, during its rebuttals, must respond with new evidence and further reasoning, but no new arguments. If it suddenly dawns on the first negative that all the affirmative's evidence is over twenty years old, too bad. These are rebuttal speeches and no new arguments can be advanced.

The **first affirmative rebuttal speech** is, strategically speaking, the most important and most difficult speech in the entire debate. Attacks that took the second negative ten minutes to present must be answered in half the time, and the first affirmative rebuttalist cannot totally ignore what the first negative has had to say, especially if definitions and/or topicality are still in dispute. In policy debate, the fire drill goes like this: First, answer challenges on definitions and/or topicality. Second, respond to second negative constructive arguments. Third, respond to key issues extended in the first negative rebuttal. In value debate, the order of priority is the same, although the nature of the issues discussed is different.

The **second negative rebuttal speech** is the negative team's last speech. While he should respond to what the first affirmative rebuttalist had to say about arguments presented in the second negative constructive speech, the second negative rebuttalist must remember that his primary mission is to give the judge a reason to vote for the negative team. This speech should cover the main arguments favoring rejection of the affirmative team's arguments, regardless of whether they were initiated by the first or second negative speaker. This is the only point in the debate where observing the division of labor between the negative speakers hurts the team.

The **second affirmative rebuttal speech** is the final speech in the debate. Like the second negative rebuttal, it summarizes the debate but from the affirmative team's perspective. The second negative rebuttalist probably established reasons why the decision should favor the negative. The second affirmative rebuttalist should respond to these, as well as pointing out things the negative team has not contested that suggest an affirmative decision. In essence, both final rebuttal speakers attempt to provide the judge with a set of rules or criteria on which to decide the debate, which favors their side's interpretation of the proposition.

BURDEN OF CLASH

As already indicated, the order of speeches reflects the exigencies of presumption and burden of proof. The order of speaking also puts certain obligations on both teams in terms of going forward with the debate. Recall that the first affirmative speech must be prima facie, otherwise the debate is over before it really begins, although the rest of the speeches will be given. The negative team must move the debate forward by **establishing clash**. The negative is obligated to respond to what the affirmative has presented in some way, even if its only argument is that the affirmative case is so far off the topic that topicality is the only thing there is to argue.

Successive speakers have the responsiblity of **maintaining clash**. Each speech moves the judge closer to making a decision by responding to what the other side has just said. The only exception might be the second negative constructive speech, which, because of division of labor, usually leaves second affirmative constructive arguments to the first negative rebuttalist. It is not sufficient merely to repeat your arguments. You must respond to your opponent's arguments to move the controversy toward resolution. Not only must arguments be presented but the points of clash between the two teams must be identified. In so doing, both sides have the obligation to make an honest effort to develop arguments that do not deceive, or distort or misrepresent what they know to be true.

CROSS-EXAMINATION

The responsibilities of the speakers and the obligations to establish and maintain clash are relevant to both traditional and cross-examination debating. You may have figured out much about speaker responsibilities from having read this book. However, cross-examination gives debaters some unique opportunities. You should approach the opportunity to ask and answer questions as a chance to advance the debate in a way that favors your side.

Cross-examination usually covers the speech immediately preceding it, although it might cover lines of argument extending through several preceding speeches. You use cross-examination for various purposes.

> Cross-examination allows you to gain information about your opponent's reasoning. What kinds of inferences link evidence to claims, and what kinds of inferences link one argument to another? If they are illogical, you can point this out in a later speech.

> Cross-examination allows you to prevent possible misunderstandings. If you are not sure whether the speaker said "million" or "billion," ask. In this way you ensure that the argument you advance in a later speech cannot be dismissed because it is based on a misinterpretation.

> Cross-examination allows you to probe for and point out inconsistencies either within a single speech or between two speakers. If you are a first affirmative rebuttalist, remember that negative teams are especially vulnerable to contradictions if they do not listen to each other. Finding the contradictions makes your task much easier.

Cross-examination allows you to advance your own position. You can ask questions whose answers point toward the conclusion you wish the judge to draw.

Notice that all these purposes represent means to an end, rather than an end in themselves. Cross-examination is used to set up arguments in subsequent speeches. No one ever won a debate with an imitation of Perry Mason during cross-examination. Debates are won in the constructive and rebuttal speeches. Whatever gains you think you may have made will be realized only if you capitalize on them in your speeches.

Preparation is as important to success in cross-examination debate as it is in traditional debate. Preparation begins with a thorough understanding of your topic. Cross-examination quickly exposes limited knowledge. Be prepared to take the role of both questioner and respondent. In terms of the first three purposes discussed here, you obviously have to listen to what your opponent is saying and decide on the spot what you need to ask. However, in regard to the fourth, you can plan a series of questions in advance. A series of questions is needed because even the dullest respondent will not readily admit to something favoring your position. If your positon is that the poor are denied access to cable television because of its cost, asking "Don't you agree that the poor are denied access to cable because of cost?" will probably elicit a no. Assuming you had the supporting evidence, you would be better served by asking the following series of questions:

The poor own just as many television sets, proportionally speaking, as the rest of the population, don't they?

They watch television just about as much as everyone else, don't they?

The majority of them live in urban areas served by cable systems, don't they?

Yet few poor people are cable subscribers. Doesn't this suggest that the cost of cable service is a barrier to access for the poor?

Even though this last question might still elicit the same answer, your position would be advanced for two reasons. First, you would have planted a seed in the judge's mind that a series of signs point to your conclusion. Second, you could always ask one more question: "OK, you tell me why the poor don't subscribe to cable?"

You may want to think twice before you ask that question. When attempting to advance your position through cross- examination, always ask questions to which you already know the answer. Your motive is to educate the judge, not yourself. Thus, if you do not know the answer to a question, it is sometimes safer not to ask it, lest you discover, too late, that you have presented your opponents with an opportunity to advance their position. While you will be fairly sure of the answers your questions will elicit, you still need to listen to the answers and adapt subsequent questions or even abandon a line of questioning if it is going nowhere.

Like the role of questioner, which allows for some prior planning, the role of respondent allows you to prepare your position. While you cannot anticipate every question that might be asked, you can anticipate the kinds of questions that will probably be asked about your affirmative case and the negative arguments you typically use. Prepare for answering by having your partner interrogate you.

Just as the various speaker positions in the debate have different responsibilities, the roles of questioner and respondent carry with them specific requirements as well. Neither questioner nor respondent may confer with colleagues during the cross-examination period. The questioner is in charge during cross-examination, asking the questions, and being careful that the respondent does not try to turn the tables. Questions should be as brief and clear as possible to encourage brief and clear responses. While the questioner cannot require yes or no responses, she need not tolerate filibustering by the respondent. The respondent should attempt to be as direct as possible but may qualify answers if necessary and refuse to answer questions that are patently unfair. If it becomes necessary to qualify an answer or refuse to provide one, it is important that the respondent explain why.

Both the questioner and respondent should remember that the debate is a public-speaking situation. Both parties should refrain from making speeches during the cross-examination period, and questions and answers should be articulated clearly and distinctly so that the judge may understand both. The most important thing to remember is to remain composed. Do not become hostile or defensive, and do not do things that would produce these behaviors in the other person.

To know what to ask in cross-examination, or what to argue in your next speech, requires not only argumentative skills but a sense of what is going on in the debate as a whole. What is your team's position? What has the other team disputed? What has the other team conceded? What has your partner said? What are you going to say? No matter how good your memory is, learning to keep a flow sheet of the debate as it unfolds is your best memory aid. A flow sheet tracks the progress of arguments during a debate and is nothing more than a specialized outline.

FLOW SHEETING

In class, you fill page after page with notes on what your professor has to say. Now suppose that you have two professors who constantly disagree with each other. The only way you can keep things straight when you study is to have two sets of notes side by side. Suddenly you realize things would be much easier if you drew a line down the middle of a page of notebook paper, and put what one professor has to say on one side and what the other says on the other. If you rewrote the notes for one class in black ink and the other in red, you could tell at a glance who said what and exactly what the points of disagreement were. You have just discovered the flow sheet.

Instead of two columns, most people divide their paper into as many as eight columns, one for each speech. Unless you are able to write very small and have very good eyesight, something bigger than the standard eight-and-one-half-by-eleven notebook paper is helpful; contest debaters often use large artist's sketch pads. Outline each successive speech in the next column to the right, placing opposite each other arguments that clash and connecting them with an arrow. If nothing is to the right of an argument, it probably means it has gone uncontested. To cram lots of information into a narrow column, use special symbols and abbreviations. You will have to develop your own because there is no standard set. For instance, one of your authors uses the acronym NAIR for "new argument in rebuttals." With a little practice you will quickly develop your own shorthand.

DEBATE JUDGES

Debates are judged and winners and losers are determined, but unlike the audiences for argumentation, which may vary considerably, the audience that counts in debate is somewhat more predictable. For the most part, debate judges are normally trained professionals, who engaged in the activity themselves as undergraduates, presently coach, or have coached debate teams, and teach courses in argumentation and debate. For debaters this means that concepts like presumption and burden of proof will not be alien to the judge of a debate as they might be to a lay audience for oral or written argumentation. Debaters are well advised to avoid "teaching" the debate judge in the same way they would the lay audience. If you intend to make a topicality argument, make it and go on. Debate judges dislike being lectured on theory, so they need not be informed of the gravity of a successful challenge to topicality. Unlike the lay audience, debate judges make a sincere effort to leave their biases at the door and judge the debate round on the basis of which team debated better, rather than which team they agreed with most. For debaters this means that an idea that could have passed unproven or undeveloped before a lay audience, because it approached the status of a premise, must be proven to the debate judge. If, for example, the topic relates to unemployment, a trained debate judge will expect proof for the notion that full employment is a national goal and listen to counter arguments that it is not a goal.

That is not to say that debate judges are bias-free. In regard to style, some judges dislike what is sometimes referred to as NDT (National Debate Tournament) style, which is characterized by rapid rates of delivery, the reading of large quantities of evidence at the expense of explanation, and the excessive use of debate jargon ("On PMA 1..."); other judges may not object to this style. The formation of CEDA was, in part, a reaction to some of the perceived excesses of NDT debate. While it is un likely that many teams have ever lost rounds for talking too fast, rate can undermine your understandability and credibility with a particular judge.

In regard to the judging philosophy that shapes their decisions, some judges of policy debate see their role as that of a hypothesis tester while others see themselves as policy makers. Some judges will not consider successfully advanced topicality arguments as sufficient in themselves to warrant voting for the negative team. Other judges have a very narrow view of the range of possible meanings for the debate topic and seem to go out of their way to accept topicality arguments as a means of register-ing their displeasure with narrow interpretations of the topic. For debaters, the only saving grace is that they have to adapt to one person only, the judge, instead of a group of people with undisclosed biases. The key is to learn the tendencies of those who judge and be flexible enough to adapt.

REFERENCES

Anabolic Steroid Restriction Act. (March 23, 1989). Washington, DC: Committee on the Judiciary, House of Representatives.

Andrews, J. & Zarefsky, D. (1989). *American voices: Significant speeches in American history, 1640-1945.* White Plains, NY: Longman.

Axthelm, P. (1988). Using chemistry to get the gold. *Newsweek,* July 25, 62-63.

Barcus, E. F. (1983). *Images of life on children's television.* New York: Prager.

Barol, B.; Bailey, E.; & Zabarsky, M. (1984). Tuning in on kiddie videos. *Newsweek,* June 25, 48.

Boller, P. F., Jr. (1981). *Presidential anecdotes.* New York: Penguine.

Brockriede, W. E. & Ehninger, D. E. (1960). Toulmin on argument: An interpretation and application. *Quarterly Journal of Speech, 46,* 44-53.

Brydon, S. R. (1983). Presumption in value topic debates: The three faces of eve. Western Speech Communication Association, Albuquerque, NM., February 19-22. Unpublished Paper.

Campbell, K. K. (1982). *The rhetorical act.* Belmont, CA: Wadsworth.

Children and Television. (March 16, 1983). Washington, DC: Committee on Energy and Commerce, House of Representatives.

Cohen, J.C.; Faber, W.M.; SpinnlerBenade, A.J., & Noakes, T.D. (1986). Altered serum lipoprotein in male and female power lifters ingesting anabolic steroids. *Physician and Sports Medicine, 14,* 131-36.

Communication Research Associates. (1983). *A workbook for interpersonal communication* (3rd ed.). Dubuque, IA: Kendall/Hunt.

Comstock, G. (1982). Juvenil crime. In Meg Schwartz (Ed.) *TV & teens.* Reading , MA: Addison-Wesley.

Cowan, J. L. (1972). The uses of argument—An apology for logic. In D. Ehninger (Ed.), *Contemporary rhetoric.* Glenview, IL: Scott, Foresman.

Crable, R. E. (1976). *Argumentation as communication: Reasoning with receivers.* Columbus, OH: Chas. E. Merrill.

Dudczak, C. A. (1983). Value argument in a competitive setting: An inhibition to ordinary language use. In D. Zarefsky, M. O. Sillars, & J. Rhodes (Eds.), *Argument in transition: Proceedings of the third summer conference.* Annandale, VA: Speech Communication Association.

Ehninger, D. E. (1974). *Influence, belief, and argument.* Glenview, IL: Scott, Foresman.

Ehninger, D. E. & Brockriede, W. (1963). *Decision by debate.* New York: Dodd, Mead, & Co.

Eisenberg, A. M. & Ilardo, J. A. (1980). *Argument: A guide to formal and informal debate* (2nd ed.). Englewood Cliffs, NJ: Prentice Hall.

Fisher, W. R. & Sayles, E. M. (1966). The nature and functions of argument. In G. R. Miller & R. Nilsen (Eds.), *Perspectives on argumentation.* Chicago: Scott, Foresman.

Golden, J. L.; Berquist, G. F.; & Coleman, W. P. (1989). *The rhetoric of western thought* (4th ed.). Dubuque, IA: Kendall/Hunt.

Gorbachev, M. (1989). Perestroika: The socialist renewal of society. *Vital Speeches of the Day, 56,* 5-7.

Hart, R. P. & Burks, D. M. (1972). Rhetorical sensitivity and social interaction. *Speech Monographs, 39,* 75-91.

Holt, F. L. (1984). An Olympic-size delusion. *Newsweek,* July 16, 16.

Japanese-American and Aleutian Wartime Relocation. (June 20, 21, 27 & September 12, 1984). Washington, DC: Committee on the Judiciary, House of Representatives.

Jensen, J. V. (1981). *Argumentation: Reasoning in communication.* New York: D. Van Nostrand.

Johnstone, H. W., Jr. (1965). Introduction. In M. Natson & H. W. Johnstone, Jr. (Eds.), *Philosophy, rhetoric, and argumentation.* University Park, PA: Pennsylvania State University Press.

Karp, W. (1984). Where the do-gooders went wrong. *Channels,* March-April, 41-47.

Koehler, J. W.; Anatol, K. W. E.; & Applbaum, R. L. (1981). *Organizational communication.* New York: Holt, Rinehart & Winston.

Korda, M. (1981). How to be a leader. *Newsweek*, January 5, 7.

LaGrave, C. W. (1975). Inherency: A historical view. In David A. Thomas (Ed.), *Advanced debate*. Skokie, IL: National Textbook Company.

Liebert, R. M.; Sprafkin, J. W.; & Davidson, E. S. (1982). *The early window: Effects of television on children and youth* (2nd ed.). New York: Pergamon Press.

Matlon, R. J. (1978). Debating propositions of value. *Journal of the American Forensic Association, 14,* 194-204.

Mills, G. E. (1968). *Reason in controversy.* Boston: Allyn & Bacon.

Minnick, W. C. (1968). *The art of persuasion.* Boston: Houghton-Mifflin.

Naisbitt, J. (1982). *Megatrends.* New York: Warner Books.

Nilsen, T. R. (1974). *Ethics of speech communication* (2nd ed.). Indianapolis: Bobbs-Merrill.

Patterson, J. W. & Zarefsky, D. (1983). *Contemporary debate.* Boston: Houghton-Mifflin.

Record Labeling. (September 19, 1985). Washington, DC: Committee on Commerce, Science, and Transportation, United States Senate.

Rescher, N. (1969). *Introduction to value theory.* Englewood Cliffs, NJ: Prentice Hall.

Rieke, R. D. & Sillars, M. O. (1984). *Argumentation and the decision making process.* Glenview, IL: Scott, Foresman.

Rives, S. G. (1964). Ethical argumentation. *Journal of the American Forensic Association, 1,* 79-85.

Roberts, R. (Trans.). (1954). *Aristotle, the rhetoric.* New York: Modern Library.

Rokeach, M. (1973). *The nature of human values.* New York: MacMillan, Free Press.

Rybacki, K. C. & Rybacki, D. J. (1991). *Communication criticism: Approaches and genres.* Belmont, CA: Wadsworth.

Singer, J. L. & Singer, D. E. (1979). Come back, Mister Rogers, come back. *Psychology Today,* March, 56-60.

Sproule, J. M. (1976). The psychological burden of proof: On the evolutionary development of Richard Whately's theory of presumption. *Communication Monographs, 43,* 115-29.

Sproule, J. M. (1980). *Argument: Language and its influence.* New York: McGraw-Hill.

Toulmin, S. (1958). *The uses of argument.* London: Cambridge University Press.

Toulmin, S.; Rieke, R.; & Janik, A. (1984). *An introduction to reasoning* (2nd ed.). New York: MacMillan.

Vasilius, J. (1980). Presumption, presumption, wherefore art thou presumption. Desert Argumentation Symposium, Tucson, AZ: March 2. Unpublished Paper.

Walter, O. M. & Scott, R. L. (1984). *Thinking and speaking* (5th ed.). New York: MacMillan.

Warnick, B. (1981). Arguing value propositions. *Journal of the American Forensic Association, 18,* 109-19.

Whately, R. (1828/1963). *Elements of rhetoric,* Douglas Ehninger (Ed.). Carbondale, IL: Southern Illinois University Press.

Wilcox, J. R. (1973). The argument from analogy: A new look. Central States Speech Association, Minneapolis: April. Unpublished Paper.

Wilson, B. A. (1980). *The anatomy of argument.* Lanham, MD: University Press of America.

Windes, R. R. & Hastings, A. (1965). *Argumentation and advocacy.* New York: Random House.

Young, M. J. (1980). The use of evidence in value argument. In J. Rhodes & S. Newell (Eds.), *Conference on argumentation.* Falls Church, VA: Speech Communication Association.

Zarefsky, D. (1972). A reformulation of the concept of presumption. Central States Speech Association Convention, Chicago: April 7. Unpublished paper.

Zarefsky, D. (1976). Criteria for evaluating non-policy argument. Western Speech Communication Association, San Francisco: November 24. Unpublished paper.

Ziegelmueller, G. W.; Kay, J.; & Dause, C. A. (1990). *Argumentation: Inquiry and advocacy* (2nd ed.). Englewood Cliffs, NJ: Prentice Hall.

Index

A

Academic argumentation
    avoiding should-would arguments in, 97
    mode of resolution in, 182
    proposition in, 24, 26-27
    proposition of fact in, 41
    proposition of policy in, 29, 45, 115
    topicality in, 116
Actual issues, 101
    selection of, 113-16
Ad hominem argument
    fallacy of, 169
Ad ignorantum argument
    fallacy of, 171
Ad populum argument
    fallacy of, 172
Advocacy
    example of policy, 86-89
    example of value, 66-68
Advocate, 15
    argumentative brief of the, 188
    burden of proof and, 19-20
    fact proposition and the, 61-62
    policy proposition and the, 80-86
    prima facie case and the, 36-37
    role in defining terms, 21
    value propositions and the, 68-72
Alliteration
    style and, 186
Allusion
    style and, 186
Ambiguity
    fallacy of, 176
Analogy
    argument from, 154
    difference from parallel case, 154
    style and, 187
    tests of, 155
Analysis, 101
    actual issues selection and, 113-16
    of the audience, 182-84
    contentions argued and, 191
    defining terms during, 107-12
    fact proposition and, 61, 63
    of an issue's history, 104-106
    locating the cause of controversy through, 102-103
    value proposition and, 75
Antithesis
    style and, 187

Appeal
    fallacies of, 171-75
    to authority, 173-74
    to emotion, 172-73
    to humor, 175
    to the people, 172
    to tradition, 174
Argument (*See also* Fields of argument)
    ad hominem, 169
    ad ignorantum, 171
    ad populum, 172
    analysis of a proposition's field of, 104
    chains of, 60
    claims and, 46
    clusters of, 60-61
    contention in, 189
    irrelevant, 168
    patterns of, 59-61, 85-86, 94
    preemptive, 62, 65
    preparing a brief for, 188-89
    reasoning and the viability of, 143
    simple, 59-60
    straw man, 168
    Toulmin model of, 46-56
Argumentation, 2
    ethics and, 6, 10-13
    historical development of, 9
    law and, 7
    limitations of, 6-7
    persuasion and, 3-5, 181
    politics and, 8
    probability and, 9
    propositions in academic, 24, 26-27, 41, 45, 115
    risk taking and, 5-6
    rule-governed behavior and, 4, 12
    topicality in academic, 116
    truth and, 4
Articulation, 196
Artifact
    as evidence, 121, 125
    tests of, 128-29
Artificial presumption, 16, 18
    fallacy of appeal and, 171
Assonance
    style and, 186
Attitudinal inherency, 38-39
Audience
    acceptance of evidence by an, 132-33
    adapting arguments to the, 182
    adapting language to the, 184-85

Audience, cont'd
    argument centered on the, 181
    burden of proof and the, 19-20
    credibility with an, 200-202
    fallacy of appeal and the, 171
    involving the, 186
    natural presumption and, 16-18
    types of, 3
Audience analysis
    fact advocacy and, 61-62
    the general audience and, 182
    instrumental communication and, 17
    managing credibility using, 202
    selection of value criteria and, 71
    the specific audience and, 183-84
Authority
    argument from, 155-56, 158
    definition by, 110-11
    fallacy of appeal to, 173
    opinion as evidence, 123
    tests of, 157
Avoiding the issue
    fallacy of, 169

                            B

Backing
    argument from parallel case and, 152
    importance of, 144, 166, 173
    in the Toulmin model of argument, 54-56
Begging the question
    fallacy of, 169
Books
    as sources of evidence, 134
Brief
    argumentative, 188
    contentions in the, 189
    examples of an argumentative, 191-96
    introduction and conclusion in the, 190
    oral argument and the, 194
Burden of proof
    audience and the, 20
    presumption and the, 19-20
    prima facie case and the, 37
    proposition and the, 20, 22, 31-32

                            C

Case
    prima facie, 36-39
Cause
    argument from, 144-46
    difference from sign, 150
    multiple, 147-48
    necessary and sufficient, 148
    tests of argument from, 146-47
Chain arguments, 60
Change
    consequences of in policy advocacy, 83-85
    counterproposals to achieve, 94
    disadvantageous consequences of, 92-93
    elements of in policy advocacy, 83
    forces that precipitate value, 114-15
    overcoming resistance to, 5
    process of value, 104-105

    propositions and, 22-24
    reason for in policy advocacy, 81-82
    refuting the consequences of, 92-93
    refuting the reason for, 91
Chiasmus
    style and, 187
Circular reasoning
    fallacy of, 169
Circumvention arguments
    inherency and, 92
Claims
    in chain arguments, 60
    in cluster arguments, 60-61
    importance of grounding, 50-51
    made in the absence of evidence, 171
    opinion evidence and, 123
    prima facie case and, 45, 49
    qualified and unqualified, 55-56, 166-67
    rebuttals in, 56
    simple and complex, 48
    in the Toulmin model of argument, 46-47, 53
    types of, 46-47
    wording of, 48
Clarity
    argumentative brief and, 189
    in language use, 185-86
Climax
    style and, 187
Cluster arguments, 60-61
Communication
    expressive and instrumental, 2
Comparative-advantage organization
    in policy advocacy, 85
Complex claims, 48
Conclusion
    in oral argument, 190
Connotative meaning
    terministic screens and, 185
Contentions
    in argument, 189
    number of, 191
Counterproposal
    policy opposition and the, 94
Credibility
    of an authority in a field, 156
    external, 200-201
    internal, 201
    management of, 201-202
    of opinion evidence, 123-24
    of scientific evidence, 123
Criteria
    analysis of the proposition and, 102, 105-106
    audience analysis and selection of, 71
    defining the, 111-12
    developed, 70
    discovered, 70
    examining the appropriateness of, 76
    necessary, 71, 113
    sufficient, 71, 113
    value propositions and, 28-29, 69

                            D

Decision rule
    presumption as a, 16-17, 64

for resolving value conflict, 69
Defining terms
adapting language and, 184
analyzing proposition of fact and, 61, 63
analyzing proposition of policy and, 83, 90
analyzing proposition of value and, 68-69, 75
argumentation and, 158
avoiding equivocation in, 176
discovering issues and, 25
methods of, 110-11
in the proposition, 21-22
rules for, 107-108
types of words which require, 109-10
Definition
argument from, 158
Definitional claims, 47
in policy advocacy, 81
Delivery
credibility and, 200, 202
use of body in, 198-99
use of visual aids in, 199-200
use of voice in, 196-98
Denial
in fact refutation, 64-65
in value refutation, 76-77
Dependent variables, 122
Descriptive statistics
as evidence, 120
Developed criteria
for evaluating the value object, 70
Dialectic, 6
Dilemma
argument from, 159
fallacy of creating a false, 170
Disadvantage arguments
policy opposition and, 92
uniqueness of, 93
Discovered criteria
for evaluating the value object, 70

E

Effect
of the value object, 71-72
Eloquence
achieving, 186-87
language and, 185
overdoing, 188
Emotional appeal
fallacy of using, 172-73
Equivocation
fallacy of, 176
Ethics
argumentation and, 6, 10-13
credibility and, 201
freedom of speech and, 12
reasoning and, 12
research and, 10-11
social responsibility and, 11
value argument and, 42-43
Evidence, 118 (*See also* Grounds; Tests of Evidence)
argument from authority and, 155
audience acceptance of, 132-33
backing the warrant with, 54

books as sources of, 134
credibility and the use of, 201
degree of precision in, 182
eloquent presentation of, 186
government documents as a source of, 135-37
grounds and, 50
how to find, 133-37
how to record, 138-39
language used in, 176
making claims in the absence of, 171
newspapers as sources of, 135
opinion as, 123-24
periodicals as sources of, 134-35
qualification of the source of, 123-24
scientific, 123
secondary sources of, 124
sufficiency of, 64-65, 76
types of factual, 119-23
Example
as evidence, 119-20, 124
definition by, 110
tests of, 125-26
Extent
of the value object, 72
Extenuation
in fact refutation, 65
in value refutation, 76-77
Eye contact, 198

F

Facial expression, 198
Fact (*See also* Proposition of fact)
analyzing propositions of, 61-62
argument from authority and, 155-56
claims about, 47
evidence of, 119-23
fields of argument which dispute, 40
policy propositions and, 30, 45, 82
proposition of, 23, 28
stock issues of, 40-41
value propositions and, 66
Fallacy, 165
of ambiguity, 176
of appeal summarized, 175
of appeal to authority, 173-74
of appeal to emotion, 172-73
of appeal to humor, 175
of appeal to ignorance, 171
of appeal to the people, 172
of appeal to tradition, 174
of attacking the person, 169
of avoiding the issue, 169
of circular reasoning, 169
of composition, 167
of division, 167-68
of emotional language, 177
of equivocation, 176
of evasion, 169
of false dilemma, 170
of hasty generalization, 166-67
of irrelevant argument, 168
of refutation, 168
of seizing on a trivial point, 170

Fallacy, cont'd
of shifting ground, 169
of using technical jargon, 178
Field experiments, 122
causal reasoning in, 146
Fields of argument (*See also* Academic argumentation;
Law; Politics)
analysis of other, 106
credibility in a, 200-201
evidence required in various, 50-51
and the general audience, 182-83
reasoning preferred by various, 144
rules of engagement in a, 182
and the specific audience, 183
value criteria and, 71
value hierarchies in, 69
which dispute fact, 40
which dispute policy, 44-45
which dispute value, 42-43
Figurative analogy, 154
Forced dichotomy
fallacy of, 170
Function
analogy and, 154
definition by, 110

G

General audience, 182-83
Generalization
argument from, 150-52
fallacy of hasty, 166-67
tests of, 151-52
Gesture, 198-99
Goals-criteria organization
in policy advocacy, 86
Government documents
as a source of evidence, 135-37
Grammar
using correct, 185
Ground
fallacy of shifting, 169
Grounds (*See also* Evidence)
argument from dilemma and, 159
insufficient, 166-67
in the Toulmin model of argument, 50-51, 53
types required in various fields of argument, 50-51

H

Hasty generalization
fallacy of, 166-67
Hierarchy
identifying an appropriate value, 69, 75
of the public's values, 103
of values, 42
Humor
fallacy of appealing to, 175
Hyperbole
style and, 187

I

Illustration
as evidence, 119-20, 124

tests of, 125-26
Independent variables, 122
Inference
argument from authority and, 156
in fact propositions, 41, 61, 63-64
Inferential statistics
as evidence, 121
Inherency
analysis and the discovery of, 106
attitudinal and structural, 39
barriers to a policy overcoming, 92
elements of, 38
minor repairs and, 91
in policy argumentation, 82, 84
prima facie case and, 38
in value argumentation, 72
Instrumental communication, 2
analogy and, 155
audience analysis and, 17
Introduction
example of, 191
in oral argument, 190
Irrelevant argument
fallacy of, 168
Issue
fallacy of avoiding the, 169-70
Issues (*See also* Stock issues)
actual, 101, 113-16
propositions and, 25-26
stock, 37, 71

J

Jargon
clarity and, 186

L

Laboratory experiments, 122
causal reasoning in, 146
generalizability of, 127
Language
ambiguity in, 176
appropriate use of, 184-85
avoiding sexist, 185
clarity of, 178, 185-86
credibility and, 202
eloquence in, 187-88
emotionally loaded, 177
equivocation in, 176
fallacies of, 176-78
style in, 185
Law
argumentation and the, 7
brief writing and, 188
burden of proof and, 19
presumption and the, 16
prima facie case in the, 37
propositions and the, 23
rules of engagement in the, 182
specific audience and the, 183
Library
cataloging of books in the, 134

computerized aids to using the, 136
guides to periodicals in the, 134-35
newspaper collections available in the, 135
reference material in the, 137
using the, 133

M

Metaphor
style and, 187
Metonymy
style and, 187
Minor repairs
inherency and, 91
Modal qualifiers, 55
Movement, 199
Multiple causality, 147-48

N

Natural presumption, 16
audience and determining, 17
Necessary cause, 148
Necessary criteria
value propositions and, 71, 113
Need-plan-advantage organization
in policy advocacy, 85
Negation
definition by, 111
Newspapers
as sources of evidence, 135
Non sequitir
fallacy of, 168
Nuisance variables, 122

O

Operation
definition by, 111
Opinion
ambiguity and equivocation in, 176
argument from authority and, 155-56
evidence from, 123-25
fallacy and the use of, 173
Opponent, 15
argumentative brief of the, 188
fact proposition and the, 63-65
policy proposition and the, 89-94
presumption and, 18, 20
value proposition and the, 75-77
role in defining terms, 21
Opposition
example of value, 73-74
example of policy, 95-97
Oral argument
credibility and, 200
presentation of, 196-97
use of body in, 198-99
use of visual aids in, 199-200
use of voice in, 196, 198
Oral style
difference from written style, 186

Organization (*See also* Pattern of argument)
brief and, 189
introduction and conclusion in, 190
and speaker credibility, 201-202
Outline
brief as an, 188-89
introduction and conclusion in, 190
rules for writing an, 189
speaking from an, 194
Oxymoron
style and, 187

P

Parallel case
argument from, 152-53
difference from analogy, 154
tests of, 153
Pattern of argument
brief and the, 189
chain, 60
cluster, 60-61
conclusion and, 190
introduction and, 190
in policy disputes, 85-86, 94
simple, 59-60
Pause, 197
Periodicals
as sources of evidence, 134-35
Personification
style and, 187
Persuasion
appeal to pity in, 172
argumentation and, 3-5, 181
Pitch, 197
Pity
fallacy of appeal to, 172
Policy (*See also* Proposition of policy)
claims about, 47
fields of argument which dispute, 44-45
proposition of, 21, 29-30
stock issues of, 44-45
Politics
argumentation and, 8
mode of resolution in, 183
propositions of policy in, 29
specific audience in, 183
Posture, 199
Preemptive arguments
advancing, 62
responding to, 65
Premises
as evidence, 121-22, 125
opinion as, 124
tests of, 129
Presumption, 15
appeal to tradition and, 174
artificial, 16, 18, 171
audience analysis and, 18, 183
burden of proof and, 19-20
as a decision rule, 16-17
natural, 16-17
prima facie case and, 36-37
proposition and, 20, 22, 31-32
proposition of fact and, 61, 63-64

Prima facie case, 36, 40
  advocate and the, 37
  claims and, 49
  fact propositions and the, 41
  inherency and the, 38-39
  policy proposition and the, 45, 80, 90
  topicality and the, 38
  value proposition and the, 43, 72, 76
Probability
  analogy and, 154-55
  argumentation and, 9
  truth and, 13
Pronunciation, 196-97
  using correct, 185
Proof (*See also* Evidence; Grounds; Burden of Proof)
  burden of, 19-20
Proposition, 20
  in academic argumentation, 24, 26-27
  burden of proof and the, 22, 31-32
  change and the, 22-24
  defining terms in the, 21-22
  of fact, 23, 28
  identifying issues in the, 25-26
  locus of disagreement and the, 21
  phrasing the, 31-32
  of policy, 21, 29-30
  presumption and the, 22, 31-32
  of value, 23, 28-29
Proposition of fact, 23, 28
  actual issues in, 113
  advocating the, 61-62
  cause of controversy, 102
  history of a, 104
  opposing the, 63-65
  prima facie case for a, 41
  stock issues of a, 40-41
Proposition of policy, 21, 29-30
  actual issues in, 115-16
  advocating the, 80-86
  cause of controversy, 103
  defining terms in the, 112
  inherency and the, 38
  history of, 106
  opposing the, 89-94
  prima facie case for a, 45
  stock issues for a, 44-45
Proposition of value, 23, 28-29
  actual issues in, 113-15
  advocating the, 68-71
  cause of controversy, 102-103
  criteria in a, 113
  defining terms in the, 111-12
  fact argumentation in a, 66
  inherency and the, 38
  history of, 104-106
  opposing the, 75-77
  prima facie case for a, 72
  stock issues for a, 42-44

Q

Qualifier
  generalizations and, 151
  in the Toulmin model of argument, 54-56
Quality

of evidence as a general test, 131-32
Question
  rhetorical, 187

R

Rate, 197
Reasoning, 144 (*See also* Fallacy; Tests of reasoning;
    Warrant)
  analogy and, 154-55
  authority and, 155-56, 158
  causal, 144-46, 148
  definition and, 158
  degree of precision in, 182
  dilemma and, 159
  ethics and, 12
  fallacies of, 166-71
  generalization and, 150-52
  inferences in, 143
  parallel case and, 152-53
  sign, 148-50
  warrant in the Toulmin model as, 52-53
Rebuttal
  in Toulmin model of argument, 54, 56
Reducto ad adsurdum
  fallacy of, 175
Reference material
  collections of, 137
  guides to, 133
Refutation
  fallacy of, 168
  policy argumentation and, 91-93
  techniques of, 64-65
  value argumentation and, 76-77
Reliability
  of evidence as a general test, 131
Repetition
  style and, 187
Research
  ethics and, 10-11
Resistance to change
  overcoming, 5
Restricted generalization, 151
Rhetoric, 9
Rhetorical question
  style and, 187
Rhetorical strategy, 182
  in conclusions, 190
  in introductions, 190
  and managing credibility, 202
Risk
  argumentation and, 5-6

S

Scientific evidence
  credibility of, 123
  nature of, 122, 125
  statistical tests of significance in, 123
  tests of, 127-28
Scientific method, 122
Sign
  argument from, 148-49

Sign, cont'd
    difference from cause, 150
    reliability of, 149
    tests of argument from, 150
Simple arguments, 59-60
Simple claims, 48
Solvency
    policy advocacy and, 84
    policy opposition and, 92
Specific audience, 183-84
Statistics, 120, 125
    descriptive, 120
    inferential, 121
    tests of, 126-27
    and tests of significance in science, 123
    using visual aids to present, 199
Stock issues
    actual issues differentiated from, 101
    fact argumentation and, 40-41
    policy argumentation and, 44-45, 81-84, 89-90
    prima facie case and, 37
    value argumentation and, 42-44, 71, 75-76
Strategy
    in conclusions, 190
    in introductions, 190
    for managing credibility, 202
    policy opposition and, 90
    rhetorical, 182
    value opposition and, 75
Straw man argument
    fallacy of using, 168
Structural inherency, 38-39
Style
    clarity and, 185-86
    credibility and, 202
    elements of, 185
    eloquence in, 187-88
    grammar and, 185
    oral versus written, 186
    pronunciation and, 185
Subissues
    stock issues of policy and their, 81-84
Subsidiary effects
    policy advocacy and, 84-85
Sufficient cause, 148
Sufficient criteria
    value propositions and, 71, 113
Symbol
    language as, 184
Synecdoche
    style and, 187
Synonym
    definition by, 110

T

Terministic screen
    style and, 187
    words as a, 184-85
Tests of evidence
    consistency of, 132
    for factual material, 125-30
    general tests of, 131-33
    for opinion material, 130

    quality of, 131-32
    reliability of, 131
Tests of reasoning
    from analogy, 155
    from authority, 157
    from cause, 146-47
    from definition, 158
    from generalization, 151-52
    from parallel case, 153
    from sign, 150
Topicality
    in academic argumentation, 116
    prima facie case and, 38
Toulmin model of argument
    backing in, 54-55
    claims in, 46-49
    grounds in, 50-51
    qualifier in, 54-56
    rebuttal in, 54, 56
    warrant in, 52-53
Transfer fallacy
    of composition, 167
    of division, 167-68
    of refutation, 168
Truth
    argumentation and, 4
    fallacy and, 165
    probability and, 13
    proposition of fact and, 28

U

Unrestricted generalization, 151

V

Vague terms
    clarity and, 186
Value change
    forces that precipitate, 114-15
    process of, 104-105
Value object
    analysis of, 102-103
    criteria for evaluating the, 69-71
    defining the, 68-69, 111
    measurement of the, 71-72
    opposing the definition of the, 75
    placement within a value hierarchy, 69
Value (*See also* Proposition of value)
    claims about, 47
    fact argumentation in propositions of, 66
    fields of argument which dispute, 42-43
    hierarchy of, 69, 75
    policy propositions and, 30, 44-45, 81-82
    proposition of, 23, 28-29
    stock issues of, 42-44
Values, 68
    credibility and audience, 202
    fallacy of appeal and, 174
    historical American, 102-103
Variable
    in scientific research, 122
    manipulation of, 128

Visual aids
    principles of using, 199
    problems caused by, 200
Vocal quality
    elements of, 197-98
Volume, 197

                    W

Warrant
    argument from authority and, 156
    backing the, 55, 166

in causal reasoning, 145
in celebrity testimonials, 173
hasty generalization and, 167
parallel case and the, 152
reasoning and the, 144
stated and unstated, 53
in the Toulmin model of argument, 52
Workability
    policy advocacy and, 83-84
    policy opposition and, 92
Written style
    difference from oral style, 186